Economic Regulation and Competition

European Business Law & Practice Series

Volume 18.

The titles published in this series are listed at the end of this volume

Economic Regulation and Competition

Regulation of Services in the EU, Germany and Japan

Edited by

Jürgen Basedow
Harald Baum
Klaus J. Hopt
Hideki Kanda and
Toshiyuki Kono

KLUWER LAW INTERNATIONAL
THE HAGUE / LONDON / NEW YORK

Published by:
Kluwer Law International
P.O. Box 85889
2508 CN The Hague
The Netherlands
sales@kli.wkap.nl
http://www.kluwerlaw.com

Sold and distributed in North, Central and South America by:
Kluwer Law International
101 Philip Drive,
Norwell, MA, 02061, USA
kluwerlaw@wkap.com

In all other countries sold and distributed by Kluwer Law International
P.O. Box 322
3300 AH Dordrecht
The Netherlands

ISBN 90-411-1968-X

Library of Congress Cataloguing-in-Publication Data is available from the Library of Congress

Kluwer Law International incorporates the imprint of Martinus Nijhoff Publishers

PREFACE

In Japan and most of the continental European economies, we are presently observing a shift from what has been labeled a 'corporatist' system to more market-oriented structures. Regulatory competition caused by the globalization of markets is increasingly placing the traditional legal institutions of these jurisdictions under severe strain. This is especially true for the services markets. Of these, the markets for financial services and telecommunications services have to adapt most urgently. These adaptations are already underway to varying extents and degrees, made possible by a mixture of de-regulation and re-regulation.

In this volume, scholars from Germany, Austria, Switzerland, and Japan lay out the theoretical foundations and means for these developments. Through critical analysis, the various contributions show what has been reached so far in Europe and Japan and what remains to be achieved in the future. These scholarly analyses and proposals were first presented and discussed with high-ranking practitioners from various institutions during a conference at Ringberg Castle, the conference center of the Max Planck Society at Lake Tegernsee, on October 24 through 27, 2001. The generous support of the conference by the *Max-Planck-Gesellschaft* (MPG), the *Deutsche Forschungsgemeinschaft* (DFG), and the *Förderverein japanisch-deutscher Kulturbeziehungen e.V., Köln* (JaDe) is gratefully acknowledged.

This book presents the revised conference papers and statements by the practitioners, along with a summary of the various discussions. It supplements the earlier conference volume *Legal Aspects of Globalization* edited by *J. Basedow* and *T. Kono* (Kluwer Law International 2000).

The editors are indebted to Ms. *Ursula Shibumi Eisele* and Ms. *Ingeborg Stahl*, both of whom participated with the greatest dedication in the editing process of this volume at the Hamburg Max Planck Institute, as well as to Ms. *Kristen Zetzsche*, who once more has smoothed manuscripts written by authors from different countries into coherent English.

Hamburg, Tokyo, and Fukuoka, August 2002

Jürgen Basedow, Harald Baum, Klaus J. Hopt, Hideki Kanda, Toshiyuki Kono

TABLE OF CONTENTS

CONTRIBUTORS

Prof. Dr. Jürgen Basedow, Max Planck Institute for Foreign Private and Private International Law, Hamburg

Dr. Harald Baum, Max Planck Institute for Foreign Private and Private International Law, Hamburg

Prof. Dr. Christoph Engel, Max Planck Project Group Common Goods: Law, Politics and Economics, Bonn

Prof. Yasuo Hasebe, University of Tokyo

Dr. Knut Hohlfeld, Secretary General, International Associations of Insurance Supervisors, Basel

Prof. Dr. Dr. Dr. h.c. mult. Klaus J. Hopt, Max Planck Institute for Foreign Private and Private International Law, Hamburg

Prof. Dr. Susanne Kalss, University of Klagenfurt

Prof. Hideki Kanda, University of Tokyo

Prof. Kôji Kinoshita, Osaka University

Prof. Dr. Johannes Köndgen, Rheinische Friedrich-Wilhelms-Universität, Bonn

Prof. Toshiyuki Kono, Kyûshû University, Fukuoka

Prof. Takashi Kubota, Nagoya University

Prof. Dr. Wulf-Henning Roth, Rheinische Friedrich-Wilhelms-Universität, Bonn

Klaus-Dieter Scheurle, Credit Suisse First Boston (Europe) Ltd., Frankfurt/Main

RD Dietrich Schilling, Federal Banking Supervisory Office, Bonn

Prof. Dr. Anton K. Schnyder, University of Basel

ECONOMIC REGULATION IN MARKET ECONOMIES

by Jürgen Basedow, Hamburg

When market regulation came under attack in the 1980s, it was still tight and comprehensive in many areas, in particular in the services sector. Market access and exit, prices, and market behavior were heavily regulated in sectors such as telecommunications, rail and road transport, postal services, the supply of electricity and gas, labor, and many professions. The rising criticism of the resulting inflexibility of large parts of the economy brought about a very thorough theoretical discussion about the concept (infra I.), the political reasons for regulation (infra II.), its justification in a market economy (infra III.), and its compatibility with binding rules of the various constitutions of international and European law (infra IV.). These discus-

J. Basedow, H. Baum, K. Hopt, H. Kanda and T. Kono (eds.), Economic Regulation and Competition, (1-24)

sions maintain their basic theoretical significance, and they may also remain important in practice insofar as the former regulations have not been modified. But speaking in general terms, one has to take into account that a broad deregulation movement has taken place all over Europe, starting in the United Kingdom in the 1980s and continuing in countries such as Sweden, the Netherlands, and Germany in the 1990s. In many instances, deregulation only partially created a delicate mix of regulatory interventions and competition (infra V.). The resulting situation is very often unclear and confusing: while governments affirm their resolve to deregulate and enforce competition policy, they use their remaining regulatory powers for purposes of fiscal or industrial policy.

I. The Concept of Regulation

Like every concept, the definition of 'regulation' is linked to its purpose and context. There are different conceptions of regulation in constitutional law, administrative law, economic law, etc. Thus, in many legal systems of English-speaking countries, the term regulation is used in a formal or technical way to indicate measures of a general purview adopted by government as opposed to parliament, although the executive usually acts under special powers conveyed by an act of parliament. In an equally technical sense, European Community law reserves the notion of regulation to secondary enactments which have direct effect within all member states. It is clear that the concept of regulation is used in a much wider and non-technical sense in this paper, which deals with its role in market economies; here it includes all types of provisions regardless of their formal origin. The way they are enforced is equally immaterial. The enforcement may be entrusted to administrative agencies, such as the Regulatory Authority for Post and Telecommunication in Germany, or to self-regulatory bodies which survey the activities of the members of a profession, but it may also be left to the judiciary; thus the regulation of the labor market is to a large extent enforced by courts of law.

Another terminological clarification relates to the contrast between what may be called general or constitutive regulations on the one side and specific or restrictive regulations on the other. The cohabitation of human beings requires rules protecting the lives, the freedom, and the property of others, and concerning the relation between the sexes, the transfer of economic resources from one generation to the next, and the binding force of promise. Without general rules of criminal law, contracts and torts, and property and family relations, autonomous individuals cannot live and work together and prosper. The less a society relies on kinship relations and the more it is constituted by the exchange between anonymous individuals, the greater is its need for common constitutive regulations of the said kind.

While constitutive regulations affect everyone, the specific or restrictive regulations usually apply only to certain groups. An important part of them aims – for specific areas – at securing satisfactory results from work based on a division of labor and coordinated via markets. They essentially restrict the freedom of contract, although sometimes at a very early stage, e.g., by prohibiting certain economic activities altogether. It is this type of regulation, i.e., the restrictive regulation, that is discussed in this context. Thus, economic regulation is here understood as meaning any restriction decreed or enforced by the state on people's possibilities of action.[1] It affects their powers to dispose over themselves, their property, and their rights through legal transactions and contracts in particular.

The preceding definition presupposes individual freedom as the basic rule that characterizes the economic order. Starting from that premise, economic interchange is brought about by decentralized decisions on production and consumption, on offer and demand which meet on the marketplace. In this perspective, the restrictions effected by economic regulations are an alien element, an exception that somehow requires explanation and justification. It should, however, be recalled that a different overall conception of the economy would entail a different view on economic regulation, too. Where the responsibility for economic prosperity is vested in a central planning authority, economic regulations would not be regarded as an exception, but rather as the general rule, i.e., as a necessary and natural instrument which serves to enforce the central plan. The collapse of the socialist systems after 1990 has given evidence of the superior efficiency gains that are to be expected from a decentralized economic order. The following analysis will therefore focus on the role of economic regulations in market economies.

II. Political Explanations

The existence of economic regulation and its steady growth have been ascribed to a great variety of reasons. Some of them explain why economic

---

1 *Deregulierungskommission,* Marktöffnung und Wettbewerb (Poeschel, Stuttgart, 1991), no. 2.

regulations are adopted and some of them explain why they should be. The explanations of the former type focus on the motivation of people acting in the political and regulatory process; they are sometimes summarized under the heading of the 'positive theory of regulation'. Explanations of the latter type do not claim to describe social reality but try to give reasons that justify state interventions by means of economic regulation in a market economy; they form part of the so-called 'normative theory of regulation' and will be discussed below in section III.[2]

Economic regulations are adopted by the legislature, government, or special agencies as the result of procedures that usually involve a great number of people: politicians, regulators, and representatives of group interests. Their regulatory activities are usually unleashed by market results that are deemed to be unsatisfactory. But it should be clear that this assessment does not flow from unequivocal or objective criteria of market failure. To a large extent, it is a political opinion formed in the course of the said procedures and subject to the influence of the aforementioned actors. It is therefore important to become aware of the incentives of all participants which have an impact on that process.[3]

Politicians are not merely agents of the common welfare. They are also pursuing particular interests and in doing so, drawing on the assistance of the machinery of state power. These particular interests are also interests in regulation which inevitably favor specific interest groups. In this way politicians win friends among those who gain by regulation: owners of companies, managers, the employees, their suppliers. If politicians succeed in passing the whole off as serving the general welfare, they do not run the risk of losing much on other fronts. The friends they win are voters, they give donations and information, and they have influence. The losers – often the consumers – are very numerous and hardly affected directly and individually; they are therefore not very articulate and so they keep quiet.

The *regulatory bureaucracy* also has its own interests relating to its budget, competence, power, and prestige. These are better served if the number of regulations to be introduced, supervised, and enforced is bigger.

---

2 For this dichotomy of the theory of regulation, see *J. Müller/I. Vogelsang*, Staatliche Regulierung (Nomos, Baden-Baden, 1979), p. 101 et seq.; *M. Fritsch/ Th. Wein/ H.-J. Ewers*, Marktversagen und Wirtschaftspolitik (2nd edn, Vahlen, München, 1996), p. 296 et seq.; *R. Weber*, Wirtschaftsregulierung in wettbewerbspolitischen Ausnahmebereichen (Nomos, Baden-Baden, 1986), p. 90 et seq.

3 The following assessment draws upon *Deregulierungskommission*, supra note 1, no. 21.

So bureaucrats ultimately become advocates of regulation. Their interests meet those of the regulated. They work with them to differentiate regulation further and further. While the regulated market actors are increasingly protected from competition, the regulators gain in influence and budget. An initiative to remove obsolete regulations can hardly be expected from the regulatory authority.

Group interests can be organized in various ways. Interests that have particular weight for each member of a group and that are concentrated in small groups can be more easily organized and thus more strongly represented than very disparate interests. It is easier for the individual member of the group to see that the group depends on him and that his input is worthwhile. This explains why producer interests can be so much more effectively transmuted into regulations that are favorable to them than consumer interests or other widely disparate interests. In addition, the particular incentives of group representatives must be taken into account. They are the intermediaries between the individuals and the political and regulatory system. The more complicated the latter, the more important is the role of the intermediaries. While the individual members of the group may be interested in deregulation, their representatives will rather act in the opposite direction.

The following conclusions can be drawn from these observations:

- The various actors pursue interests that are not necessarily identical with the common welfare and which in some instances are in outright contradiction to the public good.
- Given the wide margin of discretion which regulators have under most regulations, and given the even wider discretion of politicians, the assessment of unsatisfactory market results – which is the starting point of all regulations – tends to be distorted by private interests.
- This risk increases as the interests of the different actors coincide and form tacit alliances, which apparently they do in many instances.

It follows that a basic assumption of public law has to be questioned: the mere fact that members of parliament and officials of state authorities get their income from the taxpayer does not by itself guarantee that they promote the public good when it is in conflict with their private interests. Additional safeguards are required to attain that objective.

III. Justifications of Economic Regulation

In the first place, a theoretical reflection on the need for economic regulations in a market economy is necessary. If society shares the general belief in the superior ability of competition to efficiently allocate resources, enhance innovation and problem-solving capacities, and extend the choices available in all situations, etc., there must be valid reasons for each and every restriction of competition brought about by regulation.[4] It is not sufficient to invoke the public good as the supreme guideline of all public action. There must be strong evidence that the effects which are generally expected from competition are foreclosed by structural peculiarities of the specific market, i.e., by market failures. Five main reasons can indicate such failures:

(1) the possibility of positive or negative external effects of production and consumption;
(2) inevitable market power, in particular in the case of a natural monopoly;
(3) destructive competition;
(4) asymmetric information;
(5) opportunist behavior in the making and execution of contracts.

Some of these points merit some further clarification.[5]

A. External Effects

It is by no means uncommon that by producing or consuming goods we may hurt or benefit others. A satisfactory market result is, however, not jeopardized if those affected can themselves ensure the internalization of such external effects by means of contractual arrangements or by remedies provided by the general legal system, for example, by claims for compensation. Thus, the residents in many legal systems are required to contribute to the costs of development of a local road which will benefit them anyway.[6] And a landowner who is harmed by pollution originating from his neighbor's premises may claim damages to compensate his losses and will thereby re-

---

4 *M. Krakowski*, Theoretische Grundlagen der Regulierung, in: *idem* (ed.), Regulierung in der Bundesrepublik Deutschland (Verlag Weltarchiv, Hamburg, 1988), pp. 19, 25.

5 The following discussion draws upon *Deregulierungskommission*, supra note 1, nos. 9-13; see also *R. Weber*, supra note 2, p. 98 et seq., *M. Fritsch/Th. Wein/ H.-J. Ewers*, supra note 2, p. 74 et seq.

6 See in German law § 127 et seq. of the Construction Code (Baugesetzbuch).

establish an economic balance which also might have been achieved on the basis of a contract.[7] In both cases, externalities – positive externalities in the former case and negative in the latter – are internalized.

However, there are cases where even the best possible rule designed to achieve internalization fails. This is particularly so with regard to positive externalities in the case of public goods, i.e., goods from the consumption of which nobody can be excluded because their use by one person does not prevent their use by another. Thus, the production of safety or clean air benefits everybody who is living in a given area, regardless of whether he takes his share in the cost or not. It is obvious that the design and the enforcement of appropriate property rules that limit the inhalation of clean air or the use of safety to certain persons is either impossible or too expensive. Knowing this, nobody would contribute to the production of clean air and safety; instead, everybody would wait for others to invest and hope that he gets a free ride. In the final outcome, no clean air and no safety would be produced. External effects of this kind which cannot be internalized form a theoretical and compelling reason for special regulatory intervention by the state.

These considerations also have some bearing on financial markets. For the ability of a market to function can also be a public good, i.e., a problem of external effects. The collapse of a major bank or a large insurance company not only affects those directly concerned but many others as well – indeed, everyone – if it causes a crisis of confidence in other banks or insurance companies. Indifference on the part of depositors regarding the standing of their bank may be acceptable, but 'competition in laxity' in the banking business would not be. It is not covered by the principle of consumer sovereignty. The same applies to insurers.

B. Natural Monopolies

We speak of a natural monopoly if the production to meet the entire market demand for a good can be achieved at the most favorable cost in a single plant and with the sale carried out by a single enterprise. This is called a 'natural' monopoly for two reasons: First, monopoly production is appropriate because, for technical organizational reasons, it generates lowest costs

---

7 See in German law § 906 para. 2, 2nd sentence of the Civil Code (Bürgerliches Gesetzbuch, BGB).

for the economy as a whole. Second, if one started with several plants operated by several companies, competition would inevitably cause all of them except one to leave the market. Examples of this are the railway network, gas pipelines, harbors and airports, and the so-called local loop in telecommunications, i.e., the connection of the private user with the next switchboard.

Monopolies must be rejected because they are inefficient in optimizing supply and minimizing costs. While a regular monopoly will usually be under attack very soon in open markets and may therefore be left to the general control of abuses of a dominant market position under competition law,[8] this is different in the case of a natural monopoly. Here, competitors will not change the basic structure of the market, and the potential competition is no valid instrument to curb monopoly power. Since the incentive to abuse that power is unrestricted in every single transaction, the regulation of prices and market behavior is the only viable solution. It must, however, be borne in mind that such regulation suggests itself only with regard to those segments of the market that are characterized by a natural monopoly. In the supply of gas, for example, only the transport network can be regarded as a natural monopoly, while the production and distribution may very well be left to competition.

A related argument to justify regulation is the danger of 'cream skimming'. If the conditions for a natural monopoly are met for some sections of a market while others would allow for competition, the resulting prices would be much higher in the former than in the latter. Take, for example, the collection and delivery of mail in rural areas, which has the characteristics of a natural monopoly, and in metropolitan districts where competition by new entrants ('cream skimmers') would be possible and would force down prices. Because such differentiation is regarded as socially undesirable, it is argued that the whole market including the competitive segments should be left to a single supplier. This supplier would charge uniform rates that would not cover the high costs of the rural operations but would exceed the costs of urban collection and delivery. It follows that the plea for a regulatory monopoly that would allow cross-subsidization cannot be explained in these markets by their *economic* characteristics, but rather as results of the *political* objective of charging uniform prices regardless of the relative costs.

---

8 See art. 83 EC Treaty and, in German law, § 19 of the Act against Restraints on Competition (Gesetz gegen Wettbewerbsbeschränkungen, GWB): (1998) Bundesgesetzblatt (BGBl.) Part I, p. 2546.

Given the wide price margins that exist for all kinds of goods and services between the cities and the countryside, the objective of price uniformity for certain services may be called into question. But this is a political and not an economic issue.

C. Destructive Competition

Competition always implies the exit of the weaker market actors. In this sense, competition is always destructive. It follows that the mere possibility of market exit cannot justify regulation. This is different where suppliers of production factors (labor and capital goods) cannot adjust to changes in market conditions within a relatively short period of time. This may occur in sectors where it is difficult to use production factors elsewhere or in another way. Firm-specific skills of workers and the acquisition of ships for inland navigation are often-cited examples for such non-recoverable investment. Here it can happen that as the demand weakens, the suppliers hope to be able to force their rivals off the market by price-undercutting, thus allowing them to stay in the market without losing their investment.

In practice, the argument of destructive competition is of very limited use. On the one side, cases of irreversible costs are much less frequent than is generally assumed. Thus, the investment in aircraft requires very high investment at the initial stage of the airline business without creating irreversible costs; there is a very workable market for used aircraft. On the other side, market actors are usually aware of the long-term commitment that is required in certain sectors of the economy. A farmer cannot expect his investment to pay off each single year; it is the long-term balance that counts. The length of the relevant term changes from sector to sector, and regulation may only be justified where a response to changing market conditions is lacking even after the sector-specific period of time has elapsed.

D. Asymmetric Information

Unequal information is a particularly important rationale for regulation. The main concern here (though not the only one) is consumer protection. In general, consumers are much less informed about the products and services they purchase, and about the risks related to the contracts they conclude, than the producers and sellers. A consumer could, of course, improve his knowledge by acquiring information, asking experts, etc. But this would require expenditures in terms of time and money that would not be rational in many cases.

Why should the purchaser of a car bother about standard clauses of the contract on jurisdiction, the prohibition of set-off, or sanctions for late payment if such clauses become relevant only once in ten thousand cases? It is very rational for him to concentrate on some relevant purchase criteria – such as speed, comfort, fuel consumption, color, or the power of the engine – which he can appreciate at every occasion. If it is rational for consumers to disregard the standard conditions of contract in this process, no efficient allocation of contractual risks can be expected from them, and it would be up to state regulation to prevent inefficiencies in this sector.

Similar reasons could be given for sectoral regulations relating to financial services. Consumers cannot effectively monitor the investment practices of banks and insurance companies, nor is competition able to provide the necessary information as crashes of the financial systems in the past have shown. Similar considerations apply to the capital markets. The bias of information created by insider trading apparently cannot be coped with by the competitive process; if it is not excluded by appropriate regulation, the whole market will be threatened (see above).

As a justification for regulation, asymmetric information is difficult to handle. In practice, it exists almost everywhere, but it can be overcome by the market process in many sectors. Thus, asymmetric information can support regulation only with regard to those single aspects of markets or individual contracts where remedies cannot be expected from the competitive process.

E. Opportunistic Behavior

Many contracts in general – and all long-term or relational contracts in particular – are incomplete. They establish a certain balance of rights and duties as perceived at the time of conclusion, but they do not provide a solution for every problem that might occur in the course of the transaction. While general contract law gives an answer to some of those questions, many have to be dealt with by means of renegotiation or unilateral rights of determination. In such situations each party is tempted to distort the original contractual balance of rights and duties in its own favor. That is what we mean by opportunistic behavior.

Such situations are usually characterized by an information bias between the parties: thus, an employee usually knows his own abilities to carry out certain activities much better than the employer, who in turn is much more aware of his own business perspectives than the employee. In insurance contracts, the policyholder is in a much better position to assess the risk insured than the insurer, who in turn has a better perception of his own investment policies and the risks and profits flowing therefrom which affect the policyholder. General contract law tries to accommodate such situations of uncertainty by rules such as the adjustment of consideration in case of an unforeseeable rise of cost, the delegation to one party of the power to determine the content of the contract, the unilateral right to terminate a contract of indeterminate duration, or the duty to renegotiate in good faith. But all these rules can hardly create legal certainty and leave ample leeway for opportunistic power. This explains the long-standing trend to regulate markets that are characterized by long-term contracts in particular.

IV. Regulatory Policies in the Shadow of Binding Law

A. Limitations of Regulatory Sovereignty

The preceding analysis has shown that economic regulation may be justified in a market economy where a market failure can be established. On the other hand, the criteria for the assessment of some types of market failures are extremely vague. The finding of such market failures, therefore, is very much a matter of political discretion. This observation explains the great significance of the so-called positive theories of regulation outlined above in section II. Given the general inclination of regulators and politicians to increase regulation, it is important to study the legal limitations of economic regulation, limitations which might be enforced by the court system. Put in other words, a market economy based upon the firm belief in the superiority of competition needs the judiciary as a counterweight to the inflation of regulatory policies favored by the political and regulatory system.

This function depends upon two characteristics of the controlling legal standards:

- They must be binding upon legislators and regulatory bodies in the single states. This requirement is met by rules of public international law, European Community law, and national constitutional law.
- They must be directly applicable to the effect that courts of law can enforce them against national regulations regardless of their implementation within the national legal system.

The latter condition is fulfilled by constitutional law in some countries such as Germany where the constitutional court, in the early years, made frequent use of its powers to strike down economic regulations for violation of certain basic rights guaranteed by the constitution; more recently, its activities have become less conspicuous in this field. Public international law, and in particular international treaties such as the General Agreement on Tariffs and Trade (GATT)[9] and the General Agreement on Trade in Services (GATS),[10] might have a similar effect, but most legal systems, including the European Community, do not acknowledge a direct effect of such treaties.[11] In Western Europe, the most sensible and effective control of national regulatory provisions by the legal system flows from European Community law, and in particular from the basic freedoms and the provisions of the EC Treaty on competition,[12] all of which have been declared directly applicable by the Court of Justice.[13]

B. The Free Movement of Goods in the European Community

It is well known that the EC Treaty has established a limited number of basic freedoms which safeguard the free flow of resources within the European Community. These freedoms protect the free movement of persons, both workers and self-employed, of goods and services, and of capital and payments. Their effects cannot be described here in detail, so an exemplary look at the free movement of goods and the regime of services of general economic interest must suffice.

---

9 General Agreement on Tariffs and Trade of 30 October 1947: 55 UNTS 187 = (1951) Bundesgesetzblatt (BGBl.) Part II, p. 173.

10 General Agreement on Trade in Services of 15 April 1994: (1994) OJEC L 336/190.

11 ECJ, case C-149/96, *Portugal v. Council*: (1999) ECR I-8425, recital 47.

12 For a detailed analysis, see *J. Basedow*, Deregulierungspolitik und Deregulierungspflichten – Vom Zwang zur Marktöffnung in der EG: (1991) 2 Staatswissenschaften und Staatspraxis 151 et seq.; *idem*, Le marché unique, programme de déréglementation: (1993) Revue internationale de droit comparé 619 et seq.

13 See, e.g., ECJ, case 26/62, *van Gend en Loos v. Administration fiscale néerlandaise*: (1963) ECR 1 for the free movement of goods; case 2/74, *Reyners v. Belgium*: (1974) ECR 631 for the freedom of establishment; case 33/74, *van Binsbergen v. Bedrijfsvereniging Metaalnijverheid*: (1974) ECR 1299 for the free movement of services.

The controlling effect of the free movement of goods is most clearly demonstrated by the celebrated case of Cassis de Dijon.[14] Here, the plaintiff intended to import a consignment of fruit liqueur called Cassis de Dijon originating in France for the purpose of selling it in Germany. The Federal Monopoly Administration for Spirits refused the authorization required under German law on the ground that, according to the existing regulations, the marketing of fruit liqueurs was conditional upon a minimum alcohol content of 25%, whereas the alcohol content of the French liqueur was only between 15 and 20%. In protest of that refusal, the plaintiff invoked the free movement of goods guaranteed by the EC Treaty, whereas the German government claimed that the fixing of a minimum alcohol content by national legislation was necessary in the interest of public health and consumer protection. On the one side, such legislation was to avoid the proliferation of alcoholic beverages on the national market; on the other side, consumers had to be protected against unfair practices on the part of producers and distributors of alcoholic beverages who would lower the alcohol content in order to gain competitive advantages.

The Court of Justice did not approve this line of thought. In the first place, it held the rules on the minimum alcohol content to be a measure having an effect equivalent to quantitative restrictions in trade between member states for the purposes of article 28 EC (ex 30).[15] Such measures may be recognized as being necessary 'in order to satisfy mandatory requirements relating in particular to the effectiveness of fiscal supervisions, the protection of public health, the fairness of commercial transactions, and the defense of the consumer'.[16] The grounds advanced by the German government were, however, not accepted by the Court of Justice. In its view, the public health cannot be protected by the regulation in question if at the same time a wide range of beverages with a low or high alcohol content are freely sold on the German market. As to the argument relating to the fairness of commercial transactions, the court held that this could be much better put into effect by appropriate information concerning the alcohol content on the packaging of the goods. The court therefore concluded that alcoholic beverages which have been lawfully produced and marketed in one of the member states could be introduced into any other member state provided that the

[14] CJ, case 120/78, *Rewe v. Bundesmonopolverwaltung für Branntwein – Cassis de Dijon*: (1979) ECR 649.

[15] *Cassis de Dijon*, supra note 14, recital 15.

[16] *Cassis de Dijon*, supra note 14, recital 9.

import does not violate mandatory requirements of the latter country;[17] as a general rule, the court reserves the right to control such requirements under the principle of proportionality.

From this line of argument emerges the so-called country of origin rule which has become a core component of the constitutional structure of the internal market. It means that national regulations which almost invariably hamper the import of foreign products may come under scrutiny in the European Court of Justice. If the Court of Justice declares them to be incompatible with the internal market, they may be maintained for purely internal situations of the respective member state. But in that case, a so-called reverse discrimination would result: national producers and sellers would be more strictly regulated than their competitors from abroad who could avail themselves of the free movement of goods. It is politically difficult to explain and to maintain such a situation. It is therefore fair to say that once the Court of Justice declares a national regulation to be a disproportionate restriction of the free movement of goods, that regulation will sooner or later be repealed in most cases. The process described above has been extended to services by a similar jurisprudence of the Court of Justice.

C. Services of General Economic Interest

In more recent years, the Court of Justice has had to deal increasingly often with national regulations relating to services of general economic interest such as telecommunications and postal services or the supply of electricity and gas. Under article 86 of the EC Treaty, undertakings entrusted with the operation of such services are subject to the rules of the Treaty insofar as the application of such rules does not obstruct the performance of the particular tasks assigned to them. While the Court of Justice leaves it to the member states to define the services of general economic interest, it again subjects the national regulations to the test of proportionality, which in some cases entails the declaration that a national regulation cannot be reconciled with the Treaty.

Thus, in the *Corbeau* case, the monopoly of the Belgian postal service for the transport of letters came under attack.[18] A private supplier of postal services collected mail at the senders' premises, a service which was outside

---

[17] *Cassis de Dijon*, supra note 14, recital 14.

[18] ECJ, case C-330/91, *Corbeau*: (1993) ECR I-2533.

the scope of the activities of the national postal company of Belgium. Yet the private supplier was indicted for violation of the legal monopoly of the national postal service. The Court of Justice held that the national postal service abused its dominant position in a disproportionate way by prohibiting the private supplier from carrying out services which it did not offer itself.

The conflict between national regulations relating to services of general economic interest and the principles of competition and free trade enshrined in the EC Treaty are among the most controversial issues of Community law at present. Here again the controlling and potentially deregulatory effect of Community law becomes visible. In the sector of public services, which is strongly dominated by a tight alliance of political and economic interests, Community law appears to be the only way toward competition and more flexible structures.

V. Deregulation and the New Regulatory Mix

As pointed out before, the interests of those who are involved in the regulatory and political process tend to thwart competition by differentiating and extending regulation. If competition is to maintain its key position in the economic order, that tendency must be compensated by a continuous examination of the need and adequacy of existing regulations with a view to an eventual deregulation. It would even make sense to institutionalize that continuous scrutiny and create a permanent deregulation commission. In Germany, the Monopoly Commission is competent under § 44 of the Act against Restraints on Competition[19] to express its views on current issues of competition policy, and it has repeatedly made use of that competence to suggest deregulatory measures in certain markets. However, such opinions have a purely advisory function.

At first sight, deregulation may appear to be a one-way street, a simple repeal of pre-existing restrictions. Reality is more complicated, however. It rather amounts to a new regulatory mix than to a straight deregulation. Three different types can be discerned:

- the transition to less restrictive alternative forms of regulation;
- the combination of deregulation and regulation of information;
- the combination of deregulation and network regulation.

---

[19] § 44 GWB, supra note 8.

A. The Transition to Less Restrictive Alternatives

Numerous examples show that deregulation is not equivalent to a simple reduction of the number of provisions in the statute book. Quite the contrary, broadening the scope of competition often requires legislative measures that establish the framework for future competitive action. Take the above-mentioned example of the postal monopoly. The situation was simple as long as that monopoly subsisted: private competition was excluded by a single statutory provision, and most details relating to the operation of the postal service were left to administrative management and discretion. Thus, there were no legal rules on the number of post offices and collection points that had to be maintained in the country in order to safeguard a sufficient level of communication services. When the German constitution was changed in 1994 to allow for competition in that sector, the fear of cream skimming (see section III.B. above) gave rise to a constitutional commitment of the German federal state to guarantee 'appropriate and sufficient services throughout the whole territory'.[20] While this provision is reasonably flexible and does not harm the development of competition, the German government has felt bound to define these so-called universal services in great detail. It has issued a regulation which practically depicts the present methods of production of the German postal service.[21] It not only fixes the number of mail boxes and post offices that must be accessible to the public, but even prescribes that a certain percentage of post offices must be run by the respective company itself, thereby excluding mail franchise systems.

This regulation clearly goes over the top; it petrifies existing structures of production and thereby contravenes the spirit if not the letter of the deregulatory statute. On the other hand, the example also shows that the reasons given for existing regulations in section III. above, in this case the fear of cream skimming, continue to produce their effects and have to be coped with by new regulatory measures that form a package with deregulation. Yet the overall effect of such a package will be the substitution of the former regulation by less restrictive alternatives in most cases.

---

[20] See art. 87f para. 1 of the Basic Law (Grundgesetz) as introduced by an act of 30 August 1994: (1994) Bundesgesetzblatt (BGBl.) Part I, p. 2245.

[21] See § 2 of the Regulation on Postal Universal Services (Post-Universaldienst-verordnung, PUDLV) of 15 December 1999: (1999) Bundesgesetzblatt (BGBl.) Part I, p. 2418.

Numerous examples give evidence of such deregulatory package deals. Thus, the second coordination directive on banking[22] has introduced the country-of-origin principle on the European banking market, thereby opening the national markets for the regulatory framework of the banking business as established by the national laws of any one of the other fourteen member states. It follows that at least in some member states, the risk of bank insolvencies increases as compared with the previous situation. As a counterbalance designed to outweigh that risk increase, new regulations have been adopted at the European level, for example, a directive on insolvency ratios for credit institutions[23] and a directive on deposit guarantee schemes[24]. As the overall result of that package, however, competition has been intensified in the industry.

Another example can be taken from insurance, where premiums and conditions before deregulation were subject to an administrative control and approval prior to their use in the market. The effect of that supervision had been a far-reaching uniformity of conditions and the approximation of insurance rates. But the German supervisory office had also used its powers to prescribe certain basic standards for policies; to take an example from private health insurance, the insurers, in order to get the approval of the authority, had to submit an undertaking that they would also insure newborn children of the policyholder even if the children were handicapped or stricken with severe diseases. When the third generation of EC insurance directives forbade the requirement of ex ante approval of insurance conditions, it became immediately clear that certain basic standards of consumer protection were threatened. The German legal system reacted in a double way: a 1994 amendment to the insurance contract law introduced a fairly comprehensive set of rules on private health insurance which provide mandatory minimum standards protecting the policyholder. Moreover, the

22 Second Council Directive 89/646/EEC of 15 December 1989 on the coordination of laws, regulations, and administrative provisions relating to the taking up and pursuit of the business of credit institutions and amending Directive 77/780/EEC: (1989) OJEC L 386/1.

23 Council Directive 89/647/EEC of 18 December 1989 on a solvency ratio for credit institutions: (1989) OJEC L 386/14.

24 Directive 94/19/EC of the European Parliament and of the Council of 30 May 1994 on deposit-guarantee schemes: (1994) OJEC L 135/5.

Federal Court intensified the judicial control of standard insurance clauses,[25] which is carried out on the basis of the statute on general conditions of contract.[26]

Insurance deregulation shows that certain functions of the previous regulations can be shifted to private law, i.e., to constitutive regulations as they were defined at the beginning of this paper. One has to bear in mind, however, that the implementation of private law depends upon the willingness of private parties to enforce their rights in court. The implementation deficits that may result in consumer cases, in particular, are to a certain extent outweighed by the standing which consumer associations have under the German law on standard conditions of contract.[27] They may attack general conditions of contract without a case pending. Their actions, therefore, have an intermediate position between the administrative control, which was formerly carried out by the supervisory authority prior to the use of the conditions, and the subsequent control in the individual case, which is the traditional task of judges.

B. Deregulation and the Regulation of Information

As pointed out above, information is an important asset in many markets, in particular in the financial services sector. It follows that asymmetric information is a potential source of market failure. In former times, economic regulation tried to cope with this problem by fixing substantive standards for the goods and services that were commercialized in the respective markets or by the limitation of trade to certain categories of well-informed persons. Thus, the right of stock exchanges to admit securities to trade was used in

---

25 See, e.g., *H. E. Brandner*, Auswirkungen der EU-Richtlinie über mißbräuchliche Vertragsklauseln auf Versicherungsverträge, in: Versicherungswissenschaftliche Studien Bd. 2 (1995), pp. 67.

26 Act on the Law of General Conditions of Contract of 9 December 1976 (Gesetz zur Regelung des Rechts der Allgemeinen Geschäftsbedingungen, AGB-Gesetz), incorporated into the Civil Code (§ 305 et seq. BGB) by the Act on the Modernization of the Law of Obligations (Gesetz zur Modernisierung des Schuldrechts) of 26 November 2001: (2001) Bundesgesetzblatt (BGBl.) Part I, p. 3138.

27 See § 13 et seq. of the Act of 1976 which has been re-enacted as part of the Act on Injunctions of Infringements of Consumer Laws and other Provisions (Gesetz über Unterlassungsklagen bei Verbraucherrechts- und anderen Verstößen, UKlaG) of 26 November 2001: (2001) Bundesgesetzblatt (BGBl.) Part I, p. 3173 (Art. 3 of the Act on the Modernization of the Law of Obligations, previous note).

former times to decree far-reaching substantive conditions concerning the capitalization and company structures of the applicant corporations. A deregulation of such restrictions can be compensated to a certain extent by information requirements such as the duty of companies to publish a prospectus before going public[28] and the duty to communicate certain events to the public once they are listed.[29] In a similar line of thought, access to trade in futures, which was limited to stock exchange brokers in former times, has been liberalized and is now open not only for businessmen in general but for all individuals who have been informed about the specific risks of trading in futures.[30] Similar information requirements are laid down in European insurance directives. In particular, the third life assurance directive contains long and detailed lists of information about the assurance undertaking and about the contractual commitment, information which has to be provided to the policyholder before the conclusion of the contract and during its term.[31]

In situations of unequal information, the less-informed party very often relies on information and advice provided by intermediaries such as insurance brokers or capital market analysts. After deregulation they acquire an even greater weight for the functioning of the market. It is therefore essential that their outer appearance of impartiality and objectivity – which is the basis of their trustworthiness – either corresponds to the facts or is destroyed by appropriate information which they give to their customers before a contract is concluded as a result of their work. It is for this reason that a certain trend toward regulation of intermediaries can be observed in financial services; it is a consequence of deregulation of the main product markets. Such regulation of brokers and other intermediaries must in particular include their duty to disclose any legal and economic links they have with

28 Council Directive 89/298/EEC of 17 April 1989 coordinating the requirements for the drawing-up, scrutiny, and distribution of the prospectus to be published when transferable securities are offered to the public: (1989) OJEC L 124/8.

29 Directive 2001/34/EC of the European Parliament and of the Council of 28 May 2001 on the admission of securities to official stock exchange listing and on information to be published on those securities: (2001) OJEC L 184/1.

30 See art. 11 of the Council Directive 93/22/EEC of 10 May 1993 on investment services in the securities field: (1993) OJEC L 141/27; see also § 53 of the German Stock Exchange Act (Börsengesetz): (1996) Bundesgesetzblatt (BGBl.) Part I, p. 1030.

31 See Annex II of the Council Directive 92/96/EEC of 10 November 1992 on the coordination of laws, regulations, and administrative provisions relating to direct life assurance and amending Directives 79/267/EEC and 90/619/EEC (Third Life Assurance Directive): (1992) OJEC L 360/1.

specific actors of the main market. Thus, an insurance broker who holds himself out as somebody who could select appropriate coverage from a wide choice of different products available on the market must tell the applicant that he effectively operates exclusively on behalf of a single insurer or that he receives a particularly high premium from a given insurance company.[32] Similar considerations apply to information provided by investment brokers and capital market analysts.

C. Competition through Network Regulation

Deregulation has taken hold of several network industries, in particular telecommunications and electricity, gas and railways. A peculiarity of these sectors – though it is not limited to them – is the existence of natural monopolies.[33] It has already been pointed out that the scope of those natural monopolies is much narrower than the traditional regulation. In telecommunications, it is only the copper wire connecting the private user with the main switchboard over the last mile that can be regarded as a natural monopoly for the time being.[34] Experience has shown over the last years that competition of infrastructures is viable for other parts of the net. The same applies to the telephone and data transfer services offered in the network; it is very well possible that different service operators use one and the same net. Similar observations have already been made regarding the supply of gas and electricity; while power lines and gas pipelines usually cannot be duplicated in an efficient manner, the production and distribution of energy can very well be carried out under competitive conditions in one and the same network. In rail transport it would appear equally conceivable to admit different transport companies using one and the same railway infrastructure and yet competing with each other.[35]

---

32 See Commission Recommendation of 18 December 1991 on insurance intermediaries (92/48/EEC): (1992) OJEC L 19/32 and article 10 of the Proposal for a Directive of the European Parliament and of the Council on Insurance Mediation: (2001) OJEC C 29 E/245.

33 See above section III.B.

34 *U. Immenga/Chr. Kirchner/G. Knieps/J. Kruse*, Telekommunikation im Wettbewerb (C.H. Beck, München, 2001), p. 37; with qualifications *R. Schulz*, Der Zugang zum 'blanken Draht' im Telekommunikationsrecht: Wettbewerb im Netz oder Wettbewerb zwischen Netzen? (C.H. Beck, München, 2001), pp. 16-18.

35 Cf. *J. Basedow*, Wettbewerb in Gleisnetzen, in: Festschrift für Otto Sandrock zum 70. Geburtstag (Verlag Recht und Wirtschaft, Heidelberg, 2000), p. 13, 18 et seq.

Of course, the deregulation of the operational segments of the various markets would not put an end to the natural monopoly in each infrastructure, which would remain a kind of bottleneck, a serious obstacle to the development of competition. This is all the more so since the former monopolist in the services market is a vertically integrated company that owns the infrastructure, including the bottleneck parts. This confers great power on that company to exclude competitors from the use of that infrastructure or to discriminate against them. The most effective way to foreclose such discrimination would be a divestiture which would convey ownership of the infrastructure on a state agency or state company, while the services branches of the former monopolist could be split off and privatized as independent firms.[36] However, this solution is precluded for financial reasons in some of the said industries: German Telekom has been privatized as a vertically integrated company to the effect that a divestiture and expropriation of the bottleneck parts of the infrastructure would not be possible without a compensation worth several billion EURO. This option is unrealistic, and the same applies to the markets for electricity and natural gas. The German railway company is still entirely owned by the federal state, and an eventual split is the object of fierce debate. It appears, however, that the claim of the railway companies board that vertical integration provides ample economies of scope will finally win.[37]

Therefore, the above-mentioned potential for discrimination will subsist and can only be limited by economic regulation. It is fair to say that in these industries, competition in the services markets can only develop by means of a regulation of the network. It is not sufficient to award competitors a claim to employ that network for their purposes. That claim can easily be established in economic regulation or inferred from the so-called essential facilities doctrine which has been accepted in German and European competition law in the meantime.[38] The regulatory experience of the telecommunications sector demonstrates that there is a great variety of discriminatory strategies

---

36 *Deregulierungskommission*, supra note 1, 359, with regard to the supply of electricity.

37 See, however, the recommendations of the Advisory Board of the Federal Ministry of Transport, *Wissenschaftlicher Beirat beim Bundesminister für Verkehr*, Bahnstrukturreform in Deutschland – Empfehlungen zur weiteren Entwicklung: (1997) Internationales Verkehrswesen 626 et seq.

38 See § 19 para. 4 no. 4 GWB (supra note 8) and *J. Basedow*, Dienstleistungsmonopole und Netzzugang in der europäischen Wirtschaftsverfassung: (1997) 16 Jahrbuch für Neue Politische Ökonomie 121 et seq.

which the former monopolist may embark upon. They include the prices to be paid by its competitors, the delay of interconnection operations, the lack of collocation rooms, etc.[39] A detailed and costly regulation of a great number of specific aspects becomes necessary if competitors are to have a fair chance.

The first years of regulatory practice in Germany do not allow for much optimism. While the Regulatory Authority for Post and Telecommunications has tackled a great number of issues, the effect on competition is not very promising. In fact, market shares of competitors which rose during the first years have remained unaltered recently, and it appears that the former monopolist is slowly gaining back lost customers.[40] While some of the administrative decisions appear to have been influenced by political considerations, others have been undermined by Telekom's repeated applications for legal review, which have delayed the practical effects of the regulatory policy for months and sometimes even longer. It is difficult to see that the market may be able to function without regulation one day. It would appear instead that the model of the telecommunications market will serve as an example for future regulation in the energy and railway sectors. That regulation has to be more efficient, however, and should become independent from political considerations.

VI. Conclusion

(1) The concept of economic regulation is defined neither by formal characteristics of the legal norms in question nor by their enforcement through administrative agencies. Economic regulation is rather understood as meaning any restriction decreed or enforced by the state on people's possibilities of economic action.

(2) In this sense, the concept of economic regulation presupposes individual freedom as the basic rule of the economic order and competition as the form of its organization which promises the best results in terms of economic efficiency, consumer sovereignty, innovation, and problem-solving capaci-

[39] *Monopolkommission*, Wettbewerbsentwicklung bei Telekommunikation und Post 2001: Unsicherheit und Stillstand, Sondergutachten (Nomos, Baden-Baden, 2002), no. 110 et seq.

[40] See 'Die Telekom gewinnt im Festnetz Marktanteile zurück': Frankfurter Allgemeine Zeitung, 26 October 2001.

ties. From this perspective, economic regulation is an alien element that needs explanation and justification.

(3) The adoption of regulations requires political consensus. Considerations relating to the general welfare that are usually said to guide politicians and regulators cannot sufficiently explain their regulatory activities, however. It appears instead that those considerations are often superseded by their self-interest, which frequently meets the interest of the regulated and their representatives. Their interests are served by the extension and differentiation of economic regulation.

(4) Since, as a matter of principle, the general welfare is furthered by competition, economic regulations are justified where the basic assumption that competition produces optimal results cannot be maintained for structural reasons defined as market failures. Such market failures include external effects, natural monopolies, destructive competition, asymmetric information, and opportunistic behavior.

(5) A closer analysis of regulated markets will often reveal that the said market failures do not exist any more or not for the whole regulated market or that they do not justify regulation to the extent it actually has. It follows that the general welfare requires deregulation as a permanent task of economic policy.

(6) Since the general welfare and the motivations of those who are involved in the regulatory system are not necessarily in line with each other, it is essential to observe duties of deregulation that follow from binding rules of law. In the European Community, the basic freedoms laid down in the EC Treaty have played and still play an important role for the implementation of deregulatory policies.

(7) Regulatory changes brought about as a result of economic policy or legal pressures rarely come down to a straight deregulation. The inherent deficits that actually exist in some markets often require some kind of proactive state measures which replace the pre-existing regulations. The package of deregulation and new regulation, however, will frequently result in less restrictive alternatives as compared with the present situation. In financial services in particular, the regulation of information and of intermediaries may be a sufficient substitute for existing product regulation.

(8) Natural monopolies are usually limited to a much narrower scope than was initially assumed. It is not sufficient, however, to reduce regulation in scope, i.e., to the infrastructure networks or the relevant parts of it. The implementation of competition in the other parts will only succeed if the remaining bottlenecks are subject to a particularly strict regulation relating to access, prices, and a great variety of modalities of employment of the infrastructures.

Part 1:

REGULATION OF BANKING SERVICES

REGULATION OF BANKING SERVICES IN THE EUROPEAN UNION: A COMPARATIVE VIEW

Johannes Köndgen, Bonn

J. Basedow, H. Baum, K. Hopt, H. Kanda and T. Kono (eds.), Economic Regulation and Competition, (27-74)

I. What Is So Special About Banking Regulation?[1]

Banking is a regulated industry in every part of the world. However, among the many regulated industries, the banking industry has always been a special case. It is a special case even in relation to the rest of the financial services sector. Why is that so?

The core of banking business is accepting money for deposit and lending it to borrowers for a term. Because it is, as a matter of principle, a creditor's risk to recover if the other party defaults, the insolvency risk is by no means specific to the bank-customer relation and therefore would not be in itself an adequate reason for the regulation of deposit taking. This is true even if there is a substantial difference in bargaining power and/or information between the depositor and the deposit-taking party, as would normally be the case in a bank-customer relation. Banking regulation is not, at least not in the first place,[2] some sort of consumer protection. The key word is financial system stability. The business of credit institutions, in their dual function as deposit-taking institutions and lenders, is transforming risks, especially by transforming maturities. As lenders, banks create long-term (i.e., illiquid) assets,

1 Where not otherwise indicated, the terms 'regulation' and 'supervision', or 'regulator' and 'supervisor', are used interchangeably.

2 But see infra, II.B.2.

which they finance by taking short-term deposits. This mismatch[3] makes their business so different from other financial service suppliers, notably securities firms, which also accept their customers' monies, and it accounts for the dissimilarities between the respective regulatory regimes.[4]

There is a second point to remember that is almost as well established.[5] Most banks are members of, and agents cooperating in, a network, through which almost every market transaction in a modern economy relying on money as a generalized medium of exchange has to be channeled: the payment system. As is generally the case in a network, the failure of one single agent puts this entire network at risk of ending up in systemic failure. And once a payment system – national or cross-national – collapses, it will affect the smooth functioning of any other market in a given economy.

Again in contrast to other regulated industries, banking regulation is founded on quite a variety of objectives of different weight and character.

II. Regulatory Objectives and Regulatory Principles

A. The Overriding Objective: Securing Systemic Stability[6]

1. Prudential Regulation Proper

The business of credit institutions is vulnerable to a double market failure. First, small depositors, most of whom want risk-free deposits, are not in a position to recognize and monitor the specific risk profile of their bank. When the risk does materialize, usually in consequence of major debtors' default, account holders will run to withdraw their deposits, because each is

---

3 The mismatch is not entirely based on a 'natural law' of financial intermediation, but has to be accounted for; for some interesting hypotheses, see *M. Hellwig*, Banks, Markets, and the Allocation of Risks in an Economy, J. of Institutional and Theoretical Economics, vol. 154 (1998), 328, 337 et seq.

4 See *R. Dale,* The Regulation of Investment Firms in the European Union, in: G. Ferrarini (ed.), Prudential Regulation of Banks and Securities Firms (London, 1995), 27 (28 et seq.).

5 See, e.g., *Ch. Goodhart*, Some Regulatory Concerns, 132 Swiss Journal of Economics and Statistics, 613, 620 et seq. (1996).

6 For a summary of current economic research, see, e.g., *E. Baltensperger/J. Dermine*, The Role of Public Policy in Ensuring Financial Stability: A Cross-Country, Comparative Perspective, in: R. Portes/A. Swoboda (eds), Threats to International Financial Stability (Cambridge, Mass., 1987), 67; *Goodhart*, supra note 5, at 620 et seq.

anxious to recover his deposit at its nominal value to the disadvantage of the latecomers. That in turn may force the bank to liquidate its outstanding loans at a loss, ultimately driving the bank into insolvency. Second, a bank run, by a sort of contagion effect that cannot be neutralized by simple diversification, may trigger the risk of the bad rumors causing other ill-informed depositors to overreact and withdraw their deposits as well. What may have commenced as a seemingly isolated failure of a single institution may then grow into a general bank run and end up in a solvency and liquidity crisis of the entire financial system (domino effect). In the first place, therefore, banking regulation and supervision are designed to cope with a confidence problem. Safeguarding the banking public's confidence will guarantee the overall stability of the financial system.

Although this paradigm of 'prudential' regulation today seems widely accepted both among economists[7] and regulators, it should not be taken for granted. All empirical evidence of historical bank crises strongly suggests that such crises hardly ever occurred under a system of unregulated 'free banking', but were the outcome of defective regulation.[8] Even though the idea of 'free banking' in its orthodox version may still appear eccentric, it is to a certain extent re-emerging in the contemporary discussion about whether banking regulation should make a fundamental move toward deregulation, or at least grant more leeway for self-regulation, an approach that ultimately counts on the adaptive flexibility of, and the discipline imposed by, financial markets. Still, for the purpose of the following analysis, it seems appropriate to adopt the prevailing 'bank-run paradigm' as our point of departure.

2. The 'Unclean' Paradigm of Banking Regulation

Prudential regulation *stricto sensu* would require addressing all financial intermediaries who are vulnerable both to large borrowers defaulting and to bank runs by depositors. Historically, however, that has not always been the dominant approach. Many regulatory laws have focused on the type of business performed by a bank instead of on systemic risk. They took banking regulation for merely a division of general trade regulation designed to 'police' the banking industry. Banks had to be regulated because their

7 See, e.g., *Baltensperger/Dermine*, supra note 6, 67.

8 *F. Easterbrook*, Regulation and Responsibility: A Note on Banking, 77 Cornell L. Rev 1079; *J. Macey/G. Miller*, Banking Failures, Risk Monitoring, and the Market for Bank Control, 88 Columbia L. Rev. 1153 (1988).

customers needed to be protected against the risk of being defrauded or otherwise ill treated. For a comparative analysis, this 'unclean' approach to banking regulation is further obscured by the fact that there is no accepted functional definition of a bank for the purposes of prudential regulation. On the contrary, the notions of what constitutes a banking business vary considerably across different business cultures and jurisdictions.[9] Not only is there the great divide between systems of universal banking and systems separating commercial banks from securities firms. Even within one and the same system the notions vary over time. The German Banking Act of 1934, e.g.,[10] initially listed as typical banking transactions only deposit taking and lending, brokerage, custody of securities, and guarantees. Today, the list covers almost any financial service other than insurance.[11]

Although securing systemic stability has now come to be accepted as the primary objective of banking regulation, regulation in fact serves a host of other objectives. Some of them, e.g., combating money laundering, do not seem to affect the pursuit of the primary goal of systemic stability; consequently, the issue of conflicting policies does not arise. Others may indeed be understood as 'secondary' because in the case of conflict they have to give way to the goal of safeguarding systemic stability. Such conflicts may occur, e.g., related to the competition policy for the banking industry[12] or, if less frequently, related to consumer protection. They may also arise between prudential regulation and monetary policy if a central bank, in its function as a lender of last resort, pours additional liquidity into the monetary system solely to prevent the collapse of several larger credit institutions. This potential for conflicts is bound to have repercussions on the institutional structure of banking regulation and supervision.[13]

---

9 For the conceptual difficulties see, e.g., *G. Krämer*, Ziele, Adressaten und Risiken der Bankenaufsicht, 2000, 123 et seq.

10 Kreditwesengesetz § 1. Its time of origin notwithstanding, this law is considered to be untainted of specifically national socialist thought.

11 On the definition proper of a 'credit institution', see infra, IV.C.2.

12 See, e.g., *C. Mayer*, Regulatory Principles and the Financial Services and Markets Act 2000, in: E. Ferran/Ch. Goodhart, Regulating Financial Services and Markets in the Twenty-First Century (Oxford-Portland, 2001), 25, 28, 32.

13 *Cf. M. Andenas/I. Gebhardt*, Financial Market Regulation in Europe – Some Institutional Aspects, in: D. Hummel/R. Breuer, Handbuch Europäischer Kapitalmarkt (Wiesbaden, 2001), 151, 157-59.

B. Subordinate and Secondary Objectives

1. Banks as Agents of Public Monetary Policy

As bank lending operates to augment or constrain the credit supply of an economy, the banking system is by necessity a prime agent in the implementation of public monetary policy – another reason why the regulatory law treats banks differently from other suppliers of financial services. Apparently the need to regulate is not due here to a failure occurring in a market governed by private actors. It is justified on the grounds that banks in this function are, whether they like it or not, the extended arm of the government. How tightly credit institutions are regulated in their capacity as quasi-government agents varies in different countries. At the very least, the government agency responsible for the conduct of monetary policy, notably money supply policy (usually an independent central bank), needs to ensure the cooperation of the banking system for the purpose of financial statistics. In contrast to prudential regulation, monetary policy regulation does not directly interfere with banks' business organization and business decisions; it only sets an 'external' parameter for otherwise autonomous private decision making. On the other hand, the implementation of monetary policy goals (e.g., decreasing money supply or increasing interest rates) may well interfere with 'prudential' objectives because it affects correlated risks of the banking business, causing, e.g., depositors to demand higher interest rates, and at the same time lowering the prosperity of borrowers and thereby their capacity to service their debts.[14]

2. Consumer Protection

Consumer protection is at stake whenever the consuming public is addressed by a commercial party. Yet consumer protection in the banking business has a special coloring. Banking is a confidence business. Banks are custodians of their customers' monies. In a broader sense, any bank-customer relation is fiduciary in character, giving rise to special fiduciary duties which make it distinct from a normal arms'-length contract. Speaking in economic terms, the bank-customer relation involves all sorts of principal-agent problems. Depositors, e.g., do not know how their bank uses their deposits. Credit-

---

14 *Hellwig*, supra note 3, 329.

seeking consumers have to rely on their bank for advice about which sort or which maturity of loan might suit them.

Thus it does not come as a surprise that preventing fraudulent and abusive business practices or, more generally, the breach of fiduciary duties to the disadvantage of poorly informed consumers seems to be a concern for the regulation and supervision of securities firms rather than of commercial banks.[15] Giving financial advice to retail investors is of the essence both of the brokerage and the asset management business. By contrast, the need for customers of commercial banks to get financial advice is comparatively low. Not by coincidence is there a sustained development toward automation and depersonalization of transactions. Commercial banks take on the role of financial advisor at best (if with growing importance) when dealing with credit customers, acting in a dual capacity both as lenders and managers of their customers' liabilities. Consequently, it is the credit business in the first place where all modern jurisdictions have undertaken regulatory action.

Two other rationales that have been cited as calling for the regulation of banks do not seem to be specific of credit institutions.

3. Concern for Competition

One is the *concern about monopoly* or, more generally, about inadequate competition in the banking industry.[16] Certainly, in terms of competition the banking industry is special, because banks depend heavily on economies of scale and, in order to connect to networks, create and maintain essential facilities. Some of these networks, e.g., payment systems, may constitute natural monopolies.[17] But so do telecommunication services or power plants. On the other hand, traditional belief holds that credit institutions as a matter of principle should be sheltered from unrestrained competition, which is said to induce bank managers to engage in too risky operations. Recently this

---

15 *Goodhart,* supra note 5, 618 et seq.

16 See again *Baltensperger/Dermine*, supra note 6, at 69.

17 *Goodhart*, supra note 5, at 615; see also *J. Köndgen*, The Advent of the EURO in Germany, European Business Law Review 1999, 464, 469.

belief has been called into question, giving way to greater confidence in the operation of market discipline.[18]

4. Prevention of Money Laundering

While all the aforementioned justifications have long become routine in the theory of banking regulation, another rationale is of more recent origin (and has lately gained special prominence). It is found in the high incidence of *money laundering* via the banking system. Contrary to every other area of banking regulation, money laundering regulations neither target a bank's business activity directly, nor do they aim at safeguarding or improving the efficiency of the banking system or the financial system in general. Even more, money laundering is a concern obviously not only for depository institutions but also, if to a lesser degree, for other actors who are in the business of managing their customers' financial affairs, such as brokerage firms, asset managers, mutual funds, or even law and accountancy firms. From that perspective, money laundering regulations mandate behavior that is extraneous to the rendering of financial services. They require both money-taking professions and supervisory authorities to join forces with the government in pursuing a goal of public policy: the prevention and prosecution of criminal behavior.

These considerations aside, the effective prevention of money laundering may arguably be said to be an original concern of banks and banking regulators alike due to the detrimental effects the incidence of money laundering not only has for the affected institution but also for a financial center altogether. Still, money laundering regulation is not a cornerstone of banking regulation, either in theory or in practice. Therefore, and although money laundering regulation is certainly a topical issue, I will leave it aside in what follows.

C. Tools and Styles of Regulatory Systems

1. Contemporary banking regulation theory distinguishes between prudential and protective regulation, the former seeking to take preventive measures against crises of the financial system, and the latter to curb or remedy the

---

[18] See *R. Dhumale*, Incentive v. Rule-Based Financial Regulation: A Role for Market Discipline, in: Ferran/Goodhart, supra note 12, 59–73.

detrimental effects once a crisis has come to pass.[19] By broad consensus, the two policies are not conflicting but rather complementary.[20] All modern regulatory systems have in one way or another adopted a policy mix of prudential and protective regulation.

The repertory of *prudential tools* is extensive. It ranges from more general devices – such as controls on market entry, professional qualifications for bank officers, or disclosure and financial reporting rules – through instruments specifically targeted at the deposit-taking business – such as provisions for capital adequacy and liquidity, asset (loan portfolio) diversification, or restrictions on permissible business activities – down to the specific tools of monetary policy, most notably reserve requirements. Among the *protective measures*, deposit insurance today seems to be the one most widely institutionalized. Other devices include lender of last resort facilities or state aids (e.g., guarantees) for a troubled bank. The relative drawbacks of each prudential instrument are notorious and have provoked the search for an optimal combination.[21]

2. Aside from the aforementioned systemic repercussions, protecting the integrity of the fiduciary bank-customer relation is normally less a regulatory concern, but is left to private initiative and private litigation. Still, there are several exceptions where banking regulation, too, is targeted at curing the malfunctions in a principal-agent relation, notably if the principal is a consumer. Examples may be found in consumer credit regulations with special emphasis on mandating appropriate disclosure to consumers, e.g., through regulations of advertising, 'truth in lending' provisions, etc. Another example is regulations for banks outsourcing parts of their business to other banks, or indeed to non-regulated service suppliers.

The instruments of consumer protection differ substantially from those employed by prudential regulation. Prudential regulation, with its emphasis on early risk discovery and early risk prevention, aims at an orderly *organization* of a banking business.[22] By contrast, regulation for consumer protec-

---

19 *R. Dale,* The Regulation of International Banking (Cambridge, 1984).

20 Because the existence of protective devices, e.g., deposit insurance, is likely to reduce the probability of bank runs, too; see only *G. Ferrarini*, Introduction, in: Ferrarini, supra note 4, 1, 4.

21 Cf. the summarizing remarks by *F. Bruni*, Prudential Regulation in an Integrated Financial Market: Issues of Optimality and Credibility, in: Ferrarini, supra note 4, 89, 94–96.

22 For a more extensive discussion, see infra, II.A.1.

tion is *transaction*-centered, focusing on a bank's conduct of business. The regulatory technique then is most frequently a mixture of mandatory contract law and traditional 'command and control' regulation[23] supported by administrative or, in cases of grave culpability, criminal sanctions for non-compliance. As in other areas of consumer protection, introducing mandatory or semi-mandatory contract rules is usually preferred as the option which least restricts the freedom of economic action.[24] Thus, in jurisdictions that accept consumers wanting to early prepay a term loan, the 'command and control' solution has sometimes been to put a cap on the term which the parties may stipulate.[25] Instead, more recent legislation, e.g., § 490 subs. 2 German Civil Code (*BGB*), provides a borrower's right[26] to terminate the contract against compensation of the lender's expectation interest.[27] Administrative regulation tends to be a last resort whenever enforcement through the private plaintiff fails because he or she is poorly informed or is burdened with disproportionate litigation costs. Among administrative regulations, price controls (e.g., fixing interest rates or servicing charges) seem to have lately fallen into disrepute, but they are still in force in some jurisdictions.[28]

3. As a matter of *regulatory style*, regulatory systems may be classified by the degree to which they allow for flexibility in the system. This can be done, first of all, by granting leeway for self-regulation, constraining the regulators to a merely supervisory function. In matters of extreme complexity such as capital adequacy standards, regulators often have no choice but to restrict themselves to setting standards that are deliberately vague, and indeed arbitrary to a certain extent, leaving the implementation of such standards to the superior expertise of the professionals on the spot in each

---

23 The phrase is borrowed from *P. Cartwright*, Consumer Protection in Financial Services: Putting the Law in Context, in: P. Cartwright, Consumer Protection in Financial Services, 1999, 9.

24 See already *Basedow's* general remarks to this point in this volume, supra pp. 1 et seq.

25 For a comparative survey of mortgage prepayment laws, see *J. Köndgen*, Vorzeitige Tilgung hypothekarisch gesicherter Festzinskredite, in: Die vorzeitige Rückzahlung von Festzinskrediten. Eine rechtsvergleichende und ökonomische Analyse (Frankfurt, 2000), 1.

26 Interestingly, the German law reserves this right for every borrower, not only for consumers.

27 Measured against the interest foregone until the stipulated maturity.

28 E.g., in France, where checking accounts may neither bear interest nor earn servicing charges for the bank.

bank.[29] Flexibility is also served if regulatory powers are discretionary to a certain extent, e.g., when a decision has to be made on whether to bail out a credit institution on the brink of illiquidity or insolvency, the decision being premised on intangible factors such as the quality of the bank management.[30] Even if it comes to sanctioning grave infractions (or incompetence, for that matter), authorities tend to adopt a practice of 'graduated responses' if possible.[31]

D. *Allocation of Regulatory Responsibilities*

The question of how much flexibility a given regulatory system allows is closely related to how a system allocates and distributes the regulatory and supervisory task. Some countries entrust those functions to a single government agency, e.g., the Financial Services Authority in the U.K. Others have the primary responsibility allocated to a (mostly independent) central bank, e.g., France, Italy, or, in former times, the U.K. Still others rely on a division of labor between the central bank and a specialized supervisory entity. Germany has chosen to entrust the bulk of the regulatory and supervisory responsibilities to an all-purpose 'Federal Financial Services Supervisory Agency',[32] but leaves some selected supervisory powers (especially the right to have banks report their financial data and evaluate them) with the *Bundesbank*.[33]

Another variable is the degree of independence conceded to the supervisory agencies by the government. By a rule almost universally followed, such authorities have to report to the government, usually to the Ministry of Finance. Yet even if supervisory agencies are formally subject to ad-hoc government instructions, their outstanding professional expertise guards them against overly tight government interference. Reportedly, only once in

---

29 The empirical finding is in line with the economic theory of self-regulation; see, e.g., *A. Ogus*, Rethinking Self-Regulation, Oxford Journal of Legal Studies Vol. 15, 97 (1995).

30 *Goodhart*, supra note 5, 626.

31 See again *Goodhart*, supra note 5, 62.

32 *Bundesanstalt für Finanzdienstleistungsaufsicht* (as from 2002).

33 *Kreditwesengesetz* § 7 (as amended 2002). For further details, see *D. Schilling* in this volume, pp. 97 et seq.

nearly forty years of its existence has the German supervisory entity,[34] albeit legally an authority subordinated to the Ministry of Finance, had to comply with an express government directive.

III. The Project of European Banking Regulation: Institutional Environment and Foundations in EU Law

A. The Diversity of Institutional Structures and Business Environment of Banking in the EU

When the European Commission set out to harmonize banking regulation in Western Europe in the late 1970s,[35] they encountered in the member states a business and institutional environment of the utmost diversity. And obviously, the national regulatory frameworks in place largely reflected this diversity. I will name the most salient differences only.

Germany and the Benelux have traditionally had, and still have, so-called universal banks with very few restrictions on permissible business activities. German banks not only conduct securities business under the same roof, they have also penetrated the real estate brokerage business. The larger ones retain extensive equity holdings in industrial firms (i.e., in non-banks) with which they maintain close links. By contrast, Italian and, to a lesser extent, British banks were more narrowly specialized to the core business of deposit taking and lending.

Countries such as Austria, Greece, Portugal, and Germany have long known a large public sector[36] of institutions with very little equity capital, their solvency being guaranteed by central or local government, whereas in the U.K., Denmark, or Spain the public sector is almost negligible.[37] The capital of the largest German banks (organized as plc) was bolstered by hidden reserves as an extra safety cushion for emergency cases, whereas

---

34 Prior to 2002: Federal Banking Supervisory Office (*Bundesaufsichtsamt für das Kreditwesen, BAKred*).

35 Beginning in 1977 with the 1st Directive on the coordination of laws, regulation, and administrative provisions relating to the taking up and pursuit of the business of credit institutions, O.J. L 32/30 (77/780/EEC).

36 Prior to 1990, France also had a large public sector, but of a different kind, i.e., with a long tradition of nationalized large banks.

37 Statistical figures (as of 1988) are provided by *E.P.M. Gardener/Ph. Molyneux*, Changes in Western European Banking (London, 1990), 21.

U.K. institutions were obliged to give a true and fair view of their financial situation in their balance sheet. Another point of divergence is deposit rate regulation. While some countries pay interest rates conforming to money market rates, others pay below market rates, and France disallowed the payment of interest on demand deposits (checking accounts) altogether. Almost as diverse as the business conditions for credit institutions were the regulatory and supervisory systems in place. In France and (prior to the establishment of the Financial Services Authority) the United Kingdom, the central banks had the say; in other countries the competent authority was a subdivision of the Ministry of Finance; and Germany distributed responsibilities between the *Bundesbank* and a semi-independent federal government agency.[38]

B. Legal Foundations and Historical Context of European Financial Regulation

From its very beginning, the thrust of European banking regulation differed markedly from the policies adopted by the single member states. The founders of the Community wanted to establish a common market on the basis of a loose political federation with little supranational legislation. Obviously the banking industry in the European Community prior to the Treaty of Rome was not in a state of 'free banking', because there had long been some elaborate banking regulation in force in each member state, however fragmented and incomplete it might have seemed. Accordingly, in its early origins, European supranational regulation did not venture into novel substantive conceptions of how to combat market failures and achieve stability in the banking system. The European policy makers' mandate was of a different kind, namely, to develop and complete an internal market in financial services. In primary European law there was no explicit mandate to fulfill this task other than the fundamental freedoms embodied in the EC Treaty: the right of establishment, the freedom to provide services, and, later on, the free movement of payments and capital.[39] It took some time until

[38] Federal Banking Supervisory Office (*Bundesaufsichtsamt für das Kreditwesen, BAKred*); for the current institutional structure, see infra IV.F.

[39] On the impact of the freedoms on the internal market for financial services, see generally *D. O'Keefe/N. Carey*, Financial Services and the Internal Market, in: G. Ferrarini/K. Hopt/E. Wymeersch (eds), Capital Markets in the Age of the Euro (The Hague-London-New York, 2002), 3.

European banking regulators realized that the freedoms to supply banking services community-wide, reinforced by the principle of non-discrimination, could not thrive as long as suppliers had to comply with nine divergent regulatory regimes and were subject to dual supervision both by their home country and the respective host country. The European Commission then adopted a policy of removing at least such divergences in the national regulatory regimes which it found most disruptive to the objective of establishing a common financial market. The harmonization of banking regulation was to be achieved on a step-by-step basis, as the enlargement of the Community (with the United Kingdom, Ireland, and Denmark joining) had not only aggravated legal and regulatory diversity within the Community but also had inflated the potential for political conflict in its law-making institutions.

The primary means of achieving legal harmonization under the treaty is the issuing of directives under Artt. 94 (ex 100), 44, and 52.[40] Consequently, the Community set to work with the enactment of the First Council Directive of 12 December 1977 on the coordination of laws, regulations, and administrative provisions relating to the taking up and pursuit of the business of credit institutions.[41] It was a rather hesitant beginning. The directive provided a first definition of 'credit institutions'. It ruled out the practice of making the licensing of a foreign bank's branch or subsidiary contingent on a 'need test'. Positive requirements for authorization, on the other hand, such as capital adequacy, were kept at a minimum and stated in rather general terms. Finally, the directive sought to strengthen the commitment of member states' supervisory agencies to continual cross-border cooperation. The mid 1980s saw the passing of two directives, one introducing consolidated supervision by the home state of the parent company, the other providing rules to govern the financial reporting of credit institutions.[42]

The breakthrough of European banking regulation came about ten years later with a package of three directives. By far the most important of them was the Second Council Directive of 15 December 1989 on the coordination of laws, regulations, and administrative provisions relating to the taking up and pursuit of the business of credit institutions.[43] Along with two further

---

40 But for the more recent developments, see infra III.A.

41 Supra, note 35.

42 Directive 83/350/EEC of 13 June 1983 on the supervision of credit institutions on a consolidated basis, O.J. L 193/18; Directive 86/635/EEC of 8 December 1986 on the annual accounts and consolidated accounts of banks and other financial institutions, O.J. L 372/1.

43 89/646 EEC, O.J. L 386/1.

directives on solvency ratios[44] and on a credit institution's own funds,[45] this directive has rightly been acclaimed as the *magna carta* of European banking regulation.[46] It enacts and spells out three fundamental principles:

- the two companion principles of minimum harmonization of prudential regulation standards and of a single, community-wide recognized banking license issued by the home country ('European passport');
- the principle of home country control (or country of origin principle), enhanced by establishing institutionalized procedures of mutual notification and cooperation among the competent authorities in the member states.[47]

By tradition, attempts at harmonization of laws, be it the restatements of American law or the German Civil Code of 1900, have been more than a mere quantitative operation that would content itself with determining, as it were, the mean average on a scale of divergent national laws. To the extent that harmonization aims at discovering the 'optimal' rather than at restating the 'average' rule, it is a qualitative effort as well. The European harmonization of banking regulation is no exception to this rule. It had to break new ground. Consequently, and notwithstanding the widely acclaimed hypothesis that the 1990s have been a decade of international deregulation,[48] the venture of European banking regulation does not neatly fit the antithesis of deregulation and re-regulation. In the first place, it aimed at a reconstruction of regulation at a supranational level. Clearly, its effects have been deregulatory to the extent it was designed to, and effectively did, remove barriers to cross-border trade in financial services. Yet at the same time, the web of European regulation established more stringent substantive standards than had been in place in most member states, whether on the prudential or on the consumer protection side. To summarize: The farther European legislators proceeded on their way toward a harmonized regulatory regime, the more

---

44 Directive 89/647/EEC of 18 December 1989 on a solvency ratio for credit institutions, O.J. L 386/14.

45 Directive 89/299/EEC of 17 April 1989 on the credit institutions' own funds, O.J. L 124/16.

46 All directives concerning prudential regulation have lately been consolidated and renumbered in the directive of 20 March 2000 relating to the taking up and pursuit of the business of credit institutions 2000/12/EC, O.J. L 126/1.

47 On the 'basic choice' between host state or home state control, see *W.H. Roth*, Regulation of Insurance Services in this volume, pp. 167 et seq.

48 See *R. Dale*, International Banking Deregulation (Oxford, 1992).

they felt the need – beyond the mere completion of a common market – to develop a consistent regulatory philosophy of their own.

IV. The European Regulatory and Supervisory Framework

Measured against the accepted findings in the economics of banking regulation, the European approach at first sight seems anything but revolutionary, and may indeed be considered rather traditional. In EC banking regulation, too, we encounter the familiar repertory of deposit insurance, provisions about capital adequacy and liquidity, or loan portfolio diversification. With regard to prudential regulation, this does not come as a surprise, given the pivotal role that the policy recommendations of the so-called Basel Committee on Banking Supervision have assumed in the process of defining uniform standards for banking regulation worldwide.[49] Of course, when it comes to the details, one will discover all sorts of idiosyncratic and sometimes peculiar provisions. In addition, given the diversity of the member state regulatory schemes and their business environment, path dependencies have left their mark.[50]

This article is not the place to provide an in-depth analysis of the sometimes tedious technicalities of prudential regulation, such as defining 'tier 1' or 'tier 2' bank capital items or quantifying liquidity ratios.[51] I shall attempt instead to dwell upon those features that I think make up the distinctive profile of European banking regulation.

---

49 See, in more detail, infra, IV.A.1.

50 As highlighted by some national case studies in *G. Morgan/D. Knights* (eds), Regulation and Deregulation in European Financial Services (London, 1997).

51 See, e.g., *F. Häuser*, The Structure of Own Funds, in: Ferrarini (ed.), supra note 4, 113 et seq.; the 'Basel II' standards are outlined in *G.A. Walker*, International Banking Regulation: Law, Policy and Practice, The Hague/London/New York 2001, 573 et seq.

A. The European Law-Making Process

1. The Impact of Globalization: The Basel Committee on Banking Supervision as a Trendsetter for European Regulation

The pressure for financial market integration has never stopped at the borders of the European Union. Even more than in the field of securities regulation, the borderline between European and global banking regulation has become blurred.[52] As has already been said, with regard to the regulatory scheme for prudential regulation, the European Union has acknowledged the political leadership of the Basel Committee by adopting the Basel regulatory and supervisory framework of 1988 ('Basel I')[53] and 1997/2001 ('Basel II').[54] Cornerstones of the Basel framework were the allocation of home and host country supervision for branches and subsidiaries, the design of precise standards for capital adequacy (solvency), and the consolidation concept for the supervision of international financial conglomerates.[55] The pivotal influence of the Basel propositions has shaped not only standards and instruments of European regulation[56] but also the style of European law making in this field. The European directives inspired by the Basel Committee go substantially beyond the conventional tools of non-discrimination, mutual recognition, and free movement, which have characterized legal harmonization in other markets for services. Not surprisingly, there is little European case law relative to banking regulation.

The regulatory standards emanating from Basel are typical experts' law, with all its merits and drawbacks. The Basel Committee is composed of the central bank governors (viz. their respective delegates with the Bank of

---

52 For a recent portrayal of the Basel Committee's role in international banking regulation, see *G.A. Walker,* supra note 51, 39 et seq.; more concisely, *H.P. Tarbert*, Rethinking Capital Adequacy: The Basel Accord and the New Framework, 56 The Business Lawyer, 767, 779 et seq. (2001).

53 Transformed into European law through the Directive on Own Funds 89/299/EEC and the Directive on Solvency Ratios 89/647/EEC.

54 'Core Principles for Effective Banking Supervision', Basel Committee on Banking Supervision, Basel, September 1997; reprinted in *Walker*, supra note 51, 445; 'The New Basel Capital Accord', January 2001. The 'New Accord' comprises several documents, listed in *Walker*, op. cit., 569.

55 See already *Ferrarini*, supra note 20, at 6.

56 For a survey of the European position toward the so-called 'Basel II Accord', see infra, IV.B.1.

International Settlement) of the G-10 countries.[57] Its status under public international law is, to say the least, in the twilight;[58] by general consent, however, it lacks any official law-making power. Accordingly, although the governments of the member countries may still have some residual control over what their central bankers are doing, the political and democratic accountability of the (largely anonymous) committee members in their capacity as law makers is virtually nonexistent. The legitimacy of the standards issued by the committee is based solely on their drafters' expertise. Both in form and substance the standards are highly technical and complex. Although the committee's proposals are promulgated to the public at an early stage, it is mostly experts and interest groups, instead of governments, who raise their voice in the discussion process. When it comes to implementing the Basel standards into European directives, and, subsequently, enacting them into member state domestic law, it is once again for a handful of experts to do the job.[59] In the German Ministry of Finance, only one official is reportedly responsible for drafting the banking regulation and supervision laws. The final assent of governments and parliaments, then, is usually merely ceremonial.

As technical experts' law, the Basel standards are largely unrelated to any policies other than the concern for systemic stability. Thus, member state governments are occasionally tempted to challenge the Basel approach for its failure to consider conflicting issues of competition policy, industrial policy, or the 'general good'. When the German government, e.g., became aware that the 'Basel II Accord' might hurt credit-seeking small and medium-sized enterprises, it raised objections against the accord in the European institutions. Such intrusions at a very late stage of the legislative process may, at the end of the day, lead to unbalanced outcomes.

2. The Law-Making Methodology of the European Legislator

Law making by way of issuing directives (Art. 249 par. 3 EC) is by far the procedure most commonly applied to European banking regulation. Because

---

57 For further details, see *Walker*, supra note 51, 42; *Tarbert*, supra note 52, 779.

58 *D. Zaring*, International Law by Other Means: The Twilight Existence of International Financial Regulatory Organizations, 33 Texas International Law Journal 281, 285 (1998).

59 The same seems to hold true for the United States; cf. *Tarbert*, supra note 52, 789.

the European Parliament has a say in their enactment,[60] directives are not only endowed with adequate democratic legitimacy; they also best suit the strategy of minimum harmonization that has been a hallmark of EU law making in the past fifteen years or so.[61] Only very recently did the European Commission indicate that they have come to regard the issuing of directives as a procedure that is both too time-consuming and too cumbersome to meet the requisites of regulating fast-moving financial markets.[62] At the same time, the Commission is set, whenever feasible, to prefer initiating voluntary 'best practice' arrangements over enacting positive regulation. Recently, the project of improving transparency for mortgage loan customers was not effected through a directive but by way of a Commission recommendation to the European mortgage banks associations to work out a European Code of Conduct.[63] It is expected that any such regulation through 'soft law', while it counts on the professional expertise of the affected financial institutions, will evolve as a methodology that is both more flexible and more conducive to private decision making, hence politically more readily acceptable.

The decision-making center promoting European banking regulation is clearly the European Commission. At the level of the – subordinate but powerful – Directorates-General (DG), the coordination and supervision of the rules concerning financial services is allocated at the *Internal Market Directorate-General* (DG XV). Relative to DG XV, the mission of the *Health and Consumer Protection Directorate-General* with regard to financial services is constrained to consumer credit and e-commerce. This division of labor may account for the fact that European financial services policy over the last decade has, as highlighted both by the basic policy objectives advanced in the Financial Services Action Plan (2000) and by the Wise Men's Report,[64] tended to focus on securities regulation rather than on banking regulation, and, regarding the latter, has adopted an industry- rather than

---

60 Art. 251 with Art. 47, 55, 95 EC.

61 See infra, IV.B.1.

62 See *Financial Services Action Plan* of 11 May 1999, COM(1999) 232.

63 The *European Code of Conduct on pre-contractual information for consumers concerning home loans* was signed on 5 March 2001 by five European consumer organizations and six European credit associations offering home loans; see European Commission, press release of 6 December 2001, <http://europa.eu.int/comm/internal_market/en/finances/lending/01-1755.htm>.

64 Report of the Committee of Wise Men on the Regulation of European Markets, presented on 15 February 2001.

a consumer-oriented perspective.[65] It is indeed disputed whether and, in the affirmative, to what extent, investors should, as a matter of European law, be treated as 'consumers' of financial services.[66] The issue is not just academic. It is prejudicial for the allocation of policy-making power among DGs as well as, and more importantly, for the question of whether investors (or part of them) shall enjoy the protection of Art. 153 EC mandating an active consumer policy in the pursuit of completing the internal market.

B. *The Federal Perspective*

1. Strategic Choices: Minimum or Maximum Harmonization?

As has been said previously, under the EC Treaty harmonization of laws is the primary device to establish and complete a common market by leveling off barriers to trade resulting from divergent regulatory legislation in the member states. Prior to 1985, the Commission pursued a strategy of total harmonization. Almost from the beginning, this ambitious strategy was doomed to failure given the cumbersome decision-making procedures in the Community.[67] Therefore, as set out in the White Paper *Completing the Inter-*

---

65 On the Commission's present agenda there are only two priorities related to banking regulation: in the first place, the Proposed Directive on the Supplementary Supervision of Credit Institutions, Insurance Undertakings and Investment Firms in a Financial Conglomerate, 24 April 2001, COM(2001) 213 final.; as a contribution to bank consumer policy, see common position adopted by the Council on 19 December 2001 with a view to adopting Directive Concerning the Distance Marketing of Consumer Financial Services, O.J.C 58E/32, 5 March 2002, together with the Communication from the Commission to the Council and the European Parliament – E-Commerce and Financial Services, 7 April 2001, COM(2001) 66 final. A third project, the Commission Proposal for a Regulation to reduce bank charges for cross-border payments in euro, seems to have been aborted, as it is doubtful whether the EC Treaty confers a competence on EC authorities to regulate prices for financial services. The Commission's agenda for the close future has been updated in their Fifth Report on progress in implementation of the Financial Services Action Plan 'Europe Must Deliver on Time', 30 November 2001 COM(2001) 712 final.

66 For a discussion in detail, see *N. Moloney*, Investor Protection and the Treaty: An Uneasy Relationship, in: Ferrarini et al. (eds), supra note 39, 17.

67 See generally *P.J.G. Kapteyn/P. VerLoren van Themaat*, Introduction to the Law of the European Communities, 3d rev. ed. by L.W. Gormley (London, 1998), 776 et seq.

nal Market,[68] in 1985 the Commission reconsidered its policy and embarked on a new strategy of minimum harmonization, under which the standards embodied in a directive serve only as a floor, allowing the member states some latitude to impose more stringent rules in the process of transformation. Seven years later, the strategy of minimum harmonization was ratified through the principle of subsidiarity enacted in the Treaty of Maastricht. This is not the place to discuss the merits and demerits of minimum harmonization in general. Instead, I will focus on whether and to what extent this strategy is workable and appropriate for the specific purposes of banking regulation.[69]

It seems that the Commission's general approach to the concept of minimum harmonization has always been pragmatic rather than related to any theory. Minimum harmonization was, on the one hand, a transitory stage of harmonization with a regard to what was politically feasible; on the other, it served as a means of giving consideration to member states' particular needs and interests. In contrast to this pragmatic approach, the academic discussion tends to link minimum harmonization to the economic concept of *competition of regulatory systems*.[70] In theory, it is expected that the strategy may work to lower transaction costs in cross-border trade and, by allowing for some upward diversity, at the same time encourage regulatory arbitrage and, through the responsiveness of legislating member states, enhance the search for the best possible regulatory regime. In practice, the matter is not all that simple. Taken seriously (i.e., not merely metaphorically), the concept of systemic competition is subject to (at least) a double caveat. First, regu-

---

68 COM (85) 310 final.

69 I am here referring to the more detailed argument submitted in my former article 'Mindestharmonisierung im europäischen Bankrecht – konzeptionelle Grundlagen', in: U. Everling/W.-H. Roth (eds), Mindestharmonisierung im Europäischen Binnenmarkt (Baden-Baden, 1997), 111-139.

70 The concept of regulatory competition had its origins in American corporate law. From corporate law it spilled over to the field of securities regulation. The body of international literature on regulatory competition seems boundless; for a random choice of recent articles, cf., e.g., *R. Romano*, Empowering Investors: A Market Approach to Securities Regulation, 107 Yale Law Journal 2359 (1998); *J.P. Trachtman*, Regulatory Competition and Regulatory Jurisdiction, 3 J. Int'l Economic Law 331 (2000); *H.E. Jackson/E.J. Pan*, Regulatory Competition in International Securities Markets: Evidence from Europe in 1999, 56 The Business Lawyer 653, 661 et seq. (2001). Especially on banking regulatory competition, cf. *I. Wörner*, Europäische Bankenregulierung im Spannungsverhältnis zwischen Regulierungswettbewerb und Harmonisierungsbemühungen (Baden-Baden, 2000).

latory competition has to be 'orderly' and must not end up in a 'race to the bottom'. Second, balancing the goal of lowering transaction costs against welfare gains through regulatory competition is a task that has to be considered case by case for each different market sector. In particular, it has to take account of the degree of cross-border mobility of market actors.

As applied to banking regulation, these general tenets yield a multifaceted picture:

As a *general observation*, regulation of banking, because of its proximity to government monetary policy, seems to be less prone to systemic competition in the first place than, e.g., capital market regulation. More specifically, with the advent of the European Monetary Union (EMU), systemic competition may indeed be restricted as a matter of law. To the extent that banks here function as direct agents of monetary policy,[71] the very idea of regulatory diversity has to be discarded.

In view of *prudential regulation*, the potential for systemic competition inside the EU is first and foremost weakened by the Community policy to merely implement what has earlier been agreed upon in Basel.[72] In fact, the European regulation of capital adequacy and solvency standards, with its exactly calculated ratios and equations, is spelled out to a degree where talk of minimum harmonization is mere lip service. That aside, the overriding goal of preventing systemic failure may, under the roof of EMU, take on a multinational dimension. Systemic failure, when occurring in a single member state of a currency union, is at risk of spilling over and spreading to epidemic proportions. If systemic failure, then, becomes a matter of common concern and common counteraction, there is no point in member states seeking to cure it by their own, divergent recipes. Not only must the substantive standards be equal; the power to enforce them, too, ought to be vested to a single lead authority. For the time being, however, neither the European credit market nor the deposit market seem to have reached such a degree of maturity as to be prone to Community-wide contagion risks. Accordingly, no crisis of a larger institution with widespread financial links to other Euro-zone countries has occurred. When truly cross-border systemic crises effectively break out – most notably in the wake of the collapse of large, highly leveraged institutions with an international constituency[73] – then (given the present structure of the European banking industry) the threat

---

71 Supra, II.B.1.

72 Supra, IV.A.1.

73 Comprising the largest European, American, and Japanese credit institutions.

to systemic stability will usually be a global one, calling for global regulatory responses.[74]

A different point of view might be taken toward *protective measures*, in particular deposit insurance. Protective measures aim not only at the stability of the financial system but also at protecting the interests of bank customers. Therefore, it would make sense to have regulators (or self-regulating organizations, for that matter) compete for the best possible system for the benefit of the banking public. Although this seems to be sound policy, the EC directive on deposit guarantee schemes[75] explicitly prohibited such competition: for a period of five years,[76] it disallowed banks to export their existing superior domestic deposit guarantee schemes into the host country of their foreign branch, even though that would have made foreign customers better off than under the coverage provided by the host state scheme. The consideration underpinning this rule[77] deserves to be quoted in its full wording:

> 'Branches of credit institutions offering better coverage than credit institutions admitted in the host country might cause disturbances in the market. The amount and the scope of coverage offered by deposit guarantee schemes ought not to become an instrument of competition.'

It perplexed some observers[78] in 1997 when the European Court of Justice validated this provision and its underlying policy, dismissing an action brought by the German government.[79] The general benefits of legal harmonization, the Court argued,[80] defeated the expectations of out-of-state credit institutions to enjoy competitive advantages based solely on the regulatory regime of their home state. The argument, it is submitted, is flawed because not only does the Court mistake the 'export' of a more stringent home state regime as some sort of protectionism; it also ignores that the

---

74 The development of such responses is still in its infancy; cf. *Walker*, supra note 51, 311.

75 94/19/EC, O. J. L 135/5 of 31 May 1994, Art. 4 (1) subs. 2.

76 Expired on 1 January 2000.

77 *Loc. cit.*, 14th recital.

78 E.g. *W.-H. Roth*, Case Note, 35 Common Market Law Review 459, 473 (1998); see also *Roth*, Einlagensicherung im Binnenmarkt, Zeitschrift für Bankrecht und Bankwirtschaft 1997(8), 373.

79 *Federal Republic of Germany* v. *European Parliament and Council of the European Union*, [1997] ECR I-2405 (C-233/94).

80 *Id.*, paragraph 42.

'export prohibition' impinges upon the out-of-state bank's freedom of establishment.[81]

Still other considerations prevail for regulations aiming at *consumer protection*. Here, regulatory competition might get nowhere because the low cross-border mobility of consumers of banking services, being the 'demand side' in the market for regulations, is notorious. And if they – rarely enough – do move, they are usually ill-informed about the consumer protection laws of the host country. Consequently, regulatory competition plainly does not happen, so that maximum harmonization recommends itself as the superior strategy. A higher degree of harmonization is indeed envisaged in the most recent endeavor to harmonize the protection of consumers of financial services: the proposal of a directive concerning the distance marketing of consumer financial services.[82] The reason for this deviation from the strategy of minimum harmonization seems fairly obvious: distance selling and e-commerce of financial services is a 'business without frontiers' with maximum cross-border mobility of both suppliers and consumers. Hence the slightest discrepancy in the overall level of protection would result in regulatory arbitrage by suppliers to the detriment of consumers. Again, regulatory competition would be self-defeating and needs to be neutralized either through maximum harmonization or through conflict-of-law rules enabling consumers to retain their domestic status of protection when entering into cross-border transactions.[83]

Among students of international regulation there is an ongoing debate over whether (and under what circumstances) regulatory competition ends up in a 'race to the bottom' or a 'race to the top'. The European answer to this question is inconclusive. This is not only because, for the reasons stated above, effective competition of banking regulatory systems is slack. There also seems, notwithstanding the existence of a European single license, to be little readiness on the part of credit institutions to take advantage of regula-

---

81 *Roth*, supra note 78, 474.

82 Supra, note 65, 13th recital. The methodology adopted by the proposed directive is far from clear. By Art. 4 (2), member states may maintain, or issue, more stringent standards for pre-contractual information, a provision which seems to revert, at least with respect to this point, to the principle of minimum harmonization. By contrast, Art. 6 (3) allows member states to exclude a consumer's right of revocation for mortgage loans provided in the directive, thus deviating even from the principle of minimum harmonization.

83 As provided in Art. 5 of the Rome Convention on the law applicable to contractual obligation, O.J. C 27/36 of 26 January 1996 (consolidated version).

tory arbitrage.[84] Consequently, the dynamics in European banking regulation are driven by the European legislative institutions rather than through regulatory competition. Frequently directives aiming at minimum harmonization, after a test and review period, have been amended by corrective harmonization if the Commission felt that their substantive policy goals had not been met by the member states.[85]

2. Is Home Country Control Still a Viable Principle?

It was generally regarded as a path-breaking achievement of the Second Banking Directive that it established the principle of home country control and at the same time furnished every bank that had acquired a license in its home member state with the so-called European passport. No doubt, this is a point of no return. If any questions are asked, they point in a different direction:[86] Is home country control still a viable principle in the age of EMU and the growing emergence of international financial conglomerates?

As the European Court maintained in its judgment validating the depository guarantee directive,[87] the home state principle is not rooted in the Treaty itself; still, it has been enacted in several directives. Accordingly it may be restricted or indeed repealed by secondary Community law. More difficult is the question of whether this would be sound policy. It is not possible to give even a preliminary answer in this brief presentation; two brief remarks must do.

---

84 See, however, infra, IV.E.2., last par. By contrast, securities firms have been said to have a preference for U.K. law; see the evidence cited and reviewed by *Jackson/Pan*, supra note 70, 664 n. 30.

85 Since the legal harmonization of cross-border credit transfers (Directive 97/5/EC, O.J. L 43) did not have the intended effect of lowering bank charges for such payments within the Euro zone, the Commission proposed a Regulation on Cross-Border Payments in Euro, 24 July 2001, COM(2001) 439 final. By the same token, the Commission is working on a follow-up directive to the Consumer Credit Directive (see the discussion paper for the amendment of Directive 87/102/EEC concerning consumer credits of 25 April 2001 at <http://europa.eu.int/comm/consumers/policy/developments/cons_cred/cons_cred1a_en.pdf>), because the transforming member state laws proved to be too divergent.

86 See *Andenas/Gebhardt*, supra note 13, 151 et seq.

87 Supra, note 79.

First of all, the longer the momentum toward maximum harmonization of the substantive regulatory standards persists,[88] the more the pressure for centralized supervision by a single European body will increase. It would seem that the current fashion of urging the competent member state authorities for ever closer cooperation through improved information sharing, development of memoranda of understanding, etc.[89] cannot but be transitory. The inherent logic of progressive cooperation will eventually espouse establishing a central, powerful supervisory agency at the Community level with executive powers of its own. Repealing the principle of home state control, then, turns into an institutional issue, which will be discussed later on.[90] Secondly, the history of drafting the Maastricht Treaty[91] (creating the ESCB and the ECB) strongly suggests that the member states for the time being cannot be expected to readily yield the supervision of their banking industry to the Community. So long as the principle of home control cannot be held responsible for some major community-wide financial crisis,[92] the call to repeal it will not be heard.

C. *Other Fundamental Concepts*

1. The Separation and Re-convergence of Banking and Securities Regulation

a) Initial Stage: Sector-Specific Regulation

Unlike the American Glass-Steagall Act, the separation of banking and securities regulation in Community law was not an act of deliberate and principled policy making. Rather, and once again, this decision was dictated by pragmatic considerations. Facing a diverse landscape of financial services firms in the member states, with universal banks existing in one half and some sort of institutional segmentation in the other, the Commission did not mean to bring about extensive structural change in the European banking

---

88 As described in the preceding paragraph.

89 Cf. *Economic and Financial Committee*, Report on Financial Crisis Management, April 2001.

90 Infra, IV.F.

91 For a brief description, see *Andenas/Gebhardt*, supra note 13, 160-61.

92 As might be triggered some day in consequence of excessive borrowing from syndicated lenders by telecom-media-technology enterprises; cf. the warning by *ECB, Annual Report 2001*, p. 139.

system. In fact, the decision was one of administrative and political expediency, because the new regime could be enacted and implemented in two steps, without prejudice to existing systemic architectures in the member states.

The downside of this pragmatic approach seemed to be a useless overlap between, or indeed duplication of, substantive rules and supervisory powers, especially in member states where a system of universal banking was in place. Should capital requirements for a universal bank be defined by the rules for credit institutions or by those for securities firms? What should be the solution for financial conglomerates comprising credit institutions as well as securities firms? And how could a level playing field for (universal) banks and securities firms alike be achieved ('same business, same risk, same regulation')? Eventually, a solution was found in the principle of 'functional regulation', which for prudential purposes does not look at the institutional structure of a financial services firm but at the kind of business it is doing.[93] Technically this is implemented by placing banks under an obligation to keep both a 'trading book' for all sorts of market risks and a 'banking book' for other, especially for counter-party, risks. The former is subject to the capital requirements for securities firms, the latter to those for credit institutions. There is, however, a *de minimis* privilege for smaller institutions.[94]

b) The Need for a Consolidated (Cross-Sector) Approach

If the separation of banking and securities regulation may be said to be a typical example of path dependence, the emerging re-convergence of the two financial sectors has clearly been driven by market forces. It has frequently been observed that modern finance, after a period of classical loan-based financing, has arrived at an era of 'market orientation'.[95] This development transpires (1) in the fact that banks increasingly use novel financial techniques, thereby exposing themselves to numerous market risks; (2) in the

---

93 See *Ferrarini*, supra note 20, at 10; *H.P. Burghoff/B. Rudolph*, Bankenaufsicht (Wiesbaden, 1996), 201 et seq.

94 In a fragmented banking industry such as Germany (with a myriad of small cooperative and municipal institutions) this privilege is enjoyed by 95% of banks ('non-trading-book institutions'); see *S. Paul*, Tendenzen der Bankenaufsicht in Europa, in: Hummel/Breuer (eds), Handbuch Europäischer Kapitalmarkt (Wiesbaden 2001), 135, 137.

95 See only *Gardener/Molyneux*, supra note 37, at 28 et seq.

blurring of borderlines, especially between credit institutions and securities firms; and (3) in the proliferation of financial conglomerates, comprising not only banks and securities houses but also insurance companies.

(1) As financial intermediaries of which a principal task is maturity transformation, banks have been exposed to interest rate risk all along. The same is true for another, if less important, market risk, the foreign exchange risk. That aside, there is a growing importance of market risks in general.[96] Interest rate risks have multiplied with a higher volatility in money and capital markets. Furthermore, banks increasingly avail themselves of the techniques of modern financial engineering, especially by using derivatives. Thus, even 'narrow banks'[97] – activities largely to lending and/or deposit taking, such as mortgage banks – would supply those that restrict their business forward loans, engage in interest swap transactions, or employ other instruments designed to mitigate interest risks. Novel business activities of this kind expose a credit institution to manifold market risks, whereas traditional banking regulation restricted itself to targeting counter-party risks in the first place.

(2) Even jurisdictions with a tradition of institutional segmentation are having to cope with a transition toward a more integrated market institutional structure. Because the retail securities business normally develops as a follow-up business to deposit taking, execution of payments, and lending, there is reason to believe that all such activities are more effectively performed under the roof of a single entity. Hence, it would seem that the traditional market distinction between banks and securities houses is being demolished[98] in favor of a new divide between universal retail banks, brokerage and asset management houses for the better-off customers, and merchant and investment banks. Generally, banks move more strongly in the direction of securities and investment business activities – as highlighted by the fact that, in 2000, banks' non-interest income accounted for 52% of their total net income,

---

96 *G. Carosio*, Interest Rate Risks and Foreign Exchange Risks, in: Ferrarrini (ed.), supra note 4, 149–150.

97 For the concept of 'narrow bank', see (with critical overtones) *Goodhart*, supra note 5, 625; *Bruni*, supra note 21, 96–98.

98 For the U.K., cf. *G.A. Walker*, Banking and Financial Services in the United Kingdom: The New Regulatory Regime, in: Yearbook of International Financial and Economic Law 1998, 505, 510.

compared with less than 30% in 1996.[99] At the same time, however, this development has increased exposure to declining stock markets and resulted in a deterioration of profitability.[100]

(3) The rise of financial conglomerates is well documented, even though its kind and speed vary from country to country. While financial groups comprising only credit institutions and investment houses have existed in Europe for some decades, the inclusion of insurance firms is more recent. Group-building involves regulatory challenges that, once again, are specific to banking regulation in both kind and magnitude. The prudential risks arising in financial conglomerates are – to name but the most important ones[101] – the simultaneous use of regulatory capital in two or more entities of a group ('double' or 'multiple gearing'), the 'down-streaming' of debt issued by the parent company as equity to a subsidiary, concentration of risks due to insufficient asset diversification, or inappropriate intra-group transactions. Banking regulation has to not only cope with such group-specific risks but also to devise consistent common standards in order to ensure a level playing field for the different financial services sectors.[102]

Given the market developments described, the need for a cross-sector regulatory approach seems to be obvious. Banking regulation in Europe to date has tackled only the issue of financial conglomerates. Conglomerates having another credit institution or financial institution as a subsidiary or whose parent is a financial holding company were already made subject to consolidated supervision.[103] The proposed directive on financial conglomerates will broaden the definition of financial conglomerates to include insurance firms as a parent or a subsidiary to a conglomerate.[104] The directive adopts a complex two-tier model of supervision. The entities of a conglomerate remain

---

99 See *ECB, Annual Report 2001*, p. 138.

100 *ECB, loc. cit.*

101 For a detailed account, see *K. Neumann*, Die Aufsicht über Finanzkonglomerate (Berlin-New York, 1998), 57–198; see also *European Commission*, Explanatory Memorandum, accompanying a proposed directive on the supplementary supervision of credit institutions, insurance undertakings, and investment firms in a financial conglomerate and amending Council Directives 73/239/EEC, 79/267/EEC, 92/49/EEC, 92/96/EEC, 93/6/EEC and 93/22 EEC, and Directives 98/78/EC and 200/12/EC of the European Parliament and the Council, 24.04.2001, COM(2001) 213 final.

102 *European Commission*, supra note 101, sub 1 a.

103 Pursuant to (Consolidated) Banking Directive, supra note 42, Art. 52 (1) & (2).

104 Note 101, Art. 2 (11) & (13).

under sector-specific supervision but will, at the second tier, be made subject to 'supplementary' cross-sector supervision.[105]

Almost inevitably, the inchoate coordination of supervisory standards and of supervisory action begs the question – to be dealt with later on[106] – of whether such coordination should not be reflected in a merger of the supervisory institutions.

2. Consumer Protection: Principles and Instruments

Among the secondary objectives[107] of European banking regulation, consumer protection figures prominently while regulation to promote competition appears to be less primary. However, there are different methods for implementing consumer protection policy, both in terms of regulation and of enforcement.

Some jurisdictions delineate the scope of financial consumer protection by identifying those suppliers of financial services who shall be made subject to regulation and therefore have the status of a 'financial institution'. Defining a 'credit institution' or 'financial institution' is crucial for any regulatory system because it determinates the question of what kind of institutions a system wants to cover and, in a way, which policy goals it intends to pursue. The definition under European law goes back to the First Banking Directive of 1977[108] and is clear and simple. Any firm will be treated as a credit institution whose business it is 'to receive deposits or other repayable funds from the public and to grant credits for its own account.'[109] Conceivably, this definition was geared to the primary objective of banking regulation: namely, to achieve and maintain systemic stability.

It is tempting to contrast this narrow definition with the one given in the German Banking Act. The German definition[110] lists, besides the twin businesses of deposit taking and lending, ten other activities, each one constitutive of the status as a credit institution, from custody over the assumption of

---

105 So-called 'solo-plus' approach to supervision; see Explanatory Memorandum, supra note 101).

106 Infra, IV.F.

107 For the concept of 'secondary objectives', see supra, II.A.2.

108 Supra note 35, Art. 1.

109 Similarly, Swiss Banking Act 1999 Art. 1 defines banks as institutions who take deposits from the public by way of business.

110 *Kreditwesengesetz* (as amended 9 September 1998) § 1 (1).

guarantees down to the discounting of bills and checks. This conception of banks as financial warehouses goes back to the origins of the Banking Act in the wake of the world financial crisis of 1929/30. The guiding principle at that time was not only to prevent another systemic crisis of similar dimensions from occurring, but also to make any professional rendering of a financial service a supervised business.

What some 70 years ago looked like a rather unprincipled approach to banking regulation may today be found to follow the modern trend in banking regulation as is most conspicuous in the recent development of U.K. financial services regulation. The Financial Services and Markets Act 2000 (FSMA, s. 22) in a general clause defines as 'regulated activities' any business which 'relates to an investment', with 'investment' including any asset, right, or interest. Moreover, FSMA s. 2 (2) denominates – in contrast to the German Banking Act, which does not specify its regulatory objectives – consumer protection as one of four fundamental regulatory objectives. The implementation of this objective is enhanced by a procedural device, because FSMA ss. 8-10 involves a 'Consumer Panel' into the regulatory process.

An explicit mandate, however extensive, for regulators to protect the consumers of financial services cannot be effective if it stands alone. By the same token, the classical instruments of banking supervision such as authorization or capital and liquidity requirements do not suffice. The instrument of choice for the purposes of consumer protection is a code of conduct to which all suppliers of a given financial service have to subscribe. Remarkably, both the First and the Second Banking Directive are silent on conduct-of-business rules. In Germany, it is not only the complete absence of such a code for the banking business[111] which accounts for the almost complete neglect of matters of consumer protection by the German regulator. The prevailing interpretation of Banking Act § 6 (2)[112] also holds that, as a matter of principle, the regulator may take supervisory action only if a bank's behavior toward its customers is 'plainly illegal'.[113] Thus, the supervisory agency at

[111] Not for the securities business, to be sure.

[112] Providing that the supervisory agency has to counteract any 'abuse' (*Missstände*) which may affect the orderly performance of financial services.

[113] *R. Fischer* in: Boos/Fischer/Schulte-Mattler (eds), Kreditwesengesetz. Kommentar zu KWG und Ausführungsvorschriften (München, 2000), Einführung, p. 109. The expectations of the consumer public contrast remarkably with the legal point of view. Thus, in 2000, no less than 3422 consumer complaints were addressed to the supervisory agency; see *Bundesaufsichtsamt für das Kreditwesen*, Annual Report 2000, ch. VIII 'Beschwerden von Bankkunden'. In cases of justified complaints, the supervi-

cont. ...

no time interfered with the mis-selling of mortgages[114] by banks and their sales agents on a massive scale[115] in the late 1990s. Instead, aggrieved consumers had to rely on the courts to have their interests protected through the award of damages on a theory of civil lender liability. However, enforcement of financial consumer protection standards through costly civil liability alone may not always be adequate, notably in cases of mass fraud or if high cost barriers to litigation exist. It deserves mentioning that in the field of securities regulation, the need for complementary regulatory and supervisory action has long been recognized.[116]

If the paucity of conduct-of-business rules is a salient feature of Community banking regulation, this deficit is arguably due to the traditionally narrow European definition of what constitutes a 'credit institution', with its one-sided stress on deposit taking, which, aside from a management's excessive risk-taking in the operation of a credit institution, indeed involves little risk for consumers to be defrauded. The 'rise of consumerism'[117] notwithstanding, the focus of European financial market regulation remains on orthodox prudential regulation on the one hand and on protecting the typical securities investor on the other. Only with some hesitance did European regulators turn to harmonizing the law of financial consumer protection, leaving the problem of cross-border protection largely to conflicts-of-law provisions. Even then, however, conduct-of-business standards were enacted mostly in the guise of mandatory contract law, enforced through civil litigation rather than through supervisory action. Of the core business activities of credit institutions, solely consumer credit transactions and cross-border money transfers have been regulated. Among these, the consumer credit directive is considered outdated and too narrow in scope, because, among other flaws, it pays little regard to mortgage lending with its special problems of interest calculation, early prepayment, etc. A major leap forward is

---

sory office has adopted the practice not to take disciplinary action but to 'criticize' the behavior of the culpable institution; *loc. cit.*, p. 145.

114 Consumers were systematically misled about the quality of the financed property and the expected rent income.

115 With some 200,000 consumers affected.

116 It is remarkable, however, that even the conduct-of-business rules stated in Art. 11 of the Investment Services Directive (which was enacted four years later than the Second Banking Directive) were the result of a last-minute amendment; see *C. Cruickshank*, Is there a Need to Harmonize Conduct of Business Rules?, in: Ferrarini (ed.), European Securities Markets: The Investment Services Directive and Beyond (London-The Hague-Boston, 1998), 131.

117 *Gardener/Molyneux*, supra note 37, 55.

certainly the impending comprehensive regulation of distance selling and e-commerce in financial services.[118]

The principles of European consumer protection and the enforcement of the relevant standards do not display a clear policy profile. If any feature of the regulatory repertory can be singled out, it is the primacy of disclosure. While there is rather little transparency as to the quality and safety of deposit taking other than by way of scrutinizing a bank's financial accounts,[119] disclosure is the supreme principle of European consumer credit law.[120] It is also pivotal in the directive on cross-border credit transfers,[121] providing that a customer, prior to giving an order, has to be informed about the total of the bank's charges. Similarly, the proposed directive on the distance marketing of consumer financial services[122] (Art. 3) mandates disclosure of all relevant data about the identity of the supplier, a precise description of the product supplied, and detailed pricing information.

The more recent European regulations – in conformity with regulations other than those of financial services – require establishing low-cost and expeditious procedures for trying consumer complaints, mostly through statutory-based ombudsman schemes with compulsory membership for all authorized firms.[123]

A pending issue is whether bank customers in general (i.e., including non-consumers) may hold a supervisory agency liable for not or not duly taking supervisory action mandated by Community banking regulation. While some directives concerning the insurance markets explicitly provide for such liability, the banking directives do not. Therefore, the German Federal Supreme Court (*Bundesgerichtshof*) has referred the matter to the

---

118 See supra, text accompanying note 82.

119 With the exception that every deposit-taking institution has to disclose its membership in a deposit insurance scheme under deposit insurance directive, supra note 75, Art. 9.

120 'Truth-in-lending' standards. Other internationally proliferated remedies, such as a consumer's right of revocation or interest rate caps, are not in the directive.

121 Cross-Border Credit Transfer Directive 97/5/EC, O.J. L 43/25 of 14. February 1997.

122 Supra note 65.

123 See, e.g., directive on distance marketing of consumer financial services, supra note 65), Art. 14; U.K. Financial Services and Markets Act 2000 ss. 225-34. By contrast, Germany still relies on a voluntary ombudsman scheme; for details, see *St. Steuer*, Schlichtungsverfahren: Ombudsmann in *H. Schimansky/H. Bunte/H. Lwowski* (eds), Bankrechtshandbuch, 2d ed. (München 2001), § 3.

European Court of Justice to give a preliminary ruling under EC Treaty Art. 234 (3).[124]

D. Tools of Regulation: The Dominance of Quantitative Methods

1. As has been said earlier, the bulk of European banking regulation is clearly targeted at the risk of systemic failure. The tools of prudential regulation are in their majority of a rather traditional kind.[125] Controls on market entry have been abolished; admission procedures are more or less a formality. Among the few qualitative instruments, controlling bank management qualifications both in the licensing proceeding and on a periodical basis conforms with international supervisory practice. For the rest, the classical quantitative methods apply. The relevant solvency ratios have their origin in the first Basel capital accord and are in no way innovative. Liquidity ratios are still waiting to be harmonized, that is, they are left to member state regulation.[126] In pursuit of a general policy not to interfere with the institutional structure of credit institutions, there are few restrictions to the range of permissible business activities at the European level;[127] nor does the European law address the sensitive question of whether banks should be permitted to have industrial (non-bank) equity holdings.[128]

Further qualitative instruments will be inserted in the regulatory framework both through the proposed directive on financial conglomerates and the Basel II Accord.

- The directive not only enlarges the concept of management control by extending the requisite qualifications to persons who, as managers of a non-regulated entity, have a dominant influence over the business of a regulated entity of the group.[129] It also requires group-wide internal control mechanisms and appropriate procedures of risk management to

---

[124] *Bundesgerichtshof*, 16 May 2002, III ZR 48/01, WM 2002, 1266.

[125] For a general survey, see already supra, II.C.1.

[126] See, e.g., German Banking Act (*Kreditwesengesetz*) § 11, specified through 'principles' established by the supervisory authority consensually with the *Bundesbank*.

[127] Special credit institutions such as mortgage banks are still governed by divergent national legislation.

[128] European law does, however, place restrictions on holdings in non-financial undertakings for capital adequacy reasons; see *D. Schilling*, The Regulation of Banking Services in Germany, in this volume, pp. 97 et seq.

[129] Supra, note 101, Art. 18 (1).

be put in place[130] as a 'first line of defense' against risk concentration.[131] By the same token, compliance with quantitative capital adequacy standards is reinforced by measures to prevent the manipulation of risk buffers through inappropriate intra-group transactions.[132] Generally, the concept of 'supplementary' supervision enshrined in the directive is targeted at the overall financial condition of the group rather than at exact consolidation of its single entities.[133]

– As will be shown below, the Basel II Accord envisages granting credit institutions greater latitude in devising and administering their own risk-measuring and risk-monitoring models. By necessity this will also involve a shift from quantitative to qualitative methods of supervision. More emphasis will be put on improving risk transparency and market discipline through stringent demands on comprehensive publicity.[134] Credit institutions will be made subject to a 'supervisory review process' which requires the competent supervisory authorities to periodically undertake a qualitative review of a bank's capital allocation techniques and its compliance with the relevant standards.[135] On the other hand, the Basel II Accord seeks to curb banks' operational risks through a 'quantitative' extra capital cushion,[136] an undertaking which some commentators regard as without theoretical foundation, arbitrary, and unwieldy for any practical purpose.[137]

2. If the quantitative tools of European banking regulation are shaped largely by what was already decided at Basel, the *regulation of deposit insurance* has a distinctly European flavor. The Deposit-Guarantee Directive[138] is also based on the home country principle, that is, the costs of failures are borne by the home state. Minimum coverage is at a modest amount of 20,000 Euro because European legislators subscribed to the economic doctrine that total coverage might lead to moral hazard on the part of banks

---

[130] Proposed Directive, supra note 101) Art. 6 (2).
[131] The phrase is *Goodhart's*, supra note 5, 628.
[132] See already supra, IV.C.1.b).
[133] See Commission's 'Explanatory Memorandum' introducing the Proposed Directive, supra note 101.
[134] So-called 'third pillar'; see *Basel Committee on Banking Supervision*, supra note 54, Overview of the New Basel Capital Accord, 4 (D).
[135] So-called 'second pillar'; see *loc. cit*, 4 (C).
[136] *Loc. cit.*, 4 (B) 2 (i).
[137] *Paul*, supra note 94, 139.
[138] Supra note 75.

and make depositors indifferent toward their banks' taking excessive risks. Also remarkable is the coexistence of mandatory and voluntary (self-regulatory) deposit guarantee schemes. The directive allows private schemes (insurance type) to be carried on if they offer at least the same protection as government-sponsored schemes. Thus, mandatory deposit guaranty is kept to a state of subsidiarity.

3. The supervisory remedy of last resort, i.e., the *rescue of a failing bank by government* or by other public funding for political rather than economic reasons,[139] may also face special treatment under European law. Notoriously, such state aid is readily granted notably to publicly owned institutions.

By the traditional legal point of view, the bail-out of an ailing bank is a matter of discretion for the government (Ministry of Finance), normally acting at the request of the supervisory authority and in accordance with the central bank (in its capacity as the lender of last resort). Today, a member state government which intervenes by granting aid in the form of providing a bridge loan or a state guaranty, or underwriting a capital increase, may infringe on European competition law in two ways. First, facilitating the survival of an enterprise that has failed in a competitive environment amounts to frustrating the socially beneficial effects of free competition, no matter whether the rescuer is a private firm or the government. Prudential concerns may certainly justify compensating the depositors of the failed institution in order to restore confidence into the banking system. However, this is not sufficient reason to keep the failed institution alive for an extended period. Second, by EC Treaty Art. 88 (2) subs. 3, any state aid, for its potential to distort competition, is acceptable only if 'justified by exceptional circumstances'. State aids for the purpose of restructuring an ailing enterprise generally pass this test, if a 'private market-economy investor' would have acted in the same way. Moreover, in the case of a publicly owned company, the intervening state has to prove that a normal return may be expected from the capital invested within reasonable time.

In its ruling in the *Credit Lyonnais* case of 1995,[140] the European Commission gave (conditional) approval to the aid granted by the state of

---

[139] Which seems to have been practiced in Japan on occasion; see *Kubota* in this volume pp. 75 et seq.

[140] Commission decision of 26 July 1995 giving conditional approval to the aid granted by France to the bank Credit Lyonnais, O.J.L 308, 21. 12. 1995, p. 92.

France to the bank.[141] The Commission accepted as a principle that state aid, if granted to a credit institution in trouble with a potential for disproportionate systemic risks, may be judged differently from aid to other enterprises. This, however, must not relieve the intervening state from the burden, even if intervention may be necessary to curb systemic risks, to make sure that the solution is chosen involving the least competitive distortion. In order to be in line with the common interest, every state intervention requires, on a case-by-case basis, careful balancing of the conflicting goals of safeguarding fair competition on the one hand and financial stability on the other.[142] Finally, the Commission's approval of rescue operations is contingent on a 'coherent and realistic recovery plan' being notified.[143] The Commission will adopt 'a more favourable view of support measures' if the latter are taken by independent supervisory authorities.[144]

E. *Regulatory Styles*

1. The Dilemma of Self-Regulation in Banking

Self-regulation and supervision through self-responsible bodies, if mostly under government guidance, have long been a hallmark of securities regulation worldwide. By contrast, banking regulation has relied very little on self-regulation, even in its attenuated form of government-guided self-regulation. Historically, this fact is easily explained by the traditional conception which has it that prudential regulation is some kind of industry policing designed to prevent risk-prone bank managers from unwisely putting the financial system in jeopardy. Contemporary experience with banking self-regulation is scant, and anything but encouraging. In a bold change of paradigm that lasted for some ten years, the U.K., primarily for the purposes of securities regulation, introduced comprehensive supervision by self-responsible, non-government bodies. By the late 1990s, the British were so disillusioned at

141 Prior to the crisis that prompted the granting of state aid, *Credit Lyonnais* had been the leading European banking group in terms of total assets.
142 Commission decision, *loc. cit. sub* 3.1.
143 Commission decision, *loc. cit. sub* 3.2.
144 Commission decision, *loc. cit. sub* 3.2.

the practical outcomes[145] of this 'live experiment' that the new Financial Services and Markets Act 2000, which almost completely abolished financial market self-regulation in favor of a statutory regime, passed the Houses of Parliament largely undisputed.[146] Not surprisingly, therefore, European banking regulation as a matter of principle does not encourage self-regulation to date. And only tentatively is this antagonistic posture being mitigated. While regulatory policy seems to maintain strong reservations toward *supervision* by self-responsible bodies, it opens greater leeway to self-*regulation*.

The driving force behind this development is, once again, the Basel II Accord. Roughly speaking,[147] the new paradigm has been instilled by three factors: (1) the rapid change in financial product technology cannot be followed by slow and cumbersome public regulation; (2) there is a growing perception that the quantitative Basel I standards based on a simple risk-adjusted asset-to-capital ratio are, notwithstanding their apparent mathematical exactness, both too inaccurate and too indiscriminate[148] to provide a gauge appropriate for any given portfolio of any given credit institution; these deficiencies work as a disincentive to creating well-balanced risk portfolios; and (3) the Basel I Accord did not achieve its own objective of creating a level playing field between national markets.

With the new accord, it is primarily the shift toward internal ('in-house') risk measurement and management models that is relevant for the present purposes. Under the new policy, the quality of a bank's loan portfolio shall be judged either by an external rating agency or (especially in the case of larger institutions) through the internal rating of each borrower. The use of such internal models is highly illustrative of the dilemma of self-regulation in banking. Its obvious advantage is that the attempt to capitalize on a lender's superior expertise of the quality of its loan portfolio can lead to efficiency gains. The downside, aside from the difficulty for smaller institu-

145 Culminating in the self-regulatory organizations' failure to avert the Maxell pension funds scandal and the wide-spread mis-selling of pension plans; see *Mayer*, supra note 12, 25.

146 *H. Davies*, Reforming Financial Regulation, in: Ferran/Goodhart (eds), supra note 12, 17, 19–21.

147 There is insufficient space here for a detailed account of the Basel II Accord, and even less so because the relevant explanatory documents supplementing the new accord are both elaborate and easily accessible. For an introduction see also *Walker*, supra note 52, 569–597.

148 Especially the indiscriminate 100% weighting of all commercial credits has been severely criticized.

tions to develop the requisite expertise, is the rise of a principal-agent problem between the supervised bank and its regulator: the former has superior knowledge of the facts which the regulator needs to know to perform its supervisory task. To be sure, this problem was already existent under the Basel I quantitative standards; however, to a lesser extent, because compliance with such quantitative standards is more readily observable. In order to compensate for the aggravated informational asymmetries arising from the use of internal models, regulators may overreact by tightening their qualitative supervision standards to an extent that unduly interferes with their freedom to conduct their business as they see fit. In other words, yielding some regulatory powers to the regulated industry is likely to provoke more supervisory activity. In Germany, where, regarding *market risks*, such internal risk management models have been allowed for, empirical observations show that this prediction is not without merits.[149]

2. Rule-Centered vs. Principle-Centered Approach

The strategy of minimum harmonization leaves sufficient leeway to member states for fine-tuning and adapting their domestic regimes to their specific institutional and business environment. Just as banking business is a matter of style, no matter how fine the surface texture of its regulatory framework, so is banking regulation itself. Cultural differences are to be observed both with respect to legislation and to implementation and enforcement, i.e., banking supervision.

Indeed, European national regulations show varying degrees of specificity, with some countries relying on casuistic distinctions and on the utmost precision in phrasing a rule ('rule-centered' approach), while others deliberately prefer more indefinite wording that leaves supervisors with wider discretion ('principle-' or 'policy-centered' approach) and facilitates cooperative problem solving. Not surprisingly, a prime example of the rule-centered approach is Germany, where the Banking Act distinguishes no less than six different groups of financial services firms.[150] By contrast, the Swiss Banking Act contents itself with naming as subjects of banking regulation

---

149 *Paul*, supra note 94, 141-47.

150 See *Kreditwesengesetz* of 9 September 1998, § 1 (1)-(3d). Regulated markets, e.g., stock exchanges, are not included in this list.

solely 'banks', which it defines as deposit-taking and/or lending enterprises.[151]

Even if the texture of regulation is tight, its implementation by the supervisory authorities may, at the end of the day, still be informal and discretionary. As an example, take the U.K. where banks are not only regulated by harmonized EC rules but also by a complementary set of domestic, meticulously designed, and rather bulky regulations.[152] At first sight, this body of rules might be considered a banker's nightmare. Yet the British style of supervision is said to be rather informal and highly personalized,[153] preferring 'a flexible and differentiated risk-based approach to setting standards and to supervision'.[154] In order to keep in touch with market developments, it seeks continuous proximity to business practice, institutionalized through the establishment of a 'Practitioner Panel' with a consulting function.[155] This flexible and sometimes indeed indulgent[156] approach to a certain extent seems to neutralize the excessive technicality and complexity of the black-letter rules.

Because banks, for obvious reasons, prefer to have informal and cooperative supervisors, the style of regulation and supervision, too, may foster regulatory arbitrage. Thus, even after most of the European directives had been in force Community-wide, some Japanese and American parent banks in the early 1990s were reported to have converted their German subsidiaries into branches of their subsidiaries based and supervised in England for the sole reason of escaping the stricter governance by German supervisors.

---

151 See *Bundesgesetz über die Banken und Sparkassen* of 28 September 1999, Art. 1 (1), (2); *Verordnung über die Banken und Sparkassen* of 30 November 1999, Art. 3.

152 This observation refers to the state of the law and practice prior to the coming into force of the Financial Services and Markets Act 2000; it remains to be seen whether the new law will change not only the black letter rule but also the style of regulation.

153 Cf. *Walker*, supra note 98, 509.

154 Cf. *Walker*, supra note 98, 518.

155 See Financial Services and Markets Act 2000, ss. 8–9.

156 At least prior to the establishment of FSA, which introduced thoroughgoing investigation, intervention, and discipline to banking supervision. For the traditionally 'non-interventionist culture' of the Bank of England, see *Walker*, supra note 98, 525–526.

F. Institutional Framework: Allocation of Regulatory and Supervisory Powers

The institutional framework of European banking and regulation and supervision has to address three questions. First, it is again the federal question coming into play: 1. Should the relevant powers be conferred on a centralized body at the Community level or remain with the member state authorities, 'federalized' only through an accord mandating more or less close cross-border cooperation of the competent authorities? 2. If centralization is indeed the route to be pursued, does the (primary or secondary) Community law provide the necessary institutional arrangements? 3. At the Community level, how should the regulatory and supervisory tasks be allocated (horizontal perspective)? 4. Is it preferable to divide them among different authorities or to concentrate them in a single, all-purpose financial market supervisory authority?

1. The 'federal question' has been addressed earlier.[157] For the time being, the supervisory powers remain vested in the single member state authorities, which, however, under the Second Banking Directive[158] are under a duty to cooperate closely. The solution of the future, it has been argued above, will sooner or later be a general transfer of member state competencies to a centralized supervisory body at the Community level.

2. The institutional arrangements in the Treaty for establishing centralized supervision are not yet in place. As is well known, apart from the European Central Bank (ECB), under current European law the Community has no administrative or executive infrastructure at its disposal. The numerous committees entrusted with the tasks of financial market regulation that have recently been sprouting up[159] in the wake of the Financial Services Action Plan[160] are invariably restricted to advisory or, at best, implementing functions. Prudential supervision, to work effectively, frequently requires early and speedy executive action, e.g., by imposing cease-and-desist orders or organizing a bail-out of a distressed institution. Therefore, a supervisory authority at the Community level would need to have comprehensive execu-

---

[157] Supra, IV.B.1./2.
[158] Supra, note 43.
[159] Most notably the Committee of European Securities Regulators (CESR)
[160] Supra, note 62.

tive powers of its own. By implication, such a 'European Banking Commission' could be established only through an amendment of the Treaty.[161]

To be sure, the ECB/ESCB does have some limited supervisory functions which it administers through the national central banks in their capacity as members of the ESCB.[162] To date, however, such powers are restricted to the purposes of monetary policy and the smooth operation of payment systems. Concerning prudential functions, the Maastricht Treaty, in a typical compromise formula, required the ESCB only to 'contribute to the smooth conduct of policies pursued by the competent authorities relating to the prudential supervision of credit institutions and the stability of the financial system'.[163] With regard to the substantive scope of the prudential powers, the latter appear to be restricted to prudential functions *sensu stricto*, i.e., for the purpose of safeguarding systemic stability.[164] From an institutional and procedural point of view, the ESCB's role under this provision is merely consultative and coordinating.[165] Still, by a simplified and unusual procedure, the Council, acting in accordance with the Commission and the European Parliament, may 'confer upon the ECB specific tasks concerning policies relating to the prudential supervision of credit institutions and other financial institutions with the exception of insurance undertakings'.[166] The ambit of this enabling clause is not entirely clear.[167] Its language ('tasks concerning policies') connotes a transfer of regulatory rather than direct supervisory or executive powers. Moreover, the Council may enlarge the ECB's competencies in the field of prudential regulation and supervision only with regard to 'specific tasks', i.e., on an *ad hoc* basis, and it is indeed unlikely that the member states – the principle of subsidiarity aside – will reach unanimity in making use even of this rather limited power. In spite of this feeble basis in the Treaty, some commentators consider the ECB as the 'natural' single supervisory authority in a truly integrated financial mar-

---

161 Similarly *C. Hadjiemmanuil*, European Monetary Union, The European System of Central Banks, and Banking Supervision: A Neglected Aspect of the Maastricht Treaty, [1997] Tulane Journal of International and Comparative Law 105, 121–122.

162 Art. 14.3 Statute of the ESCB.

163 Art. 105 (5) EC; Art. 3.3 Statute of the ESCB.

164 *Hadjiemmanuil*, supra note 161, 139-44; *Andenas/Gebhardt*, supra note 13, 165.

165 Art. 25.1 Statute of the ESCB; for an account of the advisory practice of the 'Banking Supervision Committee', see *ECB, Annual Report* 2001, pp. 137–142.

166 Art. 105 (6) EC.

167 See already *Andenas/Gebhardt*, supra note 13, 164–165.

ket.[168] Be that as it may, the unanswered question remains of whether a concentration of regulatory and supervisory prudential functions with the ECB/ESCB is desirable in the first place.

3. The allocation of supervisory and regulatory powers and their institutional separation has been the subject of an ongoing debate not only within the Euro zone. Pragmatists tend to argue for allocating the prudential functions primarily with the national central banks. Because central banks normally not only operate the payment system but are also responsible for statistical return requirements, they are regarded as closer to the day-to-day business of the industry and thus in a position to act more promptly in emerging crises than a regulator, which is external to the banking system. In a way, this argument also holds true for the ECB by virtue of its running a European real-time gross settlement system (TARGET).[169] Moreover, in their role as lenders of last resort, central banks traditionally administer a prime instrument of prudential supervision in the case of a liquidity crisis.[170] Finally, the closeness of a supervising central bank to the banking system has beneficial effects for gaining information relevant to an effective conduct of monetary policy.[171]

Nevertheless, concerns against attributing broad responsibilities for pan-European banking regulation to the ECB have been raised from different points of view.

Constitutional concerns are premised on the principle of central bank independence, as enshrined in EC Treaty Art. 107. Financial market regulation and supervision, it is argued, is of essence a political responsibility performed on a discretionary basis, which therefore should be subject to executive control and democratic accountability.[172] The argument seems to

---

168 *X. Vives*, The Supervisory Function of the European System of Central Banks, 51 Giornale degli Economisti e Annali die Economia 523, 530-31 (1992); *R. Smits*, in: Groeben/Thiesing/Ehlermann (eds), Kommentar zum EG-Vertrag, 5th ed. 1999, Art. 105 no. 69.

169 Trans-European Automated Real-Time Gross Settlement Express Transfer; for more details, see *ECB Annual Report 2001*, pp. 124–126.

170 The ECB's competence to act as a lender of last resort is, however, not beyond doubt; cf. *Hadjiemmanuil*, supra note 161, 142.

171 For a summary of the advantages of banking supervision by the central bank, see *C. di Noia/G. di Giorgio*, Should Banking Supervision and Monetary Policy Tasks Be Given to Different Agencies?, International Finance, Vol. 3, 1999, 4.1.

172 *Hadjiemmanuil*, supra note 161, 146-52; similarly *Andenas/Gebhardt*, supra note 13, 169–172.

weigh heavily, because it invokes one of the fundamental principles embraced by the Maastricht Treaty. On the other hand, it has been dismissed even by jurisdictions that place a high value on central bank independence, such as Germany or (prior to the creation of FSA in 1997) the United Kingdom. There is a twofold explanation to this apparent paradox. First, and from a legal point of view, the Treaty mandates ECB independence for the purposes of conducting monetary policy only, not of performing supervisory functions.[173] Second, most jurisdictions which separate the two functions among different institutions also grant to the supervisory authorities *de facto* operational, if not legal, independence from governmental direction.[174] Vindicating 'operational independence and adequate resources' for supervisory authorities is indeed a core principle of the Basel II Accord.[175] Many of these institutions in fact resemble the Independent Regulatory Agencies established under U.S. constitutional law.[176]

The constitutional argument, therefore, has to be reversed. It is not central bank independence that rules out supervisory functions to be conducted by the ECB. In order to conform with the rule of law, supervisory responsibility need not be performed under tight governmental control; it is enough to subject it to judicial review instead. The empirical evidence with regard to merging supervisory and monetary policy powers points in a different direction: Systems with a central bank monopoly in banking supervision have been found to have a significantly worse inflation track record. Thus, it is not independence that is impairing effective supervision; rather, supervisory responsibility tends to weaken central banks' commitment to a stringent monetary policy.[177]

Little doubt exists that the transfer of regulatory and supervisory powers to central banks substantially augments the *potential for conflicts of interest.*[178] The management of reserve requirements or the pitching of interest rates, for instance, which are classical instruments of central bank policy, are instrumental both for the conduct of monetary policy and for the stability of the banking system,[179] yet situations may arise where one objective can be

---

173 But see *Hadjiemmanuil*, supra note 161, 151 (arguing for the contrary).
174 For the case of Germany, see already supra, text accompanying note 34.
175 Core Principles for Banking Supervision, Basel Committee, 1997, no. 1.
176 For details, see, e.g., *L. Tribe*, American Constitutional Law, third ed., vol. I, p. 710 et seq.
177 Cf. *di Noia/di Giorgio*, supra note 171, 3.1.1.
178 *di Noia/di Giorgio*, supra note 171, 4.2 (summarizing earlier literature).
179 *di Noia/di Giorgio, loc. cit.*, 3.2.3.

reached only at the expense of the other, requiring a trade-off with less than optimal results.[180] The data also suggest that the incidence of bank failures is significantly lower in countries with central bank supervision.[181] Undeniably, this finding is rather ambiguous because, on the one hand, it may be read as evidence of a superior skill in handling systemic crises; on the other, it may stand for a greater closeness between the central bank and the banking system, involving a risk of regulatory capture.

A final objection to be raised against broadening the ECB's competence for banking supervision is the fast-growing *importance of international financial conglomerates*. As has been observed earlier, regulatory policy has to adapt to these changing business structures through devising a core of common standards for banks, securities firms, and insurance companies. It almost logically follows that the administration of such common standards has to be entrusted to a unitary agency.

4. Among the larger EU member states, the U.K. was the first to adopt this 'single agency model' by establishing the Financial Services Authority (FSA). Britain faced the double task of centralizing the fragmented supervisory powers for the securities markets as well as for the banking system, and at the same time of shifting the responsibility for monetary policy from the Treasury to the Bank of England. Under the new regime, with respect to banking supervision the Bank of England retains only a responsibility for ensuring overall financial stability, including financial system infrastructure and the payments system, and providing liquidity assistance.[182] As a secondary objective, the single agency model aimed to improve cost efficiency for the benefit of the supervised institutions as well as of consumers of financial services.[183] The FSA enjoys almost complete operational independence, subject only to *post factum* inquiries initiated by the Treasury.[184] The Treasury's responsibility, in turn, is restricted to guidance of the overall institutional

[180] Under the institutional framework in place, the potential for conflicts of interest seems to be diminishing because the monetary jurisdiction in the Euro area has been assigned to the ESCB, whereas the supervisory one rests with the member states, which, in their majority, maintain separate supervisory authorities; cf. *ECB Annual Report 2001*, p. 136.

[181] *Ch. Goodhart/D. Shoenmaker*, Should the Functions of Monetary Policy and Banking Supervision Be Separated?, Oxford Economic Papers 1995, 539-560.

[182] For more details, see *Walker*, supra note 98, 512–520, 530–531.

[183] *Walker*, supra note 98, 512, 515.

[184] Financial Services and Markets Act 2000, ss. 14–18.

structure of regulation.[185] In exceptional situations requiring some lender-of-last-resort rescue operation, it would seem that the Bank of England will function as lead institution.[186]

In May 2002, Germany followed suit by merging the three supervisory authorities in place[187] into the Federal Financial Markets Supervisory Agency.[188] The German solution differs from the British model primarily in two respects: It subjects the new unitary supervisory agency to government control,[189] and it includes the central bank more closely in the supervisory process. At an early stage of drafting the 'Integrated Financial Services Supervision Act'[190] it had been envisaged to sharply curtail the Bundesbank's involvement in supervisory tasks. However, on demurrers by both the Bundesbank and the ECB, the final version of the act indeed strengthened the Bundesbank's position. As neither the new supervisory authority nor its predecessors have an administrative infrastructure, whereas the Bundesbank has a network of decentralized branches at its disposal, the drafters of the act eventually felt a need to rely on the Bundesbank's particular closeness to day-to-day business, which makes it more receptive to industry input. Hence, while all disciplinary and enforcement powers invariably remain with the supervisory agency, the latter has now become subject to a duty of continuous cooperation with the Bundesbank beyond the traditional obligation of mutual information sharing.[191] The duty to cooperate has been institutionalized through the establishment of a joint 'Forum for Financial Market Supervision'[192] chaired by the supervisory agency. Moreover, the Bundesbank retains a say in the rule-making process, notably in the definition of capital adequacy and liquidity standards, which is subject to its approval.

---

185 *Walker*, supra note 98, 530.

186 *Walker*, supra note 98, 531.

187 For banking supervision: *Bundesaufsichtsamt für das Kreditwesen*; for securities trading: *Bundesamt für den Wertpapierhandel*; for the insurance market: *Bundesaufsichtsamt für das Versicherungswesen*.

188 *Bundesanstalt für Finanzdienstleistungsaufsicht*.

189 At least by the black-letter rule, see *Gesetz über die integrierte Finanzdienstleistungsaufsicht* of 22 April 2002, Bundesgesetzblatt I 2002, 1310, Art. 1 § 2. Arguably, however, the new act was not designed to alter the current practice of *de facto* operational independence.

190 *Gesetz über die integrierte Finanzdienstleistungsaufsicht* of 22 April 2002, Bundesgesetzblatt I 2002, 1310.

191 *Kreditwesengesetz* (Banking Act) § 7, as amended by *Gesetz*, supra note 190, Art. 2 (9).

192 *Gesetz*, supra note 190, Art. 1 § 3.

Commentators seem to consider the single agency model as the patent solution to the exigencies of modern financial market supervision.[193] If that be true, it is hardly conceivable that the ECB will ever be assigned the role of a unitary supervisory agency at the Community level. The ECB's undisputed core competence is focused on the prudential supervision of credit institutions. Other supervisory functions, e.g., the establishment and application of conduct-of-business rules, are clearly beyond this competence. Moreover, the ECB's expertise and experience in matters of the securities markets are not beyond doubt;[194] in regard to the insurance markets they are plainly non-existent. From a constitutional perspective, the EC Treaty in its 'enabling clause'[195] is not only silent on but explicitly rules out an ECB competence in the field of supervising insurance companies. Given these economic and constitutional obstacles and the realities of policy construction in the Community, the member states cannot reasonably be expected to hand over their powers of financial market supervision to the ECB altogether. Most likely, political pressure in the foreseeable future will clear the way for the establishment of a European Securities Commission.[196] Some day, however, we may witness the creation of a novel central and unitary European Financial Services Supervisory Authority with a federalized infrastructure, fashioned after the institutional design of the ESCB.[197]

V. Conclusion and Summary

Relative to other regulated industries, the regulation of banks stands out as almost unique, comparable at best to the insurance industry. Banking is not a self-contained industry such as telecommunication or, say, nutrition or drug manufacture. Banks stand for the blood circulation of the entire economy. While regulatory policies in other industries primarily aim at safeguarding fair competition and protecting consumers, banking regulation has a single

---

193 *di Noia/di Giorgio*, supra note 171, 5.

194 However, the ECB cooperates with the Committee or European Securities Regulators (CESR) on issues of common interest in the field of securities clearing and settlement systems. Cf. *ECB Annual Report 2001*, p. 132.

195 Supra, text accompanying note 166.

196 Cf. *G. Thieffry*, The Case for a European Securities Commission, in: Ferran/ Goodhart, supra note 12, 211–233.

197 See the well-balanced suggestions by *di Noia/di Giorgio*, supra note 171, 5., 6. More skeptical is *Hadjiemmanuil*, supra note 161, 153–154.

and paramount objective, which it pursues even at the cost of other objectives such as competition policy: securing overall financial stability.

Just as regulatory policies for the banking industry are special, so are the regulatory tools. Since financial risk is less difficult to quantify than risks for public health or for consumers being overcharged by monopolies, banking regulation by tradition relies on quantitative standards. That makes banking regulation easier and more difficult at the same time: easier for supervisory purposes, which can be based on quantitative data that are easy to produce and easy to observe; more difficult when it comes to designing regulatory standards so that they optimally capture the actual magnitude of risks. For similar reasons, little room remains for self-regulation in banking.

European banking regulation in its fundamentals seems to conform with this pattern – not surprisingly, because, for prudential regulation at least, it largely traces the pioneering work performed by the Basel Committee. Clearly, European regulation has a bias in favor of traditional quantitative methods, to the disadvantage of incentive-based market discipline. More room for self-regulation is likely to open up as the Basel II Accord is being transformed into European law. Likewise, conduct-of-business rules, which to date are still in short supply, might become a suitable field for self-regulation.

European banking regulation is a federal project. Its pillars are the principles of home country regulation and supervision and mutual recognition, based on an ever-increasing body of harmonized law, with a clear focus on prudential regulation. Finally, it should be noted that European banking regulation is still a work in progress. Harmonized rules on taxation of financial products and capital income in general are still wanting, establishing a non-negligible barrier to the completion of a single financial market. The institutional framework of European regulation seems to be in a state of transition. No consensus has been reached, either in view of the organizational structure (single unitary authority or plurality) or of the desirable degree of a future central authority's independence from government. Still, in the long run there may be a compelling case for a more centralized structure.

REGULATION OF BANKING SERVICES: THE JAPANESE PERSPECTIVE

by Takashi Kubota, Nagoya

I. Introduction

Japanese bank regulators are simultaneously grappling with two great challenges, one for the future and one from the past.

For the future, the Japanese financial system is shifting from its traditional government-controlled system to a market-oriented system through the

J. Basedow, H. Baum, K. Hopt, H. Kanda and T. Kono (eds.), Economic Regulation and Competition, (75-96)

drastic reform called the Japanese version of the Big Bang.[1] Its aim is the revitalizing of Japanese financial market commensurate with the international markets of New York and London (or to win the international competition). Many measures have been taken so far, but we still need to have some legal reforms to deregulate anti-competitive restrictions, and new regulations to support the function of market mechanism in free competition.

In a challenge from the past, Japanese banks have been suffering from the non-performing loans (NPLs) problem for more than ten years since the collapse of the bubble economy. This comes from the functional disorder of the traditional system, and regulators have taken some new steps to cope with it. The NPLs still continue to hold back the economy, and the situation seems worse with the general deflation.

This paper will mainly examine the recent structural changes in banking regulation. In each aspect of (1) Financial System Reform and (2) Financial Crisis Management, Japan seems to be in the middle of a great structural shift. By showing recent Japanese regulatory history, this paper aims to find out: (1) what structural changes are going on; and (2) what issues are currently present. Then we will consider the future direction and some remaining issues.

Part II will describe the Financial System Reform. With economic and financial developments, banking regulation with strong government control has been less effective than market-oriented regulation. This chapter introduces some explanations to this structural shift of regulatory principles, and picks up two Japanese reforms for consideration.

Part III will take up Financial Crisis Management. This issue is currently more important than system reform because weak banks with NPLs cannot actively enter into new business, even if the system is reformed. This chapter will explain that the 'convoy system' based on 'industry segmentation' ceased its function in the mid 1990s, and regulators have taken several steps to cope with the NPLs.

Part IV will sum up the above and consider some remaining issues.

---

1 Since 1996 the Big Bang has aimed to conform to the three rules of (1) FREE, or a free market that employs market principles; (2) FAIR, or a transparent, trustworthy market; and (3) GLOBAL, or an international market.

II. Financial System Reform

A. *Changes of Regulatory Principle: From 'Government' to 'Market'*

1. The Shift and its Reasons

In response to increasing pressure from the financial markets, the basic Japanese banking regulatory principle has increasingly been governed by the market rather than by the government. The Big Bang reform, especially the removal of the regulatory walls that prohibited banks and securities firms from entering each other's business domains, was the major step toward the deregulation of past government control – or anti-competition – and the new regulation of market disclosure, fair trade, and safety net.

Unlike the market principle, the government principle limited the free competition of trade from entry to exit by explicit and implicit rules. Companies' entry to banks, banks' entry to securities and other financial businesses, and banks' entry to new transactions such as derivatives was strictly limited until recently. By limiting competition and lowering deposit rates below the competitive rate (the financial restraint policy[2]), the government was thought to have increased the profitability of banking,[3] and thus both the net worth and the franchise value.[4] This capture of policy-induced

---

2 For details, see *J. E. Stiglitz*, From Miracle to Crisis to Recovery: Lessons from Four Decades of East Asian Experience, in: Stiglitz/Yusuf (eds), Rethinking the East Asian Miracle (Washington, D.C., 2001), p. 509 et seq.; *M. Aoki/S. Dinç,* Relational Financing as an Institution and Its Viability under Competition, in: Aoki/Saxonhouse (eds), Finance, Governance, and Competitiveness in Japan (New York, 2000), and *T. Hellmann/K. Mrudock/J. Stiglitz*, Financial Restraint: Toward a New Paradigm, in: Aoki/Kim/Okuno-Fujiwara (eds), The Role of Government in East Asian Economic Development (Oxford, 1997), p. 163 et seq.

3 However, *A. Horiuchi* (Keizai hatten to kinyû shisutemu no kinô [Economic Development and the Function of Financial System], Autumn conference paper presented at the Japanese Association of Finance in 2000) questions the effectiveness of the Japanese financial restraint policy and thinks that the banks' high profits in the postwar period came from the good performance of borrower manufacturing companies.

4 According to *M. Aoki/S. Dinç* (supra note 2), the Japanese regulatory framework in the 1950s and 1960s was close to this mechanism. Throughout the 1960s, the deposit rate was fixed (e.g., 5.5 percent for a one-year time deposit), while the average effective lending rate (adjusted for compensating deposits) charged to all the companies listed in the Tokyo Stock Exchanges was more than 14 percent. They say cont. ...

rents by individual banks seems to have been partially conditional on their compliance with government policy, since the monetary authority controlled branch licensing as an effective instrument of punishing non-compliant banks, and the government preference included the rescue of financially distressed banks and firms by major banks and main banks to avoid social and economic instability.[5]

This government principle worked well in the economic development stage of postwar Japan. However, now the Japanese financial market and institutions are well developed, and the market principle – which allows banks to freely develop their own business – seems more effective for seeking further development than the government principle, which leads banks to certain policy goals. Thus Japan has been shifting its main regulatory principle from government control to the market mechanism, or anti-competition to pro-competition. The character of bank regulators also changed from 'absolute emperors'[6] to 'democratic umpires' of the free market. Regulators now promote both deregulation of out-of-date anti-competitive regulation, and new regulation for coping with market failures (such as disclosure requirements) and systemic risk (such as safety net and payment system oversight). Implicit administrative guidance not backed by laws is now prohibited, and the rule-making process has become increasingly open to the public.[7]

The government and the market can be rivals for controlling the financial world; why then did the government give way to the market? First, setting goals in the highly developed global financial world has become more difficult than it was in a developing domestic financial world. The government

---

that it may suggest that the rents created by deposit rate restrictions were substantial even if this spread included the default premium on loans and any other rents.

5 *M. Aoki/S. Dinç,* supra note 2.

6 *Mr. Hisato Ichimada,* the governor of the Bank of Japan (BOJ) from 1946-1954, was nicknamed 'the Pope' because of his overwhelming power derived from the fact that the BOJ was substantially the only provider of industrial funds. The BOJ policy measure called 'window guidance', in which the BOJ substantially limited the lending amount to banks at the BOJ counter, was very effective, but it was abolished with the financial liberalization trend. On the administration side, the Ministry of Finance (MOF) also had powerful policy measures backed by supervisory laws, such as permitting banks to establish branches. It was frequently said that 'they can order even the ways of using chopsticks'. However, even the MOF shifted to market-based regulation in the 1990s.

7 Japanese regulators increasingly use public consultation through the Internet and other media when important policy decisions are made.

policy has a dilemma of effectiveness and harmfulness. For example, the Ministry of Finance (MOF) prohibition of banks' derivative trading for fear of harming the domestic market eventually led to the competitive lag behind U.S. banks. Second, some banks have developed more expertise than their regulators. Third, the international 'soft law' for global regulatory coordination, such as that of the Basel Committee, has been very active in the direction of market principle,[8] and this move also affects Japanese regulatory reform. In the global world, regulators are competing with each other, and Japanese regulators also care about the evaluations of world investors. Fourth, the financial crisis and the scandal-caused antipathy against regulators provided the momentum for the reform. This momentum will be explained later.

2. Influence of this Shift to the Legal World

However, the market is not free from failures. The typical market failures include asymmetric information. Depositors, customers, and investors are much less informed about the performances, products, services, and their risks than the banks themselves. Thus adequate disclosure and explanation rules are needed to protect less-informed parties and help the market to function properly.

On the other hand, with the liberalization, internationalization, computerization, and trade volume increase, the risk of a banking system greatly increases through interconnected wire networks. One participant's failure can quickly lead to others' failure. Therefore, adequate risk management should be encouraged both in banks and payment systems as an ex-ante measure, and the safety net (e.g., depositors' insurance) for the systemic risk – the risk of destruction of a whole financial network – is also needed as an ex-post measure.

The shift from government to market can also cause an applicable law shift from administrative laws to private laws[9] in the future. The main characteristics of banking laws were administrative when the regulators were absolute emperors, but now they are becoming trade laws where freedom of

---

8 The new Basel capital regulation will respect banks' individual risk management systems.

9 This suggestion was given by *Professor Klaus J. Hopt* at the conference on 'Regulation of Banking Services in Germany, the European Union and Japan' in 24–27 October 2001.

contract governs with the regulatory change to democratic umpires. Another implication may be that this shift could also be seen when several government financial institutions in Japan were privatized. Currently the Japanese reform of special public corporations (SPCs) is drawing a line on issues of administrative and private (company) laws.[10] SPCs are founded on special legislation for the creation of – and sometimes formed as similar structures to – normal stock companies. Thus some SPCs can be a part of the government where administrative laws (e.g., the government disclosure rules) have control, and a part of the company where private laws (e.g., the company disclosure rules) govern. However, at this moment in time, a clear standard does not exist for differentiating what is government or not; this should be clarified in the future.

To promote the use of private laws, Japan needs to make clear laws and improve judicial functions. Japanese private laws have a great deal of room for legal interpretation, and judicial proceedings take much time and money. Improvements in legislation and justice seem increasingly important because the ex-post judicial function of mediating conflicts of interests will be expected to be more important than the ex-ante administrative function, as we will see in the next chapter.

B. Reform in 1992 and in 1997

Again, the reasons for the regulatory shift are considered not only to be (a) the domestic and international development of financial markets and (b) the international regulatory competition and harmonization, but also (c) an external shock to break the old system, such as the financial crisis and scandals. To consider this third element, we will examine two Japanese reforms in the 1990s.

1. The Situation in the 1980s[11]

Even before the collapse of the bubble economy, the need for some reform of the Japanese financial system was widely recognized. Compared with big

---

10 For details, see *H. Shiono* (ed.), Nihon ginkô no hôteki seikaku [The Legal Nature of the Bank of Japan] (Tokyo, 2001), p. 267.

11 *K. Egashira,* Transformation of the Financial System and the Corporate Law of Japan, speech draft for a lecture at Melbourne University in 1999.

and small manufacturers, which have survived in the global free competition, the financial industry was protected by political considerations and still is inefficient in the world market despite its huge size.

Until recently, Japanese financial business had been segmented since just after the Second World War: (1) the banking business was separated from the securities business; and (2) specialized banks such as trust, long-term credit, etc.,[12] were separated among the depository banks. The first separation modeled after the U.S. Glass-Steagall Act was mainly aimed at politically encouraging direct finance by excluding the influence of powerful banks from the securities business in Japan. The second separation was designed to facilitate the distribution of insufficient industrial funds under the control of the MOF and the Bank of Japan (BOJ). However, industrial funds became sufficient, and many new financial products related to the securities business were created in the 1980s. The banking business was becoming less profitable in Japan and therefore began to seek chances to enter into the securities business.

2. Reform in 1992[13]

The first reform was made in June 1992, allowing the segmented financial institutions to enter into many kinds of business by establishing subsidiaries whose business was different from that of the parent institution. This reform did not allow direct entry by the parent institution itself – such as banks doing securities business themselves – mainly to protect the securities industry.[14] The major concern at that time was that securities firms could not compete with banks under the same condition if banks were permitted to do securities business directly, because Japanese banks had a strong influence over their client companies due to their long business relationships.

---

12 The classification of the banks was short-term finance and long-term finance. Among the long-term finance banks, there were two types: (a) long-term credit banks that obtain funds for loans by issuing bonds, and (b) trust banks that get funds for loans by trust business, etc. Among the short-term banks, there were metropolitan banks whose borrowers were big corporations, and other small banks such as regional banks, Shinkin banks, credit co-operatives, etc.

13 *K. Egashira,* supra note 11.

14 Other reasons include (1) maintaining the soundness of banks and (2) eliminating the conflicts of interests between banking business and securities business.

Thus the bank subsidiaries engaging in the securities business were restricted to doing brokerage transactions because the brokerage of shares was almost the only source of income for small securities firms. Also, from the viewpoint of a firewall, bank subsidiaries could not underwrite bonds issued by corporations whose bond-trustees were parent banks. Banks were also not permitted to obtain subsidiaries by acquiring other financial institutions, with the exception that such an acquisition would be permitted in order to rescue an insolvent financial institution. As a result, competition among financial institutions was not encouraged.

3. Reform in 1997[15]

The second reform was proposed in 1997 as a result of the banks' continued lobbying for wider deregulation. The Financial System Reform Act, enacted in 1998,[16] provided effective measures. By this act, the new entry system to the securities business shifted from a license system to a registration system. The introduction of new financial products was also promoted by deregulation of OTC transactions of security-related derivatives and investment trust business. Moreover, brokerage fee regulations imposed on stock exchange members and various restrictions on the bank subsidiaries of securities business were abolished. In addition, this act includes reinforcement of the customer protection system, etc. These reforms comprise the major part of the Japanese Big Bang.

Compared with the reform of 1992, this reform in 1997 was much more drastic because members of segmented financial industries began to think that a serious financial crisis would really happen if they went without rapid deregulation and keener competition. Before the collapse of the bubble economy, it was assumed that the twenty major banks, four large securities firms, and five big life-insurance companies would lead their own independent industry groups after the reform. Thus each financial institution lobbied in favor of a deregulation that would be favorable to its own group, making it very difficult to reach a compromise among the various types of financial institutions in 1992. However, financial institutions still suffered from financial difficulties even after 1992, and they began looking for partners among different types of financial institutions and overseas financial institutions to

---

15 *K. Egashira,* supra note 11.

16 With the exception that the enforcement period of some measures could be postponed until March 2000 at the latest.

enter into new business. On the other hand, three big bank failures – Hokkaido Takushoku Bank in 1997, the Long Term Credit Bank of Japan (LTCB), and the Nippon Credit Bank (NCB) in 1998 – changed people's belief that the power of the banking industry might be the main barrier of the reform of 1992. This crisis paradoxically encouraged the reform.

Segmented Markets to a Liberalized Market

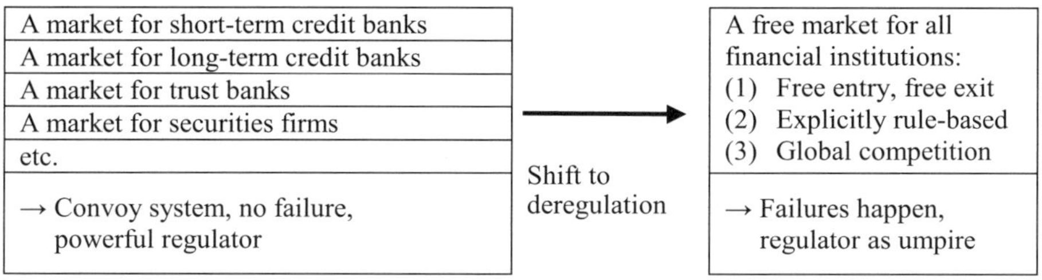

4. Scandals

Absolute power can create moral hazard. The scandal in 1995 of two high-ranking MOF officials, along with bank failures and policy failures, increased national antipathy against the MOF, and the ruling parties established the project team (PT) for reforming the MOF in February 1996. As a result of the battle between the MOF and the PT, most financial service sections were separated from the MOF as an independent agency. To make effective monitoring, a new regulatory agency called the Financial Supervision Agency (FSA) was established in 1998 by separating inspection functions from MOF. In 2000, the planning function of MOF was also merged with the FSA and it became the Financial Services Agency (FSA).[17] The FSA promotes rule-based transparent administration closely related with the Financial System Council. Though many FSA staff members are from the

[17] In July 2000 the Financial Services Agency (FSA) was established. The jurisdiction over all aspects of financial administration – including policy planning, supervision, and inspections for banking, securities, and insurance firms – has now been almost completely separated (exception: crisis management, etc.) from the MOF. With the severe criticism of MOF and BOJ scandals in 1997–98, MOF is thought to be the origin of the failure to efficiently cope with the emergence of the bubble economy and the financial instability after the bubble's collapse in 1990s.

MOF, the FSA has been trying to enhance its monitoring ability by positively recruiting skilled bankers, accountants, IT specialists, etc.

In 1998, there were more scandal cases followed by others in private securities firms and banks. Some MOF and BOJ regulators were arrested for bribery. This event was shocking to both regulators and banks. Until then, regulators' participation in parties hosted by banks was generally thought to be an effective communication tool. However, participating in such parties has been strictly prohibited since this event, and many high-ranking regulators were punished inside the MOF and the BOJ.

Though the regulators of the FSA are from the former MOF, (1) the FSA regulators were prohibited from returning to the MOF (the 'No Return Rule'); and (2) the punished MOF regulators were excluded from being FSA regulators. According to this policy, the FSA regulators do not have much professional experience, but they can start by denying the traditional ways. The MOF inspection department was not very respected, but the FSA is different. The FSA liquidated the LTCB and NCB in 1998 based on the results of the inspections. One high-ranking MOF official is reported to have criticized FSA regulators for not respecting the continuity of the former banking administration, which protected the LTCB and NCB by the traditional convoy system.[18]

5. Banks' Reactions

To survive the competition, as U.S. and EU banks do, the coalition among banks and securities firms, insurance, etc., has also been active. For example, the Industrial Bank of Japan (IBJ), the leading long-term credit bank, and Nomura Securities, the leading securities firm, co-established two new financial investment firms of derivatives and pension funds in 1998. This move further extinguishes the barriers among formerly segmented industries.

Japanese banks also began to integrate with each other to become bigger to follow the world trend of integration.[19] Some law reforms assisted this move. The merger and consolidation system was reformed in 1997. 'Share exchange' was introduced into the Commercial Code[20] in 1999. The corpora-

---

[18] *Y. Fujii*, Kinyû saisei no gosan [What Was Wrong with Japanese Financial Revitalization?] (Tokyo, 2001), p. 85.

[19] For example, U.S. Travelers Group merged with U.S. Citicorp in 1998.

[20] Shôhô, Law No. 48/1899, last amended by Law No. 149/2001.

tion division system was adopted in 2000. Regarding the Antimonopoly

Inter-Industry Coalitions and Integration Movements in December 1999

Fire Insurance	Life Insurance	**Banks**		Securities	Trust Banks
Nichido Yasuda	Yasuda	**Fuji**	**→MIZUHO Group**		Yasuda Fuji
	Dai-ichi	**IBJ**		Nomura Shin-Nihon Wako	
Nissan Taisei	Fukoku Asahi	**DKB**		Kankaku	DKB
Sumitomo	Sumitomo	**Sumitomo**	**→Bank of Mitsui-Sumitomo**	Daiwa	Sumitomo
Mitsui Nippon Kôa	Mitsui Nippon	**Sakura**		Kôei-Ishino Yamatane	Mitsui Chûô
Tokyo Marine Nisshin	Meiji	**BTM**		Nikko Kokusai BTM Personal	Nippon Mitsubishi
Kôa	Daido Taiyô	**Sanwa**	**→ UFJ Group**	Universal	Tôyô
		Tôkai		Tôkai Maruman	
		Asahi			
Fuji	Tokyo	**Daiwa**		Cosmo	

Names of bank groups as of December 2001

Law,[21] the general ban on setting up a 'genuine' holding company existed until 1997, but this restriction was lifted in order to cope with world competition by making new laws.[22] As a result, integration was promoted by

21 Shiteki dokusen no kinshi oyobi kôsei torihiki no kakuho ni kansuru hôritsu, Law No. 54/1947, last amended by Law No. 129/2001.

22 The MOF introduced a law providing for special exceptions to be applied to the mergers of banks in 1997, but this law was unpopular because it was too complex. In 1999 the Ministry of Justice introduced another bill to the Diet which provides for cont. ...

mergers (e.g., the case of setting up Mitsui-Sumitomo Bank by the merger of Sumitomo Bank and Sakura Bank), or by jointly establishing a holding company whereby they become its subsidiaries (e.g., the case of making the Mizuho Financial Group of Industrial Bank of Japan, Fuji Bank, and Daiichi Kangyo Bank).

However, the economy of size is not the answer for the revival of Japanese banking. Banks need to improve their judging ability for lending to increase promising lending of growing companies. Banks have long been accustomed to following what regulators say and avoiding taking risks, but they also have to change their ways.

C. Changes in Decision-Making Procedures

Segmentation produced different rules, markets, and products to deal with among the financial institutions, and the frequent use of strong but implicit[23] administrative guidance. Now the administrative guidance not backed by formal rules became less effective by legislating the Administrative Procedure Act[24] of 1993, and the discussions held at the meeting of advisory councils have been immediately made public in written form since 1995. In addition, the right to request the disclosure of administrative documents was provided by the Law Concerning Access to Information Held by Administrative Organs.[25]

To consider this shift, let's look at the features in regulators' decision making.

---

share exchange and is applied not only to the banks but also to all stock corporations. This promoted the setting up of holding companies.

23 It was sometimes not explicitly written, and prohibited to record on tape or notes.

24 Gyôsei tetsuzuki-hô, Law No. 88/1993, last amended by Law No. 160/1999.

25 Gyôsei kikan no hoyû suru jôhô no kôkai ni kansuru hôritsu, Law No. 42/1999, last amended by Law No. 140/2001. The purpose of this law is stated in article 1 as follows: 'to strive for greater disclosure of information held by administrative organs thereby ensuring that the government is accountable to the people for its various operations, and to contribute to the promotion of a fair and democratic administration that is subject to the people's accurate understanding and criticism'. See <www.soumu.go.jp/gyoukan/kanri/translation3.htm>.

1. 'Ex-ante' Monitoring vs. 'Ex-post' Monitoring

The Japanese traditional rulemaking style may be viewed as ex-ante monitoring, where parties with multiple interests who participate in the process serve as ex-ante monitors of legislation or administrative rulemaking.[26] During the existence of ex-ante monitoring, there was virtually no judicial challenge to legislation or administrative rules in Japan. On the other hand, ex-post monitoring, where parties litigate legislation or administrative rules, is more popular in the United States. Administrative rulemaking is more vulnerable to judicial challenge than administrative adjudication in the U.S. Ex-ante monitoring is less costly but provides fewer choices compared with ex-post monitoring. Where a regulator serves as a mediator, industry segmentation (or a specialized banking system where long-term credit banks, ordinary banks, and foreign exchange banks are separately regulated) is a necessary condition for ex-ante monitoring to work properly. However, this segmentation ceased with the Big Bang, and ex-ante monitoring now seems much less effective.

2. Adoption of 'Ex-post' Monitoring

To implement ex-post monitoring, the Japanese government needs to offer effective dispute resolution or systems for evaluating the administration. However, such systems do not seem well prepared. Although the Japanese Bankers Association started arbitration services in 1999, there are still few effective ombudsmen[27] and ADRs (Alternative Dispute Resolution). Adoption of effective financial ADRs is now under discussion in the general judicial reform in Japan. In this sense, financial reform necessitates judicial reform.

The monitoring shift from ex ante to ex post, together with the specialization of banking such as FE (Financial Engineering), IT (Information Tech-

---

[26] This classification was first made by *Professor H. Kanda* in his presentation 'Finance Bureaucracy and the Regulation of Financial Markets in Japan' in Germany in 1995, published in: H. Baum (ed.), Japan: Economic Success and Legal System (Berlin/New York, 1997) p. 365 et seq.

[27] Regional governments such as Kawasaki City adopted the civil ombudsman in 1990. In Australia, the Australian Banking Industry Ombudsman Scheme provides a free, independent, complaint resolution service for bank customers and, as of 1998, all small businesses having unresolved complaints involving up to AU$ 150,000.

nology), etc., will also change the relationship between banks and their authorities. Needless to say, major banks often have more advanced skills in banking than regulators. In such cases, the regulators' role as a mediator in ex-ante monitoring seems difficult to sustain. Thus the more rule-based, market-oriented, and transparent regulation may be needed.

III. Financial Crisis Management

A. The Collapse of the Convoy System

Segmentation also supported the convoy system with its no-failure policy.[28] For a long time bankruptcies of banks in Japan were unknown, but recently they have increased. What happened to the convoy system?

In December 1995, the former Financial System Research Council (FSRC; *Kinyû Seido Shingi-kai*) proposed the shift from the convoy system (*gosô-sendan hôshiki*)[29] to the market discipline-oriented system with more transparency. In the postwar period, it was necessary to increase bank deposits to supply industry funds to companies. To this end, banking regulators tried to make depositors feel secure through preventing banks' bankruptcies by growing major banks and letting them save the less competitive, small banks. Thus the discipline of bank management came mainly from administrative guidance rather than the market.

By the first half of the 1990s, the convoy system had already substantially ceased to function. One of the reasons is that the market became so highly competitive that the no-failure policy was difficult to maintain. The no-failure policy did not seem to stem directly from the power of the Japanese bureaucrats, but was dependent on financial industry segmentation in Japan.[30] The other reason is that major banks also suffer from their own NPLs and do not have funds to care for small banks, even if asked by the regulators.

Following the above proposal, the Japanese government adopted new measures for bank failures: prompt corrective action (PCA). PCA started in

---

[28] The policy that does not let banks go bankrupt.

[29] The system led by the MOF and the BOJ that designated major banks to help small banks out of bankruptcy. Thanks to this policy, Japanese banks had been free of bankruptcy until recently.

[30] This understanding was given by *Professor H. Kanda* at the presentation, supra note 26.

1998 and allowed regulators to promptly order banks to correct or stop bad bank operations based on their equity ratios.

B. Brief History

1. The Deposit Insurance System[31]

The Japanese Deposit Insurance Corporation (DIC) was established in 1971 based on a U.S. model. There are two options for the DIC to take when a bank stops repaying the deposit. First, the DIC may pay at maximum a principal of ten million yen (84,000 U.S. dollars) plus interest to each depositor on behalf of the bank, and the bank will be liquidated (pay-offs). Second, the DIC may ask another bank to acquire an insolvent bank and reimburse the latter's loss if this cost is less than pay-offs. These measures were not actually used until 1992, or as long as the convoy system actually worked. Big banks rescued small banks from bankruptcy without any help from the DIC because such acquisitions were thought to contribute to the economies of scale for the big banks.

However, the collapse of the bubble economy changed the system as stated above, and today no bank is willing to rescue another bank without – or even with – financial support from the DIC to reimburse their loss. This increased concern about the risk of a bank run against several small banks, and extraordinary measures were introduced in 1996 that would be in effect through March 2001 (later extended to March 2002): first, the DIC gave financial support to the rescuing bank even if it cost more than the pay-offs;[32] and second, the DIC guaranteed the deposits over ten million yen in full.

---

[31] *K. Egashira,* supra note 11, and *H. Yanagisawa,* Japan's Financial Sector Reform: Progress and Challenges, 3 September 2001, <www.fsa.go.jp/gaiyou/gaiyoue/presen/p20010903.html>.

[32] A total of 57 insolvent banks were rescued by financial support from the DIC between 1992 and June 1999.

2. 1997-98 Crisis and Public Funds Injection[33]

In 1997-98, a few banks became insolvent and major banks needed to be recapitalized. Thus two laws were enacted in October 1998: (1) the Financial Reconstruction Law,[34] which stipulates the provisions to address failed institutions; and (2) the Financial Function Early Strengthening Law,[35] which authorizes the public funds injection to banks.[36] In order to decide whether or not to inject funds, it is necessary to grasp the financial conditions correctly by comprehensive and strict examination of the appropriateness of loan classification and loan loss provisioning. The Financial Reconstruction Commission (FRC), which was established concurrently with the enactment of the Financial Reconstruction Law, may appoint and order a financial administrator to take charge of the business and property of an insolvent bank. The failed bank's bad loans may be brought according to the valuation standards of the FRC, and newly issued shares may be acquired by the Resolution and Collection Corporation (RCC). The FRC can also decide to establish a successor bank (a bridge bank) by the DIC to take the failed bank's business when it is difficult to find a bank to acquire the failed bank. The other method for dealing with a failed bank is special public management.[37]

From July to October 1998, the FSA examined all nineteen major banks and recognized the failure of the Long-Term Credit Bank of Japan (LTCB) in October and Nippon Credit Bank (NCB) in December 1998. In March 1999 they decided to inject public funds into all other major banks except one, and the Japanese banks regained stability and recovered from the near crisis in 1997 and 1998. In July 1999, the revised inspection procedures

---

33 *K. Egashira*, supra note 11, and *H. Yanagisawa*, supra note 31.

34 Kinyû kinô no saisei no tame no kinkyû sochi ni kansuru hôritsu, Law No. 132/1998, last amended by Law No. 155/2001.

35 Kinyû kinô no sôki kenzen-ka no tame no kinkyû sochi ni kansuru hôritsu, Law No. 143/1998, last amended by Law No. 129/2001.

36 The public funds for the enforcement of these two laws are 18 trillion yen (151 billion U.S. dollars) for the Reconstruction Law and 25 trillion yen (210 billion U.S. dollars) for the Early Strengthening Law.

37 This method was applied for the case of LTCB and NCB. For details, see *K. Egashira*, supra note 11. A big debate was made in 2000 concerning the guarantee clause in the consignment contract of these banks. This clause promises that the government will buy back the loans if it depreciates more than 20 percent within three years, in order to avoid the loss of the buyer. It attracted many criticisms by the taxpayers.

evolved into the *Financial Inspection Manual,* official standards that are fully compatible with the Basel Committee's *Framework for Internal Control Systems in Banking Organizations* (September 1998). In 2001, the Financial Crisis Response Council (FCRC), chaired by the prime minister, was established to address any systemic risks in the financial world, and the Japanese government was free to resort to necessary actions including additional injection of public funds.[38]

Japanese Bank Bankruptcies in 1990s

1992	Tôyô Credit Cooperative
1995	Tokyo Kyôwa Credit Cooperative, Anzen Credit Cooperative, Cosmo Credit Cooperative, Kizu Credit Cooperative, Osaka Credit Cooperative, Hyôgo Bank
1996	Jûsen, Taiheiyô Bank, Hanna Bank
1997	Hokkaidô Takushoku Bank, Tokuyo City Bank
1998	*LTCB, NCB*

Note: Italics indicate major banks.

C. Current Situation

1. Current Situation[39]

Many countries experienced the bank crises in the 1980s and 1990s, but most of them were not so prolonged as in Japan. After the recovery from the crisis in 1997, the NPLs increased again. As of 31 March 2001, major Japanese banks still have outstanding NPLs of approximately 17.4 trillion yen (146 billion U.S. dollars), which amounts to 5.7 percent of some 304 trillion yen in total outstanding loans. In spite of the above-mentioned efforts, the NPLs are even increasing with deflation. Minister H. Yanagisawa,[40] who was nominated as minister again after an interval of a few years, said, 'I believed that the time had finally come to take a step forward for the re-establishment of Japan's financial structure. However, the

[38] Currently up to 15 trillion yen has been allocated for such measures at any time.
[39] *H. Yanagisawa*, supra note 31.
[40] *H. Yanagisawa*, supra note 31.

reality has been different. The weak Japanese economy only allows me to devote most of my time to again initiating and implementing policies to ensure the financial soundness of the nation's financial institutions'.

The Durations of Bank Crises

Australia	1989-1992	Canada	1983-1985
Denmark	1987-1992	Finland	1991-1994
Italy	1990-1995	New Zealand	1989-1990
Norway	1987-1993	Sweden	1990-1993
U.S.A.	1980-1992	U.K.	1991-1992

The Japanese government is therefore urging banks to implement final disposal of their NPLs as their first priority. The banks are expected to finally dispose of loans classified as 'in danger of bankruptcy' or worse within two or three years. Moreover, the function of the RCC will be expanded to be able to engage in trust business on banks' behalf, which will provide supplementary measures to dispose of NPLs. The government estimates that the ratio of NPLs to total loans outstanding at the major banks will decrease to below four percent by March 2005. Currently the government is trying to (1) increase an allowance (maximum of 15 percent) for 'need attention' loans to construction, real estate, and sales and (2) make the RCC's acquisition of NPLs easier.

2. Some Arguments

However, the opposition parties and some analysts say that the aggregate of NPLs is actually much higher than that indicated by the banks' own disclosures. Some bankers argue that allocating sufficient provisioning for all the potential bad debts would lower the banks' capital adequacy ratios. Others insist that an additional injection of public funds would be required because the NPL amounts have been increasing since 1998 as a result of the general deflation,[41] not bad bank management. Whether the NPLs are bigger or not, we have to take effective measures to reduce them by identifying bad banks

[41] According to this theory, deflation causes substantial increase of debt and price-down of assets of the industries including construction, real estate, services, etc., which results in the increase of banks' NPLs.

and growing good banks through the injection of public funds of the least necessary amounts.

There is another issue peculiar to Japan. According to Egashira, 'borrower protection' is very controversial because of the following reasons.[42] With bank insolvency, depositors as well as borrowers suffer serious difficulty from Japanese financial practices because they usually borrow money consistently from one bank. In other words, they do not borrow money from many banks on a project-by-project basis. Accordingly, they are very concerned about the prospects for smooth financing after the transfer of the business of their failed lender bank. Furthermore, in relation to the insolvency of Japanese banks, this practice of continuous relations between the lender and the borrower has also led to the amount of bad loans of the failed bank gradually increasing after the insolvency of the bank, because borrowers who lose their pipeline of finance go bankrupt one after another. This concern is especially important in cases of insolvent regional banks whose borrowers are primarily comprised of small and medium enterprises.[43] However, there is also merit in this aspect of Japanese finance. Under this Japanese corporate finance framework, unlike the project finance system, losses can be covered by the debtors' retained earnings and their current profits from other profitable business.[44]

IV. Toward the Future

A. Summary

Based on recent Japanese regulatory history, the structural changes and current issues may be summed up as follows.

1. With economic and financial developments, banking regulation with strong government control has been less effective than market-oriented regulation. Current regulatory principle in Japan is shifting from

---

42 *K. Egashira*, supra note 11.

43 The failure of Hokkaido Takushoku Bank, which was not nominally classified as a regional bank but centers its business mostly in Hokkaido, adversely affected the economy in Hokkaido. Many economists criticize the regulators for not having saved Hokkaido Takushoku Bank when they saved LTCB and NCB, which were classified as long-term credit banks that primarily invest funds in large companies all over Japan.

44 See *H. Yanagisawa*, supra note 31.

government to market or anti-competition to pro-competition. Regulators are now promoting both deregulation of out-of-date anti-competitive regulation, and new regulation for coping with market failures – such as disclosure requirements – and systemic risk – such as safety net and payment system oversight.

2. The reasons for this shift are not only (a) domestic and international development of financial markets and (b) international regulatory competition and harmonization, but also (c) external shocks such as financial crises and scandals that broke the old system. Big bank failures in 1997 and the scandals in 1998 caused the crash of traditional Japanese financial industry segmentation, which eased drastic reforms such as the Japanese Big Bang.
3. This shift from government to market will also change the character of the regulator from emperor to umpire, the applicable laws from administrative laws to private laws, and the interests coordination method from ex-ante administrative mediation to ex-post judicial trial or alternative dispute resolution (ADR). Thus this financial system reform will also prompt the law and judicial reform.
4. The traditional Japanese safety net was the convoy system, where the leading bank in the segmented financial industry would rescue the failing bank under implicit administrative guidance. However, such a system cannot work anymore because segmentation has been reformed; even the leading banks suffer from a large number of NPLs and cannot rescue the failing banks. Thus Japanese regulators have been trying to prepare the new transparent safety net, such as empowerment of the DIC, applicable to the new market-oriented system. Further public funds have been injected into banks, and bank liquidation procedures have been prepared.
5. The NPLs issue is currently more important than the system reform because weak banks with NPLs cannot actively enter into new businesses even if free entry is newly allowed. In spite of the efforts taken by banks and regulators, the NPLs are increasing with deflation. The Japanese government is urging banks to implement final disposal of their NPLs as a first priority.

B. Toward the Future

Even if the economic impact of NPLs may be huge in some years, the shift from government to market will surely continue because the traditional system does not work anymore. Then what will be the regulators' future role after establishing a safety net and a market-oriented mechanism?

As shown below, the regulatory response to banks' risk-taking behaviors has been changing from domestic administrative control to international self-control assessed by the market. Under the liberalized financial market, banks can take various risks that are highly complicated and hard to manage compared to before. Thus current regulators encourage banks to adopt certain risk management measures. However, some banks have more advanced risk management skills than their regulators, and such skills should be respected. Therefore, the future regulatory system will move to self-control of risks assessed by the market. To implement market function of assessment and to avoid emergence of the systemic risk, regulators' inspecting role will remain.

The Regulatory Response to Banks' Risk-Taking Behaviors

Postwar System	**Current System**	**Future System**
Domestic Control	Global: Basel 1→Basel 2→Banks' Self-Control	
Regulators restrict banks' risk-taking behaviors.	Regulators allow banks' risk-taking behaviors and let the banks take their own responsibility.	
Financial risk management measures did not develop highly because the risk was limited and not as complicated as today.	For the banks' risk, regulators order banks to adopt certain risk management measures such as 'value at risk'.	Banks can choose their own risk management measures. The market and regulators check the banks' risk management process.

Financial systems consist not only of banks but also of the payment systems. The retail payment system closely relates to consumers; the wholesale payment system is the bottleneck, and important from the systemic risk concern. Regulation in this area should also be developed, and this paper will introduce two Japanese issues for consideration.

The current Japanese banking laws have at least two retail and wholesale payment issues to consider: (1) whether or not the money order business monopolized by banks should be open to other companies; and (2) whether or not the legal relationship in the large-value payment system that is currently governed by general private laws should be governed by special laws.

Regarding the first issue, Articles 2 and 3 of the Banking Law[45] exclusively allow banks to engage in money order business. For example, the U.S. PayPal service, which enables you to send your money by email at a lower cost than by bank transfers, is not offered by a bank but by a payment provider. However, U.S. PayPal had to start its Japanese business as E-bank, an IT specialized bank, in the autumn of 2001. Though an IT specialized bank is easier to establish than a normal bank, the provisions have been criticized as the obstacle for the development of payment services.[46] In fact, normal Japanese companies have already started issuing travelers' checks, credit cards, and debit cards, which can be considered to be violating the provisions. I think that lifting the restriction on further competition and innovation in payments may be needed for consumer wealth and global regulatory competition. The remaining regulatory issue will be to secure the safety of such new payment services from the point of consumer protection.

The second issue is mainly concerned with the validity of multilateral netting *without* having a central counterparty, which is still uncertain, especially under the insolvency laws. Though the bilateral netting or multilateral netting *with* a central counterparty is clearly valid, some foreign large-value payment systems adopt this multilateral netting *without* a central counterparty and allow overseas remote access. If a Japanese participant directly deals in a foreign system and goes bankrupt, the Japanese bankruptcy procedures based on Japanese law might negate the validity of foreign multilateral netting and damage the system and other participants. To avoid this, Japan should legislate a law of validating multilateral netting together with finality and governing laws, by referencing the EU Finality Directive in 1998.

---

45 Ginkô-hô, Law No. 59/1981, last amended by Law No. 129/2001.

46 See *S. Iwahara*, Ginkô no kessai kinô to kawase gyômu no haita-sei [Bank's Payment Functions and Exclusiveness of Transfer Business]: Gendai kigyô rippô no kiseki to tenbô [Legislative History and Perspective of Modern Enterprises] (Shôji Hômu Kenkyû-kai, Tokyo, 1995).

THE REGULATION OF BANKING SERVICES IN GERMANY

by Dietrich Schilling, Bonn

I. General Statement

A. The German Banking Act

The legal basis for the regulation of banking services in Germany is the Banking Act (*Kreditwesengesetz*, Credit Institution Act). The banking busi-

J. Basedow, H. Baum, K. Hopt, H. Kanda and T. Kono (eds.), Economic Regulation and Competition, (97-108)

ness is getting more and more complicated, and so is the German Banking Act with its supervisory regulations. But it is an exaggeration when the chairman of the Deutsche Bank is quoted in the newspaper as saying that he thinks there are only about 150 people in the world who really know the German Banking Act.

B. Development of Banking Supervision in General

Regulatory rules for the banking business are mostly the result of banking crises. Whenever a large bank collapses, new banking supervisory rules are established. At times even the whole organization of supervision has been changed, as in the case of the establishment of the Financial Services Authority (FSA) in Great Britain to succeed the Bank of England as the Banking Supervisory Authority after the collapse of the Barings Bank.

In addition, supervisory rules have to be changed to accommodate changes in the banking business. In a rapidly changing environment of banking markets and innovation in techniques (asset backed securities, derivatives), the supervisory systems need to be reviewed to ensure that they take sufficient account of potential risks.

The situation in Germany can be characterized as a sound banking system with only smaller banks going bankrupt in the past fifteen years. Germany has had remarkable continuity in its economy, so there was no pressure to change the banking regulatory rules from this side.

Since 1961, when the Federal Banking Supervisory Office/FBSO (*Bundesaussichtsamt für das Kreditwesen*/BAKred) was established as the German banking supervisory authority, there have been six amendments to the Banking Act. All the reforms of the Banking Act since 1988 were caused by the adoption of new EU directives and not by a banking crisis. These directives set minimum standards that have to be adopted in national law. The result is very complex banking supervisory rules that are often hard to understand.

C. The Future of Banking Supervision in Germany

Two issues may fundamentally change German banking supervision:

- The proposals from the Basel Committee, which are known as 'Basel II', will establish new standards for capital adequacy of banks.

- A new organization of the financial supervisory system in Germany with only one supervisory authority based upon the model of the British FSA. Up to now there have been three separate supervisory authorities in Germany:
  - for banks and financial institutions, the Bundesaufsichtsamt für das Kreditwesen;
  - for insurance companies, the Bundesaufsichtsamt für das Versicherungswesen;
  - for securities trading businesses, the Bundesaufsichtsamt für Wertpapierhandel.

D. Rules about Financial Crisis Management in the German Banking Act

The German Banking Act gives the FBSO enough power and the necessary organization to manage a crisis. But first of all, banking supervisors must try to prevent a financial crisis. Up to now there has been no crisis in Germany that has been able to threaten the banking system. The year 2001 was a very bad year for German banks, characterized by high costs, low operating results, high risks, and high-risk provisions. But this follows several years of good results and a long period of stability in the stock markets. As a result, the major banks were able to make all the necessary risk provisions and can be regarded as well capitalized. While the German banking supervision is satisfied in this respect, the banking business is still a more intense focus of supervision now. In a situation of weak earnings, the managers of banks are often more aggressive and tend to take more risks in their business with higher margins.

E. General Obligations of the Supervisory Law

The aim of supervisory law is to reduce the danger of bank failures, although even the best rules cannot prevent single bank failures in a liberal financial market.

1. Reasons for Bank Failures

In most cases in the past, banking crises were the result of credit risks. Therefore, the credit risk has to be the main focus of banking supervision.

But other risks – especially the operational risk, the market risk, and the liquidity risk – have also been of importance and should not be neglected.

Banks tend to have a collective misunderstanding of the market. In a booming economy, banks are eager to lend money; in a recession, they want their money back. But then the borrowers do not have enough liquidity, because their earnings in a recession are too small. This is a real danger for the economy as a whole.

It is quite normal in a weaker economy for non-performing loans on the bank balance sheets to increase. Well-capitalized banks will be able to make the necessary risk provision and have enough liquidity to be able to pay their creditors if they want their money back. Therefore, banking regulators have to force banks to raise their capital to maintain their standard as a well-capitalized bank.

2. Reasons for the Stability of the Banking (Regulation) System in Germany

There are various reasons for Germany's stable banking system:

- A sound economy with no deflation and inflation.
- A universal banking system.
- An effective supervisory system with two supervisory bodies closely working together: the FBSO and the Deutsche Bundesbank with its branches.
- An extensive deposit insurance system. (This makes a banking system safer, establishes confidence, and thus prevents runs on the banks in case of a crisis. Deposit insurance systems are often criticized: some people say that it makes banks greedy for risks, and once deposits are protected, depositors have no reason to keep an eye on what banks are doing. I do not agree with this view.)
- The German accounting system, which serves more as a protection for the creditors than the interests of the shareholders. The accounting system not only allows but often forces the banks in several cases to a cautious undervaluation of assets.
- The tax law, although it is often criticized. The tax law must be seen in combination with the accounting system, which allows hidden reserves due to the undervaluation of assets.

Now, however, the German banking system is under pressure. One point (as mentioned above) is the weak economy and the lower operating income of the banks. Another point is the change in the banking business itself, which is getting increasingly complex and difficult to understand. Even managers of banks are more and more dependent upon specialists.

Banks have invested large sums of money to develop risk measurement methods (models). But do all these new risk models for both market risks and credit risks really work well? That must be evaluated by the supervisors. Because the major source of financial debacles of banks are management failures, our main focus must be the management of the bank itself and its risk management procedures.

F. Concentration in the Banking and Financial Business

In the past there were some remarkable mergers and takeovers, not only in Japan but also in Germany and in other countries. Some mergers have been between banks, others have been between banks and insurance companies. These financial conglomerates are getting bigger and bigger and so becoming a real challenge for the supervisory bodies. Some say that these mergers have formed stronger banks. But the economy of size cannot be the only answer in a banking crisis. The merger of two weak banks will not create a strong bank. It has been proven that many mergers are not successful.

G. Economic Situation of Banks in Germany

Due to the present weak economy, non-performing loans are increasing. It is expected that all the major banks will be able to make the necessary risk provisions. As a result of these high-risk provisions, banks are getting more and more cautious in their lending business. In consequence, they are sometimes criticized and politicians are talking about a credit crunch.

H. Two Examples of Rules in the German Banking Law to Keep Risks Lower

Banks may not grant loans higher than 25 percent of their (liable) capital. All large loans (from 10 to 25 percent of the capital) may not exceed eight times their (liable) capital.

In the EU, a bank (which by EU definition is a deposit-taking credit institution) may not hold a participation in an enterprise whose share of the amount of nominal capital exceeds 15 percent of the capital of the bank. The combined shareholdings may not exceed 60 percent of the capital. But this means only participations in non-financial enterprises. There are no limitations for participations in insurance companies, credit institutions, leasing or factoring companies, and so on.

I. Adoption of EU Law

Since 1988 Germany has adopted several EU directives into the German Banking Act. That often has meant new regulatory standards. Some of them are influenced by U.S. regulations, and some by other countries.

Japan has also adopted foreign (U.S.) standards, and Professor Kubota has criticized this 'eager chase after the global standard'. In consequence, he demands that 'Japan should start to consider not accepting or adapting to the 'global' standard, but making its own standards the global one'. Could this really be the solution for Japan's banking system?

There is no doubt that the German banking law has also become more and more complicated by adopting all the new EU directives. But they are acceptable compromises, though they might not always consider the special need of a single country. What else could be done? We live in a global economy. All the major banks are thinking globally. Some of our banks are earning nearly half or more of their profit outside from Germany. For example, the Deutsche Bank announced that 25 percent of their income in the year 2000 was earned in the United States. The banks and the whole financial system need the Untied States because it represents the largest financial market in the world. So there is no choice: we all have to accept global (U.S.) standards, especially for accounting. But for banks with only local business, it might be useful to think about the proposal of Professor Kubota. They will need no global standards if the local standards are better. And, indeed, they often are.

II. Banking Supervision in Germany and International Harmonization of the Law

The Federal Banking Supervisory Office is entrusted with the supervision of credit institutions and financial services institutions in Germany.

Banking supervision was introduced in Germany as a result of the dramatic banking crisis in 1931. At first, banking supervision was carried out by the German Reichsbank (the Central Bank). After the Second World War banking supervision was first decentralized, but in 1962 it was centralized again in the FBSO on the basis of a new Banking Act (Kreditwesengesetz, KWG).

Compared with its original wording, the KWG has so far undergone six substantial amendments. The most important amendments of the KWG and the supervisory standards have been the result of years of intensive (and in the end successful) efforts to harmonize the *fundamental* banking supervisory regulations at the international level. It was also necessary to integrate forms of supervision into the German supervisory law that are foreign to the liberal German understanding of supervision.

Within one decade, different rules about more intensive control in particular have converted the German banking supervisory law, which used to be relatively simple and clear, into a complex regulatory framework that is difficult to understand and sometimes regarded as 'overregulation'. But the international harmonization of supervisory law is the banking supervisors' essential response to the progressive integration of the major financial centers to form one global market:

- We need cross-border coordination of the activities of individual national banking supervisory authorities.
- To protect the multi-linked world financial system against uncontrollable crisis, sound supervisory minimum standards must be established in all major financial centers.
- No country may be allowed to provide its banks with unjustified advantages in international competition by establishing or maintaining inadequate supervisory standards.

In the EU member states, the harmonization of banking supervisory law was achieved by the issuance of a variety of EU directives which contained binding standards to be observed by the member states in the formulation of their national supervisory law.

Beyond the EU area, the Committee on Banking Supervision in Basel is concerned with the worldwide coordination of banking supervisory measures and the harmonization of the most important banking supervisory rules. The so-called Basel Committee gives 'recommendations' which, although not legally binding, have in most cases soon obtained international recognition and have also served as a model for the EU legislation.

A. Subjects of the German Banking Supervision

Supervision applies especially to all enterprises regarded as 'banks', because they carry on any of the *twelve* types of banking business listed in Sec. 1 (1) KWG. These enterprises must have a license from the FBSO before taking up their business activities. Any conduct of banking business without a license constitutes a criminal offense.

A specialty of German banking law is the cooperation between the FBSO and the Deutsche Bundesbank. The Deutsche Bundesbank has no specific sovereign functions in the supervision of banks. All intervention powers vis-à-vis credit institutions are monopolized by the FBSO. The special value of the involvement of the Deutsche Bundesbank lies in the fact that it considerably increases the effectiveness of supervision. The FBSO has no substructure and no regional network, but the Deutsche Bundesbank has a network of branches all over Germany. This guarantees better insight into the local circumstances of banks.

The Bundesbank is further involved in the examination of the reports by the banks. All important issues about banking supervision are discussed between staff members, the FBSO, and the Bundesbank as well. All banking supervisory decisions to be made by the FBSO are also issued by mutual agreement.

A very substantial role in German banking supervision is played by private auditors, not only by carrying out the audit of the annual accounts of the banks, but also by carrying out special audits ordered by the FBSO. For these special audits, the FBSO has not built up its own team of auditors. It is questionable whether the FBSO could produce results of the same quality if the often difficult on-site examinations were carried out by its own employees.

The objective of banking supervision is quite clear: to prevent a banking crisis, because this may infect the economy as a whole. The main functions of banks are to collect the savings of people and enterprises in the form of deposits, and use these to give loans to other economic units to finance their investments. A deadlock in the bank's supply of credit would therefore cause serious losses to the national economy.

A crisis in the credit system is especially likely to occur if the bank's creditors, which include a large number of people, gain the impression that the safety of their deposits is no longer guaranteed. So a depositor protection scheme is of great importance and can assist the work of the banking supervisors. While the schemes of the savings banks and credit cooperative banks in Germany aim to guarantee the continued existence of these credit institutions, the deposit guarantee fund of the private banking industry in Germany protects the non-bank customers of insolvent member banks by guaranteeing each deposit up to 30 percent of the liable capital of the bank concerned. This ensures that customers will get back 100 percent of their deposits. Membership in this fund is voluntary, but nearly all private banks are members for competition reasons. (Some say that this system is too costly, and if a large bank were to collapse the whole guarantee system would collapse as well.)

As part of the EU harmonization law, a new (further) compensation scheme was established in 1998. The compensation is limited to 90 percent of the deposits and the equivalent of 20,000 Euro.

B. The Regulatory Framework of the German Banking Act (KWG)

The conception of supervision underlying the KWG is a liberal one that seeks to exclude any influence of banking supervision on the business decisions of banks, leaving them with a large amount of scope left for the free development of their business activity. This conception follows our knowledge that 'supervisors are not the better bankers'.

The supervisory function of the FBSO, therefore, consists merely of examining after the fact whether the bank management fulfilled the requirements of the laws and regulations. The appropriateness of business measures must be left to the bank's discretion in a free-market system, and out of the supervisors' judgment as a matter of principle.

The core of the KWG consists of general provisions concerning the bank's internal structure and rules of conduct with respect to its business activity. Risk-limiting minimum requirements regarding the liable capital, liquidity, and diversification are an important part of the regulatory framework.

Reporting duties (often monthly reports) must be fulfilled by the banks together with the examination power, which enables the FBSO to monitor compliance with these standards. If insufficiencies are discovered, the FBSO has the power to avert danger.

For the credit business, from which most credit institutions' losses still arise, the German banking law has established only general principles to reduce risks. The basic characteristic of a sound credit policy is seen in a broad credit diversification.

Pursuant to the EU Large Exposure Directive of 1992, credit exposures to a single borrower over 10 percent of a bank's liable capital (large exposures) have to be decided by all managers. No single exposure may exceed the limit of 25 percent (or 20 percent in the case of exposures to subsidiaries or parent companies). All large exposures may not exceed 800 percent of the liable capital.

Large exposures must be monitored at the same time on a consolidated basis by consolidating the exposures to one single borrower or to a group of affiliated borrowers.

C. Interventions by the FBSO

As an example of a case where intervention would be called for, if the internal structure or the business operations of a bank gave rise for concern, the FBSO would take the necessary countermeasures pursuant to Sec. 45, 46 KWG.

If the discharge of a bank's obligations to its creditors – and particularly the safety of the assets – is endangered, the FBSO may revoke its license. The safety of the assets is deemed to be endangered if the credit institution suffers a loss amounting to one half of its liable capital or a loss amounting to more than 10 percent of its liable capital in each of at least three successive financial years and thus proves to be permanently unprofitable.

Before revoking the license, however, the FBSO normally orders a temporary moratorium to block the business operations of the banks. This moratorium gives the owner of the bank the chance to reorganize.

D. The Future of Banking Supervision in Germany

In Germany, we have three supervisory authorities:

- the Federal Banking Supervisory Office BAKred, Bundesaufsichtsamt für das Kreditwesen),
- the Federal Insurance Supervisory Office (BAV, Bundesaufsichtsamt für das Versicherungswesen),
- the Federal Supervisory Office for Securities Trading (BAWe, Bundesaufsichtsamt für Wertpapierhandel),

and (with different tasks in banking supervision) the Deutsche Bundesbank with its branches.

A draft for a new supervisory law, which is presently on its way through parliament, would create one new authority by merging the three supervisory bodies.*

One point in favor of this new structure is that banks often have large stakes in insurance companies and vice versa. Another point is that both institutions are partly working in the same or similar business areas. Other countries already have this 'super-regulator' model, e.g., Great Britain with the FSA. It is expected that a merger of these three supervisory bodies will create synergy effects and so reduce costs.

E. The Revision of the 1988 Basel Accord

The so-called Basel Accord governs how banks manage risks on their balance sheets.

Although capital is the cornerstone of sound banking and the assessment of capital adequacy lies at the heart of national systems of banking supervision, there were considerable differences in the concepts and methodologies employed by the supervisory authorities in assessing and controlling the capital adequacy of banks in different countries.

In 1988, regulators from the G-10 countries agreed that there must be international rules for the capital of banks in accordance to their risk-weighted assets.

Up to now, these capital adequacy rules were simple but effective. They required banks to hold capital equal to at least 8 percent of their risk-weighted loans to non-banks. But there were many exceptions. Government debts from OECD countries required no capital. Non-OECD sovereign debts had some capital requirements, but fewer than for any private sector loans. Loans between banks also entailed modest capital requirements. The meaning was that a bank with less than 8 percent in capital reserves was under-capitalized.

These capital rules had two key aims:

– To ensure that the world's lenders maintained an adequate cushion of capital to protect them against bankruptcy.

---

* *Note by the editors*: The law went into force 1 May 2002; the new central supervisory agency is the 'Bundesanstalt für Finanzdienstleistungspflicht' (BAFin).

- To ensure that banking supervisors did not offer their own banks an unfair advantage in lending markets by allowing them to operate under less strict standards than those set by regulators of their competitors.

But these old-fashioned crude measures of limiting and classifying risks meant, for example, that banks had to put aside less capital against a loan made to a 'banana republic' than to a blue-chip company. As a result, regulators discussed proposals for capital requirements that reflected the true credit risk of loans.

The suggested new capital rules under the name of Basel II will revolutionize banking supervision. Instead of setting a fixed ratio (8 percent) of capital to so-called risk assets, the new framework of about 560 pages will allow the most sophisticated banks to use their own measures of risk to calibrate the amount of capital they must set aside.

Various large banks already use credit risk models, not only for a better knowledge of their risks but also for the pricing of loans. The higher the risk for the bank is, the more a borrower has to pay for a loan.

Of course, the risk models need to be tested over a longer period. They also must pass an assessment by the regulators. Only after successfully passing this process will a bank be allowed to use its own risk-measurement model to determine how much capital the bank needs in relation to the different risks, e.g., credit risks, market risks, and operational risks. A new feature will be that according to Basel II, 'operational risks' should also be cushioned by capital.

The timetable for the implementation of the new Basel II capital scheme stretches to the year 2005. This seems to be a very demanding and ambitious schedule for both the banks and the supervisory authorities.

Part 2:

REGULATION OF EXCHANGE AND INVESTMENT SERVICES

NEW CHALLENGES FOR STOCK EXCHANGES, INVESTMENT FIRMS, AND OTHER MARKET PARTICIPANTS

by Susanne Kalss, Klagenfurt

J. Basedow, H. Baum, K. Hopt, H. Kanda and T. Kono (eds.), Economic Regulation and Competition, (111-150)

I. General Remarks

Capital markets and stock exchanges are functional centers with the duty of providing firms with capital. They are playing a central part in every market economy (key market[1]). An efficient financial system is crucial for sustained economic growth. The change and permanent reshaping of global financial markets is accelerating. The analysis and discussion concerning the most appropriate legal framework to meet new demands is not only important for the stock exchange, its members and clients (brokers, issuers, and investors), and the capital market itself, but the whole economy of a state and an economic area. Questions regarding the reform of the traditional legal regulations are guided by considerations of how to improve the economic function of the market system so as to ensure the efficient allocation of control in all enterprises concerned, i.e., to ensure a working system of corporate governance.[2] It is the main task of the state to create the appropriate legal framework for the optimal proper working of the market economy.[3] Generally the duties of the state will depend on the extent to which a market economy has already developed and how much market-regulatory intervention is necessary, or at least beneficial.

A. The Changing Role of Different Market Participants under Different Circumstances in Transition

The new situation is the present result of several significant and interrelated developments which can be traced back to various reasons and are mutually reinforcing and partly dependent on one another.[4] The major trends are as follows:

---

1 *Stefan Grundmann*, Ein Binnenmarkt – ganz ohne Schuldvertragsrecht?, Europäisches Wirtschafts- und Steuerrecht 1999, 1; see also Financial Services Policy Group of the EU, Strategic Paper (1998), p. 15.

2 *Susanne Kalss*, Different Stock Exchange Interest Groups, in: Ferrarini/Hopt/Wymeersch, Capital Markets in the Age of the Euro (The Hague, 2002).

3 From a macroeconomic point of view, see *Carmine Di Noia*, Customer-Controlled Firms: The Case of Financial Exchanges in: Ferrarini/Hopt/Wymeersch, supra note 2.

4 *Harald Baum*, Capital Markets and Possible Regulatory Responses, in: Basedow/Kono (eds), Legal Aspects of Globalization (The Hague, 2000), p. 78; *Susanne Kalss*, supra note 2; *Bernhard Rudolph/Heiner Röhrl*, Grundfragen der Börsenorganisation aus ökonomischer Sicht, in: Hopt/Rudolph/Baum (eds), Börsen-

cont. ...

- Innovation and progress in information and communication technology.
- Institutionalization and professionalization of market participants.
- Intermediation and simultaneous disintermediation.[5]
- Structural change in the landscape of offerors of trading facilities (alternative trading systems and international alliances between stock exchanges and/or trading platforms).
- Globalization of the trading in securities and offering related services as the *mobility* and internationality of market participants (*brokers* and other *financial services, issuers* and *major investors)* is increasing due to technical support.
- An increasing importance of equity financing accompanied by the creation of new financial products and investment strategies.
- Policy and regulatory activities to facilitate cross-border capital flows, market access, and innovation in exchange services by deregulation.
- Introduction of the Euro in Europe.

All of these forces are interrelated. The most important factor has been technical innovation, i.e., the increase of capacities of data processing and the proliferation of information and communication technologies. The innovation process has promoted the transnational execution of investment services without lack of time and without the increasing of costs. Professional market participants are playing a leading role in designing the new market landscape; they have the intellectual and financial means to use both the technical possibilities and the regulatory freedom. Trading with cost reduction capacity is increasingly seen[6] as a key factor by investment service companies interested in knowing which trading institution makes use of it. By developing new financial products, they are therefore creating demand for more sophisticated trading possibilities and pushing for further deregulation at the same time. New technical opportunities, internationalization, and broader access to the offer of financial services have created a new competitive situation that has in turn enforced dynamic forces of structural changes. An important contribution to the development of the market is the availabil-

---

reform. Eine ökonomische, rechtsvergleichende und rechtspolitische Untersuchung (Stuttgart, 1997), p. 146 et seq.

5 *Peter Nobel*, Börsenallianzen und -fusionen, in: Lutter-Festschrift (Köln, 2000), p. 1485 et seq.; *Johannes Köndgen*, Mutmaßungen über die Zukunft der europäischen Börsen, in: Lutter-Festschrift (Köln, 2000), p. 1415.

6 *Otto Loistl*, Die Entwicklung des Wertpapierhandels – eine aktuelle Momentaufnahme: (1999) Wirtschaftspolitische Blätter 629.

ity and accessibility to the Internet, which opens a broad range of different services.[7]

B. Regulative Answers to New Economic Challenges

1. Need for Regulation

The new economic background is urging a reasonable and open reaction of the legislators and demands generally adequate measures

- to remove uncertainty about the regulatory response to any implications for the wider securities trading environment;
- to determine the competent authority (on the international and national level) to assure a quick and well-reasoned decision;
- to grant a level playing field for all competitors on the international – at least on the European – level;
- to identify the law applicable to the pertinent activity; and
- to raise the acceptance of the regulations and to ease the implementation and compliance therewith.

The less developed a market and a national economy, the less clear are regulations, the weaker are backing arguments, and the slower are decisions of authorities covered by a veil of uncertainty[8] – all poison for a market that is accustomed to making decisions within extremely short periods of time and characterized by flexibility and the ability to adapt to new economic demands and snap opportunities. Advanced economies and developed markets are therefore based on a well-shaped legal framework containing both material requirements and formal procedures that stimulate but do not suppress economic innovation and initiative.

---

7 Special Internet-related questions are not the topic of this article. Legislators have reacted in various fields, including the E-Commerce Directive and a proposal of the distant offering and selling of financial services. For a discussion of stock-exchange services via the Internet, see Baum, Paper presented at the Conference August 2001; *Klaus Riemer/Friedericke Häuser*, Internet und Börse: (2001) Neue Zeitschrift für Gesellschaftsrecht 385 et seq.; *Ulrich Florian*, Wertpapierhandel im Internet (München, 2001).

8 Compare Economist, 17 September 2001, referring to a study of the world bank.

2. Different International and National Activities

a) International Initiatives

The harmonization accomplished by the European securities directives is outdated and insufficient to deal with the issues raised by the pan-European markets.[9] Considerations to promote the integration of the European financial market had already begun in the very early stages of the Community and were based on a lucid study (delivered by a group of experts headed by Mr. Segré).[10] After difficult negotiations among the member states, the listing directives were set into force about twenty years ago, followed by other directives regulating the continuing disclosure of financial data, insider dealing, and the disclosure of a prospect before a public offer of a security. Finally, the Investment Services Directive regulated the requirements for market participants, regulated markets, and granted to a certain extent the European passport for investment firms. With the exception of the ISD, the directives came into force about twenty years ago; the ISD has now been in force for more than eight years.

The new economic landscape has made necessary a rethinking of EU policy on regulation in financial services and capital markets law in general;[11] various institutions have realized the urgency and are contributing in different ways to the discussion. These institutions represent a broad spectrum, including

- the European Commission
- OECC (Paris)
- UNIDROIT (Rome);

more or less 'semi-official' associations such as

- IOSCO and FESCO;

expert committees such as

---

9 *Guido Ferrarini,* Securities Regulation and the Rise of Pan-European Markets: An Overview, in: Ferrarini/Hopt/Wymeersch, supra note 2; *Guido Ferrarini*, The European Regulations of Stock Exchanges: New Perspectives: (1999) Common Market Law Review 569 (570).

10 *Europäische Wirtschaftsgemeinschaft*, Der Aufbau eines europäischen Kapitalmarkts – Bericht einer von der EWG-Kommission eingesetzten Sachverständigengruppe (Segré Report; Brussels, 1966).

11 See *Guido Ferrarini*, The European Regulations of Stock Exchanges: New Perspectives, supra note 9, p. 569 et seq.

- the wise men of Lamfalussy[12]
- the high level group of experts for company law;[13]

and supplemented by

- interest groups.

The organizations and institutions mentioned are not competing in being the first to set up regulations and standards, but they are trying to cooperate and take a mutually supportive approach by splitting and supplementing the drafting and preparing work and focusing on different matters. Proposals to reconsider financial law and regulation in this field in general were put forward on different official and semi-official levels. It will be sufficient to mention some concepts, proposals of regulation, codes of conduct, and other considerations dealing with the establishment of an adequate framework for the rapidly developing market. Three years ago the European Commission published an action plan on financial services and launched a multi-faceted process of reformulation of the framework of the European market for financial services.[14] FESCO was the European outlet of the worldwide IOSCO and stood for the European Forum of Securities Commissions. Since then, FESCO has been transformed into the European Securities Committee, which acts as an advisory body to the Commission.[15] The main tasks of this organization are to improve the standards for different market participants, to intensify the cooperation of the national surveillance authorities, and to raise the efficiency of enforcement of financial services law. Unidroit, an international private institute (not only for Europe) with the purpose of pre-

---

12 *The Committee of Wise Men*, Final Report on the Regulation of European Securities Markets (Brussels, 15 February 2001 – Lamfalussy Report 2001).

13 IP/01/1237 from 4 September 2001. The expert group is dealing in particular with company law issues, but the main aspects are closely connected with the capital market.

14 (1998) COM 625.

15 (2001) COM 1493 final; *Jens Fürhoff*, Die Rolle der nationalen Aufsichtsbehörden bei der Vollendung des europäischen Kapitalmarkts, Conference June 2001 at Frankfurt/Main. The Committee of European Securities Regulators (CESR) was established in September as an independent body. Its main tasks are to improve the coordination among securities regulators, to act as an advisory group to assist the EU Commission by preparing the drafts and the implementing measures on Community level, and to ensure more consistent and timely day-to-day implementation of community legislation.

paring and drafting international conventions, has chosen capital markets issues as one of its main working fields for the next five years.[16]

b) National Initiatives

On the national level, legislators are demonstrating their ambition to be as fast as the European and other international rule makers in establishing a new framework for the financial markets that is more or less open and interrelated to the ongoing developments on the international level.

In Germany the parliament is going to set in force three important pieces of law in the field of financial markets: the Fourth Financial Markets Promotion Act,[17] which includes the modernization of the law of stock exchanges and other trading systems; the Act on the Establishment of One Supervisory Authority,[18] which merges the different authorities responsible for different market participants and activities (insurances, banks, investment firms, and issuers) into one legal body vested with the responsibility for controlling all market participants; and finally the parliament has already approved the Takeover Act after a consultative process with a great deal of discussion lasting more than eighteen months.[19]

In Austria the parliament has already passed the Financial Market and Supervisory Act,[20] which will establish one central supervisory body responsible for the main supervisory tasks of the financial market. The new supervisory body will start its work in April 2002. The Takeover Code was set in force about three years ago and shaped closely to the then-current version of the draft of the Takeover Directive. The mere existence of the act played an

16 *Herbert Kronke*, Ziele – Methoden, Kosten – Nutzen: Perspektiven der Privatrechtsharmonisierung nach 75 Jahren Unidroit: (2001) Juristenzeitung 1149 (1154); see also <www.unidroit.org>.

17 <www.bundesministerium.de> (14 November 2001); see also (2001) Zeitschrift für Bankrecht und Bankwirtschaft 507; *Jochen Mues*, Anmerkungen zum Börsengesetz nach dem Diskussionsentwurf für das Vierte Finanzmarktförderungsgesetz: (2001) Zeitschrift für Bankrecht und Bankwirtschaft 353 et seq.

18 <www.bundesminsterium.de> (August 2001).

19 <www.bundesminsterium.de> (November 2001); for a first overview, see: *Holger Fleischer/Susanne Kalss*, Das neue Wertpapiererwerbs- und Übernahmegesetz – Materialienband mit Einführung (München, 2002).

20 Federal Gazette 2001/97; for a first overview, see: *Ernst Brandl/Rainer Wolfbauer*, Finanzdienstleistungen nach dem Finanzmarktaufsichtsgesetz (Wien, 2001).

important role for many transactions (only the largest deal in Austrian history between Bank Austria and Hypo-Vereinsbank should be mentioned), so one can conclude that the act has passed the test of practical impact with honors. Nevertheless, considerations are underway to rethink some specific regulations (such as the obligatory cash offer and the relation between merger and takeover) to adapt the act more closely to market needs.

3. New Approach to Rule-Making

As already stated, the pace of development and change is continuously accelerating. Therefore, it is important to find stable and confidence-creating regulations that simultaneously keep their flexibility so that they can be amended and accommodated to new requests without following long decision-making procedures. Therefore, the final report of the expert group under Lamfalussy drafted not only proposals for changes in the material law, but also in the fields of the rule-making and implementing process and the enforcement of rules. The expert group proposed a four-level approach: (a) framework principles, (b) implementing measures, (c) cooperation, and (d) enforcement in order to make the regulatory process for EU securities legislation more effective and transparent. The multilateral approach – in particular, the separation of principles and technical details – is one of the most important steps toward developing the adequate framework in time. Political compromise must be found only for the general principles; technical measures and definitions on the lower level are far more flexible and therefore easier to adapt to new emerging requirements.

However, the difficulties of this approach lie with the understanding of Art. 202 of the European Treaty. According to this regulation, the European Council is entitled to delegate rule-making powers to the Commission. But the European Court did not find a clear-cut line to determine how many details and regulations the Council has to formulate, and how much power may be shifted to the Commission and – as a result – to the working groups of experts;[21] in consequence, each principle and each regulation is in danger of being rendered subject to a long-lasting court procedure, which undoubt-

---

[21] See only EC 23/75 (Rey Soda); EC 16/88 (Commission/Council); EC 291/86 (Central Import Münster) EC C-240/97 P Atlanta/Council-Commission); for a short analysis, see *Hix* in: *Jürgen Schwarze* (ed.), Kommentar zum EG-Vertrag (Baden-Baden, 2000), Art. 202 EGV text number 12 et seq.

edly weakens confidence, not only in this kind of regulation but, far more, in the European capital market as such.

At the moment, the European Commission seems to be following this approach only along a special kind of zigzag course: while the considerations for the consultative paper to change the ISD stress that the special mechanism of the Lamfalussy Report will be applied, the Commission reveals in the general introduction of the proposals for the Prospectus and Disclosure Directive[22] and the Insider Dealing and Market Abuse Directive that the proposals of the two directives were published at that time because the Commission did not want to be obliged to apply the new complex and time-consuming decision- and rule-making process that was suggested and advised in the Lamfalussy Report. The ongoing rule-making process will be split into different mechanisms. The Commission argued in the Market Abuse Directive (even before totally applying the recommendations of the wise men)[23] for the 'new' Investment Service Directive (ISD) and consequently for the following regulatory measures that it will seek to give effect to recommendations of the Lamfalussy Group regarding the appropriate format of EU legislation, particularly the distinction between:

- core principles enshrined in foundation legislation (level 1);
- detailed, legally binding technical implementing measures that may need to be adapted to changing business and regulatory practices (level 2). The revised ISD will carefully delimit the matters that may be the subject of such measures;
- matters where informal agreements between supervisors may be sufficient to result in a homogeneous approach to regulation and supervision of investment business throughout the EU (level 3).

4. More Transparency and Democratic Opinion Screening

While the procedure of drafting a proposal for a directive or any other act of Commission was characterized in the past by a rather clandestine and 'closed-shop' procedure – and therefore open and prone to the one-sided influence of lobbyists and interest groups – the general approach to finding a red thread for the main issues has changed. Following a recommendation from the report of the wise men, the Commission has already taken this path:

---

22 (2001) COM 280.

23 (2001) COM 281, 5 final.

in an increasing number of projects, the public, interested persons inside and outside different pressure groups, and expert committees are invited to participate in the thinking and planning period by submitting ideas, concepts, critiques, and proposals to the Commission by mail, fax, or other media. Therefore, at an early stage the public is involved in the rule- making process; interested persons can inform themselves about ongoing projects and their progress. The Commission starts the rule-making procedure by transmitting general considerations and different questions to the market participants by mail so that not only the responsible authorities or the selected interest groups will get the opportunity to file their opinion, but everybody who is interested in the regulation of financial markets.[24] Different interests can then be included in the drafting process at a stage where they really can be considered even in the draft version of an act.[25]

C. Basic Considerations

To be able to analyze newly emerging regulative requirements under the changing technological and economic circumstances, it is first necessary to become familiar with the optimal functioning of the market and the safeguarding of the different interests under the changing circumstances. At the first step it is helpful

(1) to identify the different participants and their interests present on the market,
(2) to examine their traditional position and describe the current changes,
(3) to draw up the pending regulative challenges and present proposals for adequate regulations.

Before starting the analysis in more detail, one has to stress that the most striking questions and challenging fields of material capital market law are the same now as ten or fifteen years ago. The Magna Carta of the whole

---

24 Commission; <www.europa.eu.int/comm/int> Consultation Document of the Services of the Internal Market Directorate General; on transparency obligations of issuers whose securities are admitted to trading on a regulated market; consultation on amendments of ISD.

25 But there remain doubts. Some member states are concerned that practitioners are not being properly consulted about early drafts: Economist, 3 November 2001, p. 68.

capital market law is the *equal treatment* of the *market participants.*[26] On the one hand, regulators have to shape general concepts and single regulations in line with this basic principle; examples of explicit rules are Art. 3 of the final draft of the Takeover Directive, section two of the Austrian Law on Takeovers, or section 3 para. 1 of the German bill on takeovers. According to these regulations, all holders of securities of an offeree company of the same class are to be given equivalent treatment. As important as the explicit rules are the more general approaches by the regulators to assure the same conditions for all market participants acting under the same circumstances. Examples are the disclosure rules, access to special trading facilities, establishment of an investment firm, and consequently access to markets in general. On the other hand, the leitmotiv of equal treatment is the red thread for the market participants as well as for the competent authorities to interpret single regulations in order to assure a sound and fair operating market. *Information asymmetry* – between issuer and investor, or intermediary and investor, or among other market participants – and the *conflicts of interests* of intermediaries (opportunistic behavior) or other firms contributing to the market process can be identified as the most important phenomena of disturbing the market process.[27] Under the umbrella of the basic principle of equal treatment, these two main fields require adequate general concepts and individual supplementing regulations. In order to establish a sound and operating framework for the market,[28] these two aspects are dominating the efforts of the regulators on the international and national level. During the last year the knowledge and sensibility about these phenomena have risen so that regulators are ready to set or improve regulations. Examples are the recent proposals by the European Commission dealing (a) with the drafting and disclosure of a prospect and (b) with market abuse (insider dealing and market manipulation).[29] According to the drafters of the directives, all investors and market participants who are ready to put money in the financial market must be placed on an equal footing. On the other side, the general acceptance for this kind of rule has also risen so that the implemen-

---

26 *Stefan Weber*, Kapitalmarktrecht (Wien, 1999), p. 351 et seq.; *Holger Fleischer*, Zum Begriff des öffentlichen Angebots im Wertpapiererwerbs- und Übernahmegesetz: (2001) Zeitschrift für Wirtschaftsrecht 1563 (1568).

27 See generally *Jürgen Basedow* in this volume.

28 For the European perspective, see: *Peter Mülbert*, Konzeption des europäischen Kapitalmarktrechts für Wertpapierdienstleistungen: (2001) Wertpapier-Mitteilungen 2085 (2094).

29 See below: Commission (2001) COM 281 final.

tation of the rules will be supported not only by the public but even by the market participants.

Apart from these core issues of regulation, which are strongly related to the daily market mechanism, the regulators have to face the *challenges* and newly weighted regulatory requirements arising from the *new technological environment* and the *internationality* of trading and other connected services. For example, regulators must find a new definition of a stock exchange or a regulated market and think about whether and under which conditions alternative trading systems (ATS) should be rendered subject to regulations equal or at least similar to those applying to stock exchanges. Concerning internationality, one has to think about the determination of the competent authority (either in the home or in the host country) and the intensity and technique of cooperation. Is the current contribution of tasks efficient, or must some or at least key competences be shifted and pooled to one central authority? After making a snapshot of the general regulatory developments on the European and selected national level (Austria and Germany), some questions out of these two main fields will be dealt with more in detail.

The main task of regulators is (1) the implementation of sound and adequate rules to assure the same availability and access to market information to all market participants, and to avoid conflicts of interest or – at least – put them under adequate regulations, and (2) to transmit these general concepts to new market situations that are characterized by technological progress and the international scope of activity. The objects of the regulations have remained the same: only equal treatment of market participants will assure an operating financial market as the core of the national and international economy. But the single steps to meet these requirements have become more complex and volatile.

II. Market Participants

The relevant groups on the market are: A. the firms offering financial services, B. other services for the market, C. the issuers, and D. the investors.

A. Firms Offering Financial Services

The term 'financial service' covers a broad range of different activities that are connected with the transfer of securities and other investment opportunities. Many possibilities have opened up for credit institutions or investment service enterprises to provide accompanying services. Apart from organizing shares issues (IPO Management), trading in securities is a key activity, along with research, preparing information, and other complementary services. Investment service companies look after their own interests as investors while simultaneously acting as service providers. Until recently, research and portfolio management were important. Now, trading with cost-reduction capacity is increasingly seen[30] as a key factor by investment service companies interested in knowing which trading institution makes use of it. The common denominator of the different activities is their more or less close relation to the capital market, although their tasks and contribution to the functioning are very different. Therefore, the group is quite inhomogeneous and can hardly be put under *one* regulatory framework. The contribution of the different core and auxiliary services for the market is undergoing a remarkable change so that the importance and the necessary regulatory approach can often only satisfy for the moment.

1. Stock Exchanges

Exchanges and connected services (in particular clearing and settlement) are the backbone of modern financial markets. Their regulation is closely linked to the law applicable to the other main market participants, the financial intermediaries and issuers.[31] The role and consequently the qualification of stock exchanges have changed during the last decade. Stock exchanges today are not to be seen as a 'simple market' or a 'market surveillance authority', unilateral and definitive in prescribing the rules, but as a qualified enterprise, i.e., a firm providing particular financial services.[32] The stock exchange

---

[30] *Otto Loistl*, supra note 6, p. 629.

[31] *Guido Ferrarini*, The European Regulations of Stock Exchanges: New Perspectives, supra note 9, p. 569.

[32] *Klaus J. Hopt/Harald Baum*, Börsenrechtsreform, in: Hopt/Rudolph/Baum (eds), supra note 4, p. 402; *Klaus J. Hopt*, Europäisches Kapitalmarktrecht – Rückblick und Ausblick, in: Grundmann (ed.), Systembildung und Systemlücken in Kerngebieten des Europäischen Privatrechts (Tübingen, 2000), p. 324; *Susanne Kalss*, Beginn und Beendigung der Notierung eines Wertpapiers, in: Aicher/Kalss/Altendorfer (eds), Grundfragen des Börsenrechts (Wien, 1998), p. 256 et seq.; *Susanne Kalss*, Anlegerinteressen – Der Anleger zwischen Vertrag, Verband und Markt (Wien, 2001), p. 53 et seq.; for the Austrian legal position up to now, see *Susanne Kalss*, Österreichisches Börsen- und Kapitalmarktrecht, in: Hopt/Rudolph/Baum, supra note 4, p. 1192.

offers a special kind of financial service (trading services), among which the establishing of a trading facility for securities at the disposal of clients and the guaranteeing of fair price calculation are of central importance. Trading in securities at fair terms is reflected by optimal liquidity, informational efficiency, and minimal trading costs (including costs of settlement).[33] The good produced is a special good in the form of a public utility.[34] The price information produced by the stock exchanges not only benefits its users, but also other participants in the market. The change of stock exchanges from public institutions to private firms is characterized by three essential proceedings: change of legal form, demutualization, and going public.[35]

(1) the change in the legal form without giving up the principles of a cooperative,
(2) demutualization, meaning the conversion into a (typical) profit-oriented business enterprise,
(3) and finally going public, making the shareholder's structure more flexible and less individualized.

Going public is the last step in this development, so that the exchange company definitely stops acting as a non-profit organization and is no longer run for the interests of the exchange's members but for profit. Thus, stock exchanges are increasingly behaving like normal firms. Going public offers stock exchanges access to the capital market and therefore a medium- and long-term basis of refinancing (which is necessary to invest in electronic networks and other capital-intense activities) and creates a greater financial scope. An IPO keeps all strategic options open: the stock exchange can elect to go it alone or to join forces or include selected new strategic and/or international investors, including the risk of being taken over as the different attempts toward the LSE have shown during the last months.[36]

---

33 *Johannes Köndgen*, Ownership and Corporate Governance of Stock Exchanges: (1998) Journal of Institutional and Theoretical Economics 227; *Johannes Köndgen*, supra note 5; *Klaus J. Hopt/Harald Baum*, supra note 32, p. 168; *Jochen Mues*, Die Börse als Unternehmen (Baden-Baden, 1999), p. 28.

34 *Carmine Di Noia*, supra note 3.

35 *Susanne Kalss*, supra note 2.

36 *Harald Baum*, Technological Innovation as a Challenge for Exchange Regulation, paper presented at the conference on regulation and e-commerce in Miyazaki, Japan, 27–29 July 2001; see further *John F. Coffee*, The Coming Competition among Securities Markets: What Strategies Will Dominate, <http://papers.ssrn.com/abstract/283822>.

In contrast, going public furnishes the stock exchange itself with the necessary resources for a takeover – either on the same level or on another level of the vertical ladder of financial services connected to stock exchanges (clearing and settlement or different software houses). The internationalization of the shareholder structure can contribute to a more international orientation; therefore, the stock exchange is no longer restricted to the existing static group. However, the process of going public can open new fields of conflicts of interest. The IPO can lead to conflicts of interest with the major shareholders: generally it is the exchange's best clients who tend to be the shareholders. One could argue that shareholders are interested in a strong return owing to high transaction costs, and banks as clients have to insist on low fees for themselves and their own clients, otherwise they will migrate from an exchange to alternative trading facilities. Nevertheless, you have to keep in mind that banks and other financial institutions have a primary interest in the fast and cost-effective settling of their orders, regardless of where the cost reduction and profit derive from. Another conflict of interest may arise out of the fact that the 'Stock Exchange plc' is listed at its 'own' business, i.e., stock exchange. The conflict between neutrality (supervisory authority) and self-interest is even more advanced in comparison to the pure profit-gaining interest by operating the stock exchange as a business. The only and most efficient means to suppress any doubt of incorrectness will be maintaining the highest standards of disclosure and quality of listing material (i.e., shares) and completing the shift of competence to another neutral entity for decisions about admission and for fulfilling the continuing supervising tasks.[37]

The days when national stock exchanges had a position like a monopoly in the national market are nearly a thing of the past.[38] Stock exchanges are competing fiercely with other system providers (stock exchanges and electronic networks); nevertheless, the geographic advantage and the higher liquidity leaves space for smaller players to find niches.[39]

Going public and the openness to the international market for corporate control not only affect the stock exchange as a company, but these market developments have great influences on the whole web of contractual relationships between the stock exchange and issuers on the one side and market

---

37 The conflict between neutrality (supervisory authority) and self-interest is even more advanced in comparison to the pure profit-gaining interest by operating the stock exchange as a business.

38 *Peter Nobel*, supra note 5, p. 1488; *Susanne Kalss*, supra note 2.

39 *Johannes Köndgen*, supra note 5, pp. 1406, 1407.

participants on the other side. Examples of questions include the regulation of access; the determination of preconditions for being listed; the competence of final decision and judicial review; the change of listing rules; and the merger of stock exchanges or cooperations similar to mergers[40] in terms of the listing requirements and other contractual obligations and rights.

One decade ago, the question 'What is an exchange?' was posed in a dramatic manner; it was repeated some years ago with extended considerations that took into account the technological progress. During recent years, many proposals have been presented without a satisfying approach having been developed; however, a consensus does exist that the definition must be flexible and able to be applied to a broader range of services.[41] Stock exchanges could be defined as the type at the top of a multi-level regulative system of trading systems (platforms).

These short hints show that stock exchanges must be subject to regulations adapted to the new economic and political situation. The core goal is (1) to find a suitable definition of the stock exchange and a borderline to other trading facilities. Stock exchanges are not the only trading systems, in stark contrast to non-organized trading opportunities. They are only one – albeit still the most important – of a broad range of different facilities of the diversified trading infrastructure. Stock exchanges could be defined as the type at the top of a multi-level regulative system of trading systems (platforms). (2) In a second step, the fields of regulation to which operators of the stock exchange are subject for general business must be identified. Typical examples that can be enumerated include establishment, access, license, running of the business, continuing obligations and duties, ownership structure, and governance questions.[42] (3) In a third step, the regulators have to submit a legal framework for structural changes – such as takeovers – or cooperations, such as contractual arrangements, takeovers in the close sense, similar transactions, or other qualified international cooperations. The current concept of the ISD (Art. 15) as a legal basis for a transnational trading network[43] can be developed and improved. At least in the future,

---

40 See, for example, *Peter Nobel/Michael Blair*, virt-x: a real European Stock Exchange: (2001) Schweizerische Zeitschrift für Wirtschaftsrecht 217.

41 See the most recent study by *Ulrich Wastl/Christian Schlitt*, Abkehr vom klassischen Börsebegriff – Chance für einen Neuanfang de lege lata: (2001) Wertpapier-Mitteilungen 1702.

42 *Susanne Kalss*, supra note 2.

43 *Guido Ferrarini*, in: Ferrarini/Hopt/Wymeersch, supra note 2.

even the supranational *Societas Europa* (European Public Company)[44] can be used for the establishment and operating of a transnational stock exchange.[45]

2. Alternative Trading Systems

During the last decade, new trading systems of securities have emerged that offer similar services to the stock exchange. The coming up of these private and proprietary trading facilities confirmed the need to define a stock exchange on the one hand, but on the other to find a borderline between alternative trading systems similar to stock exchanges and other trading or trade-connected services. According to a proposal of the FESCO,[46] an ATS can be defined in a broad manner as an entity which, without being regulated as an exchange, operates an automated system that brings together buying and selling interests – in the system and according to rules set by the system's operator – in a way that forms, or results in, an irrevocable contract. The definition captures any trading functionality, regardless of whether that functionality operates bilaterally or multilaterally. It captures not only ATSs that contribute to the price discovery process through the matching of priced orders and the lifting of quotes, but also includes crossing mechanisms that match buying and selling interests at a reference price determined elsewhere, e.g., on an exchange .

3. European Approach for Trading Systems

As a result, the European Commission recently stated in a consultative paper that ATSs do not constitute a homogenous group.[47] Depending on the product they offer (typical exchange services include the dissemination of pre-trade information, order routing, price determination, matching and confirmation, reporting and documentation, dissemination of post-trade infor-

44 OJ L 294/1 from 10 November 2001; the proposal for the SE was passed by the European Parliament in early October 2001.

45 See also *Peter Nobel*, supra note 5, p. 1511.

46 FESCO, Working Paper: ATS – September 2000; <www.eurofesco.org>.

47 Commission, Communication from the Commission to the European Parliament and the Council: Upgrading the Investment Services Directive, 16 November 2000, 13.

mation, and clearing and settlement),[48] various types of electronic facilities can be distinguished:[49] passive electronic bulletin boards, active electronic bulletin boards, order-routing systems, day trading centers, crossing systems, proprietary trading systems, and electronic communication networks.

Depending on the pertinent definition of an ATS, some of these can be classified as ATSs, while others are clearly not.[50] Currently the ISD defines the term 'regulated market' in order to draw a distinction to OTC markets, but it does not focus on the changing trading infrastructure.

It is, therefore, an important task for European and national legislators to distinguish among the different services and to formulate adequate preconditions and requirements to set up such businesses on different levels. Expressed in a rather simplified form, these range from a kind of 'stock exchange light' regulation to pure registration rules; the more remote the services are from matching and price-creating activities, the more liberal and less restrictive they could be.

Following the recommendation of the FESCO, the Commission is proposing an open approach by creating a new category of market institution and introducing a new definition of 'organized market'[51] to distinguish between client order-matching services provided by investment firms/banks on a discretionary basis, and organized single-capacity trading arrangements matching multiple trading interests in financial instruments. One of the regulative questions is how to qualify and treat order-matching brokers and dealers. Obviously it is difficult – if not impossible – to draw a clear-cut line for the various activities. Definitions cannot be found by fixing one or another aspect, but by combining and weighting different criteria in a case-by-case assessment of core functionality.[52] In view of the consequences of widespread internalization of order flow for the broader market system, order-matching brokers and dealers could also be regulated in the future as

48 *Hilmar Klenke*, Börsendienstleistungen (Berlin, 1998), p. 108.

49 *Harald Baum*, supra note 36; see in particular *Ruben Lee*, What Is an Exchange? (Oxford, 1998); see also *Martin Oppitz*, Die Börse (Wien, 1996).

50 *Harald Baum*, supra note 36.

51 Not to be confused with the definition under German law. At the moment, under German law the definition of *Organisierter Markt* is equivalent to the European Regulated Market: see *Klaus J. Hopt*, Zum Begriff des Geregelten Markts nach der Wertpapierdienstleistungsrichtlinie – am Beispiel von Eurex, in: Festschrift Schimansky (2000), pp. 631, 633 fn. 2.

52 *Walter Wilburg*, Bewegliches System (1952).

investment firms.[53] This definition would limit categorization as an 'organized market'. Organized markets are offering only single-capacity trading infrastructures, whereas intermediaries *owe duties of care directly to clients*. The definition should limit categorization as an organized market to those systems or platforms that comply with a number of criteria (e.g., matching orders concluded on the system and according to the rules of the system;[54] multiple buy and sell interests on both sides of market;[55] continuous or regular basis; prices for securities quoted on the system reflect the interaction of supply and demand for that security on the system).[56] Firms not meeting these cumulative conditions would be able to seek authorization as an appropriately licensed investment firm. Consequently, operators of organized markets should also require a license and be subject to a special supervisory regime.

Under current law, the regulations on 'regulated markets' have the greatest impact on the development of the internal financial market.[57] The technique of remote membership according to Art. 15 para. 4 ISD grants access for investment firms without physical presence as they are organized on the basis of an electronic system. On the one side, Art. 15 ISD offers the European passport for intermediaries, but at the same time also the passport for screen-based trading systems. The ISD has established a mutual recognition system that even permits the formation of a transnational pan-European market.[58]

Consequently, the focus of EU legislation in the area of trading infrastructures will be on 'regulated markets', which will be positioned within the concept drafted at the top level or the inner circle of trading facilities; they

---

53 Working Document of Services of the Securities and Organised Market Unit F/3, Internal Market Directorate General (2001).

54 The definition would exclude systems that merely allow identification of the other side to a trade and that leave counterparties to conclude final agreement.

55 A distinguishing feature of organized markets are that they provide for continuous interactive confrontation of all interested purchasers or sellers of financial instrument potential prices. The automated proprietary order books of banks or dealers are excluded as the bank or system is accessible only to the client base of the system, and the system is a counterparty for every trade, trading only where it is to its own advantage.

56 Working Document of Internal Market Directorate General; Securities and Organised Markets Unit F/3.

57 *Guido Ferrarini*, in: Ferrarini/Hopt/Wymeersch, supra note 2.

58 *Guido Ferrarini*, in: Ferrarini/Hopt/Wymeersch, supra note 2; *Johannes Köndgen*, supra note 5, pp. 1401, 1411.

are drafted as a qualified subset of 'organized markets'. The category of regulated market can be described as a special form of organized market with additional qualifications, i.e., (a) safeguards regarding the operation of the market (licensing system, supervising, ownership structure, fit and proper test, and governance) and (b) the instruments admitted to trading on the market.[59] The regulatory rationale is that this category of trading arrangements should be characterized by strict controls regarding the quality and constitution of the instruments that are admitted to trading. These controls may take the form of obligations (e.g., disclosure) imposed on the underlying issuer and/or party sponsoring admission to trading. Under this concept, issuers and trading participants (broker-dealers) will be subject to special duties in order to guarantee a certain level of quality of the traded 'products'. The element 'quality of admitted and traded instruments' makes the close connection between trading service and traded product obvious: the normative link shows the necessity to harmonize the approach of the listing and disclosure directives with the concept of the ISD.[60] The preconditions of the official market (implicitly semi-official market) as the qualifying elements must be given up in favor of the common regulative elements of the regulated market.[61]

4. National Regulations

In Germany the government just recently published the governmental draft of the Fourth Financial Markets Promotion Act, in which new regulations dealing with new kinds of trading systems are included, at least to a certain extent. Under the new law (Art. 37i of the drafted version of the Act on Securities Trading [WpHG]), the regulations about trading systems will distinguish whether the different systems fulfill the qualification as a regulated market under Art. 13 ISD or not. Regulated markets outside Germany that are offering the possibility to trade in Germany by establishing terminals

---

59 Working Document of Services of the Securities and Organised Market Unit F/3, Internal Market Directorate General.

60 For the current – hardly understandable – situation (in Austria): *Susanne Kalss*, Kapitalmarktrecht, in: Potacs/Holoubek, Handbuch des Wirtschaftsaufsichtsrechts (Wien, 2002).

61 *Guido Ferrarini*, in: Ferrarini/Hopt/Wymeersch, supra note 2; See the already undertaken shift in the Proposal for a Prospectus Directive and the consultative paper of the Disclosure Directive.

will only have to submit a notification to the Germany supervisory authority, whereas other businesses offering similar services will have to file for a license. However, the German regulations will be restricted on international aspects of offering trading facilities; the bill lacks rules about the broad range of different trading facilities, and therefore does not react in full to the dramatically changed trading infrastructure. In Austria quite the same can be observed: only one article of the Stock Exchange Act is directed toward those trading facilities situated in another member state of the EU. These first national attempts at regulation seem quite restricted and a little disappointing. Obviously the national legislators are observing and awaiting the European development.

5. Investment Firms in General

Although the Investment Services Directive was set in force only eight years ago, many regulations must be changed and adapted to the new technical and policy environment to enable investment firms to truly offer their services within the whole community. According to the discussion documents published by the European Commission,[62] adjustments are pending that seek to make further progress toward a single passport for investment firms, entitling them to provide a specified range of investment services at home as well as in the other member states.

Different aspects have to be considered: (a) broadening of the list of core investment services; (b) enlargement of duties of firms offering special services; and (c) concentration of surveillance competence in the home country of the investment firm. Only a few aspects will be mentioned here.

The basket of investment services that are important for the development and sound operation of the European financial market is growing; therefore, an enlargement of the list added to the ISD has to be considered. Examples include information services close to brokerage and investment (order routing, bulletin boards, and introducing brokers).[63] From a completely different perspective, it could be useful to consider the qualification of professional

---

[62] (2000) COM 729; also (2000) COM 722; *Nicole Hammes*, Die Vorschläge der Europäischen Kommission zur Überarbeitung der Wertpapierdienstleistungsrichtlinie: (2001) Zeitschrift für Bankrecht und Bankwirtschaft 498 et seq.

[63] Working Document of Services of the Securities and Organised Market Unit F/3, Internal Market Directorate General.

investment advice as a single core investment service (to pave the normative way to avoid conflicts of interest on the European level).

According to the considerations of the Commission, investment firms that are offering order-matching services very similar to market-forum services (internal matching executed by brokers) should be subject to customized application of supervisory requirements (strengthening the obligation for these investment firms performing transactions outside the scope of 'regulated markets' to report such a transaction to a 'regulated market' immediately after its conclusion).

Finally, the competences of authorization and supervision are concentrated with the competent authorities in the country of the establishment of the investment firms (home country). The concept was already formulated in the current version of the ISD, it was well established even before in the directive about undertakings for collective investment in transferable securities (UCITS), and it is going to be extended to management companies.[64] In the meantime, this concept has been elaborated and realized in particular by the E-Commerce Directive.[65] Two considerations have to be put forward in advance: investment services offered via the Internet are subject to the directive (Art. 2),[66] and the directive establishes in Art. 3 the core principle of home-country regulation and control[67] for services offered via the Internet. Although this principle is contested,[68] it seems at least consequent to follow this concept under the genuine investment services directive as well and to transfer the responsibility of control generally (even for the conduct-of-business rules) to the home state authority. The focus of the competence

---

64 *Brigitte Haar*, Venture Capital Funding for Biotech Pharmaceutical Companies in an Integrated Financial Services Market: Regulatory Diversity within the EC: (2001) European Business Organisation Law Review 585, 596 et seq.; *Gralf-Peter Callies*, Heimatstaatprinzip und Europa-Pass (single license principle) im europäischen Finanzmarktrecht: Wettbewerb der Finanzdienstleister oder der Finanzplätze?: (2000) Europäisches Wirtschafts- und Steuerrecht 432 et seq.

65 OJ EC 2000 L 178.

66 *Gerhard Spindler*, Internationale Kapitalmarktangebote und Dienstleistungen im Internet: (2001) Wertpapier-Mitteilungen 1689, 1690; *Ulrich Florian*, supra note 7, p. 333.

67 'Each Member State shall ensure that the information society services provided by a service provider established on its territory comply with the national provisions applicable in the Member State in question which fall within the coordinated field'.

68 See, for example, *Gerhard Spindler*, Emissionen im Internet, Kapitalmarktrecht und Kollissionsrecht: (2001) Neue Zeitschrift für Gesellschaftsrecht 1058, 1059.

of the home state authority urges a continuation of the harmonization process concerning licensing and investor protection requirements. The smooth and well-developed parallel regulation of market forum services on the one hand and trading services on the other hand (codes of conduct and disclosure regulations) has high priority, therefore. One of the most significant and important steps ahead is the new approach to regulate insider dealing and market abuse.[69] The Proposal of a Directive on Market Abuse[70] offers an amended definition of insider dealing and puts market manipulation (distortion of the price-setting mechanism and dissemination of false and misleading information)[71] under punishment and further sanctions (disclosure to the public by the competent authority).

However, simple regulation is not sufficient; instead, the whole concept must provide for adequate implementation and control. The home country concept requires close cooperation between the home and host country authorities. Even with harmonized rules for investor protection and codes of conduct provided, there still remain substantial doubts that the authority where the investment firm is domiciled lacks knowledge about the different markets all over Europe and the behavior of the investors abroad. It might be presumed that the infringement of regulations against investors in another marketplaces does not attract the attention of the home authority in the same way as of the local authority. On the other side, the means of prosecution could be more suitable for the home country authority. Obviously member states with strong marketplaces, a high concentration of marketplaces, and a powerful supervisory authority (UK) must have promoted this regulatory approach. For their purpose they did a good lobbying job, but will it serve the sound operating and development of the European market?

B. *Other Services for the Market*

1. Financial Analysts

Apart from the proposed steps by the European Commission, the role of other players offering important services to the market should be analyzed. The role of financial analysts and the influence of their research reports and

---

69 *Thomas Goldmann*, Marktmanipulation und Insider-Geschäfte: Neue europäische Tatbestände: (2001) Österreichisches Bankarchiv 783.

70 (2001) COM 281 final.

71 See Annex B of the Propsosal (2001) COM 281 final.

buy-hold-or-sell-advises have to be reconsidered. Should – and if so, in what way should – they be rendered subject to special regulations? Different areas of regulation might be access to the profession, compliance with special duties, privileged access to and use of confident information of issuers,[72] and consequently liability toward the company investigated and toward third parties who are acting according to recommendations included in research reports of the analysts. However, conflicts of interests are the most striking aspect to be regulated. Ownership of shares of the investigated and recommended corporations and the relationship of the research staff and the investment department of the banking houses[73] have to be reconsidered. The role of analysts during the coming down of the new economy, the ongoing recommendations, and the slow information of the market have attracted the attention of regulators, who have begun to consider special regulations, at least concerning the last two aspects. General codes of conduct for all financial business and general in-door compliance regimes for investment firms are obviously not sufficient. Different kinds of questions must be distinguished: Should a restriction of access and a special kind of license be introduced? Should only the analysts or also members of their families or affiliated companies be forbidden to hold securities of a company within the working field of the analyst? Who should control these regulations? Are general regulations by law – or at least on the level of a directive by the securities commission – necessary and reasonable, or are regulations by professional self-regulating bodies sufficient to create substantial confidence by the investors and the market? The SEC recently declined to set regulations and pushed the ball into the court of self-regulating bodies. The shift was justified by the argument to raise the acceptance of regulations among analysts,[74] but the argument of higher acceptance and therefore simpler implementation seems too weak; obviously the Securities Commission has no convincing concept to tackle this stream of influence and possible irritations for the market. At least a code of conduct and adequate sanctions after lacking compliance must be set in force; a common European approach under the new financial market regulatory concept should be the first step. In Germany a code of conduct by the self-regulatory body of analysts (*Deutsche Vereinigung von Finanzanalysten*) failed in October 2001.

---

72 *Tim Drygala*, A step ahead of the crowd – Zur selektiven Information von Finanzanalysten nach amerikanischem und deutschem Kapitalmarktrecht: (2001) Wertpapier-Mitteilungen 1282 et seq.

73 Financial Times Deutschland, 27 September 2001, p. 19.

74 Financial Times Deutschland, 27 September 2001, p. 19.

2. Rating Agencies

The same holds true for rating agencies. Rating agencies are said 'to be hardly strangers to conflicts of interest'.[75] For the last decades they have received their fees to a great extent from the companies they rate. They even have a small regulatory role today under Austrian law.[76] According to different proposals, they should be entrusted with more tasks regarding public offerings of bonds and other securities for which a prospectus need not be published.[77] Under U.S. law, rating agencies play an increasing role in the supervision of money-market funds which have to carry top or near-top ratings from the SEC-approved agencies. The assessment of the rating agencies is gaining importance in Europe and Austria as well, so that one has to think about similar regulative measures as mentioned above. In particular, a system of restricting the access and the offering of the service and codes of conduct should be considered as these services are gaining importance and influence on the market. Additionally, clearly formulated rules dealing with the liability toward the rated companies and toward third persons[78] could contribute to clarify the role of these institutions. Finally, the importance of the assessment of the rating agencies should be recognized legislatively by imposing on the issuers of securities the duty of inserting the assessment of a rating agency into the prospectus or another disclosure document. The duty will lie with the issuer, although the assessment is only market data and only connected to the issuer; the rating agency should be obliged to deliver its assessment immediately to the issuer.

C. *Issuers*

1. Market Position

The number and significance of issuers is rising because of the increasing demand for equity and the simple technical choice of different issuing and trading facilities including different locations of stock exchanges. The tradi-

---

75 Economist, 9 June 2001, p. 86.

76 See *Stefan Weber*, supra note 26.

77 *Christian Nowotny*, Anlegerschutz bei Anleihen: (1999) Recht der Wirtschaft 717.

78 *Susanne Kalss*, Kapitalmarktbezogene Haftungsansprüche: (2000) Österreichisches Bankarchiv 641 et seq.

tional single relationship between issuer and stock exchange will be replaced by changing and parallel relationships between the issuer and different operators of trading systems, ranging from traditional stock exchanges to alternative trading systems and Internet-based networks domiciled in different countries. Double and triple listing at different market operators is becoming more and more common and is accelerating the process of loosening a singular and exclusive permanent relationship between the issuer and one stock exchange. The new situation requires a complete overhaul of the rules that regulated the previously static relationships.[79]

2. Multiple Listing

The simultaneous listing at several stock exchanges (multiple listing) must be simplified, i.e., multiple listing has to be encouraged by a stimulating regulative framework.[80] An important set of regulations must deal with the access to trading facilities, the change between stock exchanges or other trading systems, and the partial or complete delisting of issuers. In other words, the flexibility of issuers must be promoted in order to enable them to opt at least for the moment or a restricted period of time for a perfectly designed market operator to reduce the cost for raising equity.[81] The listing process must therefore be standardized and the requirements (in particular the prospectus) for a listing harmonized – at least for special market segments or at qualified trading facilities. The shift from one trading facility to another or the reduction of listings by the issuer must be facilitated. The more types of trading facilities within the categories of the organized or the regulated market that are recognized,[82] the more complex the system will be and the more attention the legislators have to dedicate to a sound and reasonable regulative framework.

Several variations need to be distinguished. These might include the shift of securities onto a market or market segment of inferior quality (from official trading to over-the-counter market) or another trading facility or market forum and the complete or partial withdrawal from the stock exchange or

79 *Guido Ferrarini*, in: Ferrarini/Hopt/Wymeersch, supra note 2; *Susanne Kalss*, The Capital Markets in the Age of the Euro (2002).

80 Proposal for a directive on the prospectus to be published when securities are offered to the public or admitted to trading; (2001) COM 280 final.

81 *Brigitte Haar*, supra note 64, p. 585 et seq.

82 See the proposals of the Commission in the consultative paper for the ISD.

similar trading facility. In addition, a distinction between different foreign stock exchanges or trading facilities domiciled in various countries within and outside the European Union must be made.[83] Partial withdrawal means the termination of the quotation on one particular stock exchange. It does not mean the termination of the quotation of a part of the shares (stock class) of a company. Simple delisting has to be regulated by market regulation as well as by company regulations. At this stage, an important impact of regulating this complex system of interrelated relations can be observed: if one small wheel is turned, there will be potential consequences for other market participants, and it is therefore necessary to think about additional regulations from different perspectives (such as the issuer or trading facility).

3. Corporate Governance Standards of Issuers

In turn, the issuers have to contribute also to make the flexible system function. Internationally oriented investors are not restricted to one country or economic area, but they are looking and acting on the international floor. As a result, over the last few years there has been a proliferation of international comparisons of financial and corporate systems. Apart from disclosure duties, corporate governance standards[84] should also be stated. During the last decade, a creeping separation of private companies and companies with publicly listed securities has already begun.[85]

There is a mounting interest in the way in which financial and corporate systems work in different countries or economic areas. Analysts observing and interpreting the market are especially interested in aspects such as instruments to measure performance and the efficiency of companies' management, and the barriers triggered in general by agency problems and controlling costs. The existence of such a code contributes to an easing of

---

[83] *Klaus J. Hopt/Harald Baum*, supra note 32, p. 418; *Susanne Kalss*, in: Aicher/Kalss/Oppitz (eds), supra note 32, p. 264 et seq.

[84] *Klaus J. Hopt*, System und Entwicklung des Kapitalmarktrechts, in: Grundmann (ed.), supra note 32, p. 330; see also the recommendation of the European Parliament concerning takeovers (2001). Communication of the Commission with regard to establishing a high-level expert group for company law issues: DN: IP/01/1237 (first feature for the second stage of work).

[85] For an Austrian perspective: *Susanne Kalss*, Special Duties and Responsibilities of Companies with Publicly Listed Securities: (2000) International and Comparative Corporate Law Journal 385 et seq.

the market process by raising the comparability of companies and establishing the parameter of the assessment, thereby decreasing the information and transaction costs.[86] For this reason, the European Commission has twice proposed investigating the need for basic principles all over Europe or formulating at least general guidelines in order to be prepared to face the challenge of the competition of legal and economic orders.[87] Stimulated by privately drafted and later officially recognized codes, special duties and additional requirements have been established for publicly listed companies.[88] Apart from the first wave of codes – in particular in the UK (Cadbury, Greenbury, Hampel, and Combined Code), France, or the Netherlands during the last year – and the more general approach by the OECD,[89] Germany launched some codes with different approaches.[90] After the first wave, the list of proposals published by the Governmental Commission (headed by Professor Theodor Baums) is the most important paper;[91] the report of the expert group is now the basis for shaping a law on the one side (by the ministry of justice) and a code of best practice on the other side (by an expert group headed by Mr. Cromme). Drafts of both have already been published.[92] In Austria, until now only special duties regarding the information flow within issuers were published by the supervisory authority which

86 *Uwe H. Schneider/Christian Strenger*, Die Corporate Governance Grundsätze der Grundsatzkommission Corporate Governance: (2000) AG 106 et seq.; *Theodor Baums* (ed.), Regierungskommission Corporate Governance (Köln, 2001).

87 *Eddy Wymeersch*, Gesellschaftsrecht im Wandel: Ursachen und Entwicklungen: (2001) Zeitschrift für Gesellschafts- und Unternehmensrecht 294, 320 et seq.

88 See the excellent overview on the homepage of the European Corporate Governance Network: <www.ecgn.ulb.be/ecgn/codes>; see also *Fabrizio Barca/ Marco Becht* (eds), The Control of Corporate Europe (Oxford, 2002).

89 OECD, Corporate Governance Principles: *Ulrich Seibert*, Vorbemerkungen zu den OECD-Principals: (1999) AG 337 et seq.

90 For a comparison, see only *Rene Theisen*, Corporate Governance – Eine neue Leitkultur für die Unternehmensführung?: (2001) Zeitschrift für Rechnungslegung und Treuhandwesen (RWZ) 157. Until July 2001 the most recent and officially established commission was the so-called Baums Commission (headed by Professor Baums); it will be continued now by the Cromme Commission (chaired by Mr. Cromme) with a twofold task: to formulate a corporate governance code and to contribute to the drafting of an amendment of the corporation act.

91 *Theodor Baums* (ed.), supra note 86.

92 <www.bmj.de>.

will be come in force in April 2002.[93] According to a recent study of a consultancy firm,[94] Austria is one of the very last countries of Europe where a code of corporate governance has not yet been established. The homepage of the European Corporate Governance Network at the University of Brussels cannot give any more information either.[95] However, during the last year an 'Austrian Corporate Governance Code' was drafted by an expert group under the auspices of the professional body of accountants (*Institut für Wirtschaftsprüfer*); this draft was first presented to the public at the annual meeting of the accountants in October 2001[96] and will be the basic document for further discussion.

Although important initiatives have been started and the member states are ambitiously developing and approving codes of conduct, one must keep in mind that figures are more important than the existence of codes and the testified compliance with their regulations.[97] Therefore, the European Union must especially keep its eye on disclosure standards for accounting information, prospectus, and continuing information.

4. Current Legislative Measures

Currently the regulations dealing with multiple listing of securities at stock exchanges or other trading facilities in more than one country and at market segments of different quality are quite complex and insufficient. The mechanism of partial mutual recognition of the prospectus and additional national requirements is not able to ensure a single passport for issuers throughout the whole community, but this rather burdensome procedure is not resulting in a satisfying outcome. Regulative steps for issuers must be coordinated with those directed toward the market infrastructure. The legislators must determine the parameters and conditions for the issuers dependent on their

---

93 Verordnung der Bundes-Wertpapieraufsicht: Emittenten Compliance Verordnung. Amtsblatt der österreichischen Finanzverwaltung, 121. Stück, Nr 210 vom 4. Oktober 2001.

94 Börsenkurier 13 September 2001, p. 1.

95 <www.ecgn.ulb.be/ecgn/codes>.

96 Institut für Wirtschaftsprüfer, Austrian Code of Corporate Governance (2001); Annual meeting at Baden, 13 October 2001; *Susanne Kalss/Christian Nowotny*, Ein Code of Corporate Governance für Österreich?, in: Institut für Wirtschaftsprüfer, Jahrbuch für Wirtschaftsprüfer 2001 (Wien, 2002).

97 See *Bernhard Großfeld/Josef Hoelzenbein*, Cyberlex als Unternehmensrecht: (2001) Neue Zeitschrift für Gesellschaftsrecht 779, 781.

'market status': either admitted to a regulated market or only publicly offered.

The considerations to create a European Passport first presented by *FESCO,*[98] then included in the recommendations of the Lamfalussy Report, and finally realized by a recent proposal of the Commission[99] fit in well with the new approach. The proposal will harmonize the different practices and differing interpretations based on distinct traditions within the European Union regarding both the content and the layout of the prospectus.[100] An enhanced level of harmonized disclosure requirements will provide for equivalent investor protection within the Union. Harmonization on the one side means simplification for the compliance of the issuers so they do not need to undergo more than one procedure and file duplicate sets of different sets of documentation or respond to numerous additional national requirements. The most important features of the current proposal are:[101]

- Enhanced disclosure standards fitting better to accounting standards;
- Alignment of disclosure standards for the public offer and admission to trading;
- Separation of the information into three documents: registration document, securities note, and summary;
- Continuing duty to update information relevant for investment decisions;
- Electronic disclosure (Internet);
- Introduction of obligatory checking and approving of an authority (giving up of simple registration or review by experts[102]);
- Simple notification of approved prospectus by the competent authority;
- Concentration of the responsibility with the home competent authority.

Apart from the 'initial information', i.e., information related to the first public offering or the admission to a regulated market, continuing disclosure duties are as important. Therefore, the European Commission has launched a harmonization initiative in addition to the prospectus directive proposal that would set a common standard for the continuing disclosure duties of compa-

---

98 <www.eurofesco.org> (2000/2001)

99 (2001) COM 280 final.

100 *Jens Fürhoff/Corinna Ritz*, Richtlinienentwurf der Kommission über den europäischen Pass für Emittenten: (2001) Wertpapier-Mitteilungen 220 et seq.; *Brigitte Haar*, supra note 64, pp. 585, 596 et seq.

101 (2001) COM 280 final.

102 Section 8 of the Austrian Capital Market Act (1991).

nies admitted to a regulated market.[103] Companies whose shares have only been publicly offered will currently not be rendered subject to further obligations; the discussion paper of the Commission does not seem to redress this lack of information. The Commission is willing to raise the frequency of interim reports, render them subject to a special review by experts, and finally shorten the period between the end of the reporting period and the time of disclosure. Moreover, the Commission is suggesting an upgrade to the ad-hoc disclosure requirements. There is no further suggestion for adapting the disclosure of major shareholdings, which should be supplemented during the consultation procedure because there are still loopholes, for example, concerning concerted actions or options.

D. Investors

Investors, i.e., the present and potential future holders of securities, are another group whose importance has been increasing during the last years. Investors are interested in a diversified and liquid market (depth of the market) that guarantees a range of attractive investment possibilities, low transaction costs, and high standards of transparency and publicity, on which investment decisions are based. The market is characterized by an easy access to market facilities from the technical point of view: Is it appreciable from the legal point of view and under which conditions? Institutional investors often play a multi-fold role: they act as investors and as issuers, but also as brokers at the same time. Obviously conflicts of interest must arise. How should they be tackled?

In general, the significance and negotiating power of investors have been increasing because of their concentration in a limited number of very large financial centers and the subsequent easier access to technical opportunities. Investors as a whole have been strengthened simply because worldwide trading in securities is concentrated in the hands of only a few investment banks, i.e., the influence shifts to the benefit of the investors. Due to the disintermediation of the trading systems by technical facilities (Internet) or by simple independent access regulations, investor access to trading facilities has become much easier.

---

[103] European Commission; Internal Market Directorate General: Consultation Document on Transparency Obligations by Issuers Whose Securities Are Admitted to Trading on a Regulated Market; see <www.europa.eu.int/comm/ internal_ market/en/finances/mobil>.

Investors do not represent a homogenous group; instead, they are a fragmented group of people and businesses. The fragmentation of the different groups makes it necessary to find criteria for a categorization to establish adequate regulations for each group in order to secure a reasonable protection of the different investor types on the one hand and a sound and efficient functioning of the market on the other. Over-regulation has to be avoided as well as the lack of adequate measures in favor of investors. The need for regulation and the kind of protective measures differ.[104] Stock exchanges and other trading facilities have to offer different services to satisfy ever-changing needs and to ensure that the development of niches and segmentation are possible in order to provide the best possible services. Moreover, there is a need for different protective mechanisms and standards. The ISD has already established the basis of different regulatory levels in line with the typical need of a group defined by law. As a consequence of the fragmentation progress, regulations will have to offer different regulative measures to different categories of investors.[105] It is therefore one of the main tasks for regulators now to find clear-cut definitions for the various group in order to offer the most adequate set of regulations. According to proposals by the FESCO, the Commission has already launched a discussion to find satisfying definitions and to link them with fine-tuned sets of law. Especially in the field of information, different developments, and plans on a European level, FESCO and the Commissions have already presented their future plans,[106] which are now also part of the consultative paper for the amendment of the ISD.[107] National legislators also have worked to develop the categories and a sound concept to raise the confidence of the investors to be qualified in the correct manner.

---

104 *Klaus J. Hopt/Harald Baum*, supra note 32, pp. 438, 445.

105 See *Günter Birnbaum/Wolf Kopp-Colomb*, Die Harmonisierung von Wohlverhaltens- und Complianceregelungen auf europäischer Ebene durch FESCO bzw CESR: (2001) Wertpapier-Mitteilungen 2001, 2288 et seq.

106 FESCO: <www.europefesco.org>

107 *Nicole Hammes*, supra note 62, p. 498 et seq.

III. Shifting and Bundling Supervisory Matters

A. General Considerations

After the first wave of regulation of financial services law, a development toward a centralized supervisory body is visible, at least at the national level. The old structures are changing. The UK set an example when it introduced a single all-powerful regulator, the Financial Services Authority, to watch over the financial market.[108] The FSA became the statutory regulator at midnight on 30 November 2001.[109] Apart from this famous shift from a multi-level supervisory structure executed by different self-regulating bodies to the single Financial Services Authority, the trend toward a one-shop authority can be observed in other countries (Finland and Sweden) and in the continental member states of Germany and Austria as well, where traditionally a patchwork of different authorities and state departments has worked for better or worse during the last years.

B. Efficient Authorities

The main motive for this reform is clear: a broader constituency for each regulator is expected to reduce inefficiencies in Europe's fragmented markets. Fragmentation along national borders diminishes the depth and liquidity of the markets and persistently increases the cost of capital in Europe in comparison to the U.S. Of equal importance is the national separation of the markets, which makes it more difficult for entrepreneurs to find venture capitalists and start-up funds.[110]

The discussion of regulatory reform in Europe has a short history because the whole regulatory development has quite a short history. Most European

---

108 *Holger Fleischer*, Der Financial Services and Markets Act 2000: Neues Börsen- und Kapitalmarktrecht für das Vereinigte Königreich: (2001) Recht der Internationalen Wirtschaft 817 et seq.; *Michael Blair*, Blackstone's Guide to the Financial Services & Markets Act 2000 (London, 2001).

109 Economist, 17 November 2001, p. 81.

110 *European Commission*, Communication of the European Commission, Risk Capital: A Key to Job Creation in the European Union; European Commission, Progress Report on the Risk Capital Action Plan (Brussels, 18 October 2000); Lamfalussy Report, Final Report on the Regulation of the European Securities Markets (Brussels, 15 February 2001) pp. 10 et seq.; *Brigitte Haar*, supra note 64, p. 596.

regulators have not been established for long, and change in the financial markets has been slower than on the international – in particular, on the U.S. – level.[111] Financial markets are complex webs of bundles of relations and closely interrelated mechanisms. A supervisory body is able to meet its controlling and supervisory tasks efficiently only if the institution takes advantage of highly developed technical equipment; however, even more important is having human knowledge and the skill to understand the mechanisms in order to be able to foresee coming developments, to react, and to do timely preparation work.[112] Knowledge can be used in the most efficient manner when specialists of different fields but similar phenomena and problems (for example, insurance and hedging funds, pension schemes, and life insurances) work together in close networks that offer an institutional framework, the legal background of confidence and mutual support, and personal contact. Qualified staff is expensive. The increasing quantity and quality of controlling tasks as well as the costs of efficient work promote the pooling of supervisory tasks by one more or less independent body which acts in line with the general guidelines of an efficient supervision of the financial markets: sound functioning of the market protection of the interests of the market participants, in particular of the investors.

C. Shift of the Role of the Stock Exchange

Although stock exchanges act as firms, they are still – at least in Austria (section 64 of the Stock Exchange Act) or in Germany – in charge of certain supervisory matters, such as the admission of securities to the market, the review of disclosure duties, and the tracing of market manipulation (partly also insider dealing). Investment service companies look after their own interests as investors and at the same time act as service providers. There is an evident conflict of interest between the stock exchange (as a firm) in charge of promoting its trading system, attracting new listings, and pushing its revenues out of the business and at the same time exercising control over its clients (like an independent supervisory authority).[113] This pending con-

---

[111] Economist, 3 March 2001, p. 67.

[112] See official considerations by the Austrian legislator: 640 Beilagen zu den Stenographischen Protokollen des Nationalrats 21. Gesetzgebungsperiode. Preface.

[113] *Eddy Wymeersch*, The Harmonisation of Securities Regulation in Europe in the New Trading Environment, (2000) Working Paper 2000-16 Financial Law cont. ...

flict of interest requires a redefinition of the tasks of the public supervisory body and the role of stock exchanges as market organizers.[114] The supervisory body has to take over the controlling tasks in relation to the stock exchanges and keep them under control like other investment businesses.

D. *Increasing Number of Tasks and Intensifying of International Cooperation*

Apart from the economic consideration and the obvious need to solve the control-profit gain conflict of stock exchanges versus market participants, other regulative developments must be kept in mind. According to the recommendations of the Lamfalussy Report and the new approach of the European Community, it is not sufficient only to formulate principles and to set regulations; instead, there must be provision for the adequate implementation and sanctioning of the new or amended duties. The Market Abuse Directive explicitly states that member states have to designate a single regulatory and supervisory authority with a common minimum set of responsibilities.[115] The range of tasks of the supervisory bodies will be enlarged enormously. The gaining of tasks and responsibilities will be taking place on different front lines: (a) broadening of traditional financial institutions; (b) expansion to new services closely connected to the financial services and capital market (trading systems, information services); (c) intensifying or introducing of control of disclosure documents for issuers of securities (prospectus, interim reports); (d) establishing and extending control to special transactions of companies whose shares are listed or at least publicly offered (takeover, thinking about a merger, demerger, and similar transactions[116]). The final draft of the Lamfalussy Report did not promote a central European authority (Super SEC) entrusted with the task of the national authorities, but instead suggested a network of specialized national authorities. The shift of

---

Institute, p. 6; *Vincent Boland*, Stock and Derivatives Exchanges: Financial Times, 28 March 2001, p. 1.

114 *Eddy Wymeersch*, supra note 113, p. 6; *Vincent Boland*, supra note 113, p. 1; *Guido Ferrarini*, in: Ferrarini/Hopt/Wymeersch, supra note 2.

115 (2001) COM 281.

116 See the first considerations: *Peter Doralt*, Übernahme, Verschmelzung, Konzern und der City Code: (2000) Der Gesellschafter 197 et seq.; *Susanne Kalss*, Aktuelle Fragen des Übernahmerechts – Erfahrungen aus Österreich, Paper presented on 24 September 2001 in Frankfurt.

exchanges as national entities to international operating businesses, the international market access of other trading facilities, and the transnational offering and trading of securities cause a broad range of difficult jurisdictional and supervisory problems[117] that have to be managed by this kind of network.

E. National Problems of Implementation

However, these regulations of the new European approach are confronting heavily national constitutional borderlines and are shaking the traditional concept of the structure of authorities and the administrative apparatus. As already mentioned, different proposals on the European level regulate that for the supervisory tasks, a national supervisory body will be entrusted which will be competent for the firms domiciled in that country. The European legislator does not set any more restrictive framing, but obviously the regulations assume the existence of independent bodies equipped with qualified technical and human resources, flexible and open for new developments and suitable for quick international cooperation. How to fulfill these expectations and requirements lies with the responsibility of the single member states. For Germany, with its traditional federal system and multi-layer supervisory system, it is exactly this task that is extremely difficult. It is difficult for Austria as well, with its constitution that is based on the principle that the whole administration will be organized so that central matters will be allotted to the ministers heading their government department in an autocratic manner. The main instruments are the ministerial order on the one side and the duty of the civil servants to comply on the other.

According to a recent judgment of the Austrian Constitutional Court (12 December 2001),[118] legislators are not allowed to establish new and separate legal entities and entrust them with all kinds of supervisory or administrative tasks; instead, they must observe the strict borders set by the constitution (with the position of the ministry as head of the department, its

---

[117] See only *Uwe H. Schneider*, Internationales Kapitalmarktrecht: (2001) Die Aktiengesellschaft, 7.

[118] VfGH (Constitutional Court) Geschäftszahl 269/01. Constitutional Court from July 2001, 15. B 1695/99-12; *Heinz-Peter Rill*, Grenzen der Ausgliederung aus der unmittelbaren Staatsverwaltung: (1986) Österreichisches Bankarchiv 748; *Ernst Brandl/Rainer Wolfbauer*, supra note 20, p. 12 et seq.; see also Constitutional Court 14473/1996

right of leading and ordering the whole field of administration, and its responsibility toward the parliament). The court made clear that the tasks of the supervisory body must not be shifted from the ministry to another separate body; in particular, supervising and punishing tasks must not be removed from the centralized administration. Financial services is by far not the only matter at stake, but it is a typical example; telecommunications and public procurement are facing the same regulative difficulties. The disintegrating process of the old-fashioned constitution created at the end of World War I and the requirements of an increasingly complex, globally acting, and technology-based administration cannot be bridged by pragmatic solutions and the establishment of a specialized authority. At least under the Austrian jurisdiction, they are more sophisticated. Tasks and structural and regulative requirements have grown beyond the constitution. The Austrian legislators have left the opportunity to broaden the space for a more liberal interpretation by entering the European Community. The new supervisory body (*Finanzmarktaufsicht*), which was established by the *Finanzmarktaufsichtsgesetz* in August 2001 and which should start to work in April 2002 at the latest, first has to pass the constitutional exam. The legislators have to use the time to reformulate the law already in force by April 2002. Only a small amount of time is left to find a satisfying solution by keeping only a few tasks with the separate body; perhaps in Austria the concept of supervising the capital market as a whole has to be reconsidered.

IV. Liability of Market Participants

Sanctions of duties have to be effective, proportionate, and dissuasive. Remember the often-repeated formula by the European Court of Justice. Liability has become more and more a driving – or at least supplementing – force in the shaping of a sound operating of the market and the adequate protection of investors by promoting a high level of duty of care. Developed liability of market participants toward investors for negligent errors and omissions stands for high quality and a positive signal of the whole market.[119] The market realizes that it can rely with greater assurance on information documents of the issuer and other market participants. Gatekeepers such as investment advisers, auditors, rating agencies, and other 'escorting services' are performing high diligence as they face liability

[119] See *John F. Coffee*, supra note 36.

issues. Standards of best practice of market participants have therefore been elaborated.

However, at the same time liability is damned as a disturbing if not destructive obstacle to a continuous market development. Market participants, intermediaries, and special firms are said to be pushed outside the market or forced to give up special services because they cannot bear the risk. This kind of argumentation is often presented by discussing the liability of auditors, but it can be seen as a typical pattern. 'Keeping the flood gates shut' is an often-repeated phrase to establish shelters for the auditors and other professionals against the claims of disadvantaged investors.[120] Can a rule really be justified that limits the liability to five million ATS (0.4 million Euro)[121] although the damage caused by a misleading or omitting statement caused damages approaching 100 million Euro? The amount of damages suffered due to information deficits for the raising of capital or IPO will often be significant – at least in total. The existence of this badly adjusted liability rule can only be explained by historical reasons. In the 1930s, accountants had to be protected against the hidden dangers of low-quality balance sheets. This new service was carried out by a young profession with a lack of sufficient personal resources, and without aggregated experience and education to raise the level and to manage the new task. The liability-limiting regulation was thought to be an introductory rule for the interim only. After seventy years of experience, the same considerations no longer count.[122] Another focus must be the design of an appropriate procedure framework[123] (bundling of claims, class action) to enforce the claims reasonably because quite often the loss by most individual plaintiffs is likely to remain limited.

---

120 See the Comparative Study: *Jaap Spier* (ed.) The limits of expanding liability (The Hague, 1998); for a summary of the arguments, *Susanne Kalss*, Die Haftung des Abschlußprüfers gegenüber Gläubigern, Gesellschaftern und Anlegern: (2002) Österreichisches Bankarchiv (in print).

121 For the audit of the accounting documents from 2002, the law distinguishes between private and publicly listed companies and negligence and gross negligence.

122 *Susanne Kalss*, Die Rechtsgrundlagen kapitalmarktrechtlicher Haftungsansprüche: (2000) Österreichisches Bankarchiv 641 et seq., 558; see also *Klaus J. Hopt*, Stellungnahme zur Aktienrechtsreform 1997: (1997/spezial edition) AG 46.

123 *Susanne Kalss*, Anlegerinteressen, supra note 32, p. 229; more generally the fundamental study by *Jürgen Basedow/Klaus J. Hopt/Hein Kötz/Dietmar Baetge* (eds), Die Bündelung gleichgerichteter Interessen im Prozeß (Tübingen, 1999).

The gaining of tasks and duties (review of interim report) of the auxiliary services must be accompanied by an increase of responsibility. One of the striking and pending tasks is to find a well-adjusted system of liability that is a stimulating but not paralyzing tool.[124] Liability caps, obligatory insurance, and individual contributions to compensate damages are first steps toward developing a concept. Adequate insurance coverage must be available to an acceptable premium level. Thinking on a European level might be more useful than along national borderlines.

The shaping force of liability for the behavior of market participants is heavily supported by the Fourth Promotion Act of the Financial Market in Germany.

In general, private law should be applied to strengthen the enforcement of market duties, particularly disclosure obligations. The long list of detailed information for contracts concluded by means of communication technologies can also be mentioned as regulations on the prospectus and listing particulars. Apart from liability claims, investors are entitled to withdraw from the contract or the offer if some substantial information about the investment product is missing.[125] Another example is the principle of 'comply or explain' in the field of corporate governance; companies are accepting codes of best practice by volunteer action. To create a stimulating network for the market, therefore, the legal framework must consist of the optimal mix of public and private law instruments driven by the self-interest of market participants and public responsibility.

V. Final Remarks

The European capital market is facing a tremendous structural change. Legislators on the international and national level have to elaborate stable and flexible instruments to be able to stimulate development and to guarantee the protection of different interests. The establishment of duties and obligations is as important as the organization of a supervisory network and additional private enforcement.

---

124 *Susanne Kalss*, supra note 120.

125 For some examples under Austrian law, see: *Susanne Kalss*, Anlegerinteressen, supra note 32, p. 184 et seq.

REGULATION OF EXCHANGES AND INVESTMENT SERVICES: A JAPANESE PERSPECTIVE

by Hideki Kanda, Tokyo

I. Introduction

Legal and regulatory developments in the Japanese financial sector have been – and still are – experiencing rapid changes at a high pace. This is no surprise: information technology and global competition have made this area highly changeable, and corresponding legal and regulatory responses are called for almost every day.

J. Basedow, H. Baum, K. Hopt, H. Kanda and T. Kono (eds.), Economic Regulation and Competition, (151-164)

It is not easy to present the trends in this area of law and regulation in recent years in distinctive terms, but three elements can be pointed out as general characteristics behind the recent developments. First, in Japan, the force for change in regulation can still be viewed as a result of domestic events. Since the 'bubble' burst in 1991, the Japanese banking sector has been suffering a previously unheard-of crisis. Several banks went bankrupt, and various rescue measures are still underway today. Second, pressure from outside Japan also has begun to influence rulemaking and change in the Japanese financial sector. It is common for various international standards to be developed at various levels. These standards, unlike traditional treaties or conventions, are not law themselves, but national regulators or supervisors generally implement these rules into national regulations, so that these 'soft' standards often become 'hard' rules in individual countries. Third, the importance of private law is ever increasing. This may be a natural result of deregulation, because parties now have more freedom in creating and offering financial products than ever, so that basic private law issues become the subject of direct attention when such new financial products are created and marketed.

In this paper, I will review various developments in the regulation of exchanges and investment services in Japan. First, I will look at a drastic reform plan known as 'Japan's Financial Big Bang'. Second, I will look at developments in 2000 and 2001. And third, I will examine implications of these developments to the Japanese economy.

II. Japan's Big Bang Reform

A. Background

The 'bubbles' in the Japanese stock and real estate markets burst in 1991. Stock prices dropped more than 60 percent between 1991 and 1995, and land prices recorded a similar drop, driving the Japanese economy into recession. As a result, financial institutions and financial markets in Japan lost their competitiveness. In Japan, the process of deregulation and an appropriate response to the rapidly changing environment in world financial markets have been delayed because the Diet and the government had to spend – and continue to spend – an enormous amount of time attempting to resolve the banking crisis. The Big Bang program, announced by the prime minister in November 1996 and aimed at remedying this delay, has two notable characteristics: (1) its reforms are drastic and extensive in scope, and (2) the timetable is specific and quick.

B. Selected Items of the Big Bang Reform until 2000

While this is hardly the place to describe in detail the entire contents of the Big Bang program, several items of the reform relating to regulation of exchanges and investment services are worth mentioning.[1]

1. Lifting the ban on pure holding companies[2]

The Anti-Monopoly Act, which prohibited 'pure holding companies' per se, was amended in 1997, and relevant statutes in the financial sector were amended in response to this change. A pure holding company is defined as a company that has more than half of its assets comprised of shares of other companies. Thus, a financial group may emerge with a holding company structure where banking, insurance, and securities businesses are offered through subsidiaries under the centralized management of a holding company. In fact, the Daiwa Securities Group established a holding company structure in April 1999. Also, a big banking group called Mizuho Financial Group was established in September 2000 in which the Industrial Bank of Japan, Fuji Bank, and Daiichi Kangyô Bank set up a common holding company. After this, many consolidations were made in the financial sector, and as a result, several financial conglomerates are emerging in Japan.

2. Establishment of new regulatory bodies[3]

In June 1998, a new agency called the Financial Supervisory Agency (the 'FSA') was established and given power to regulate banks, securities firms, and insurance companies. This power was transferred from the Ministry of

---

1 For a detailed analysis of Japan's Big Bang reform, see, for example, *T. Hoshi/ H. Patrick* (eds), Crisis and Change in the Japanese Financial System (Boston, Kluwer Academic Publishers, 2000).

2 Effective December 1997 for non-financial firms and March 1998 for financial institutions.

3 Effective 22 June 1998.

Finance to the FSA. Also, in December 1998, a new agency called the Financial Reconstruction Commission (the 'FRC') was established in addition to the FSA, with responsibilities for licensing and other regulatory activities in the financial sector. The FSA implemented financial regulation. The creation of this new regulatory structure suggests that the style of financial regulation in Japan will also change from consensus-based regulation to rule-based regulation. On 1 July 2000, the Planning Bureau of the Ministry of Finance and the FSA were consolidated into the Financial Services Agency (new 'FSA'). The FRC disappeared in January 2001.

3. Abolishment of the fixed commission system of securities brokers[4]

Although the effect of this deregulation has not yet been fully felt, this will inevitably make the securities brokerage industry more competitive.

4. Entry into the securities business: from licensing to registration system[5]

The entry level became lower for the securities industry. This change accompanied the abolishment of the prohibition on securities firms engaging in non-securities activities. The number of securities firms may increase remarkably.

5. Regulation of PTSs[6]

A new regulatory framework for proprietary trading systems ('PTSs') was introduced. Such a system typically undertakes to match buy and sell orders via a computer system, but it does not amount to a securities exchange. Japanese regulation did not have a regulatory framework for such systems, treating them merely as brokers. The new regulation requires authorization by the regulator, thus locating such systems between exchanges and brokers. The authorization standards were liberalized in 2001, and there are two such systems today in Japan, one for shares and the other for debt securities.

---

4 Partly effective April 1998 and fully effective 1 October 1999.

5 Effective 1 December 1998.

6 Effective 1 December 1998.

6. Sale of mutual funds by banks[7]

In 1998, only four percent of the U.S. $10 trillion in individuals' financial assets in Japan were invested in Japanese mutual funds. Sixty-five percent were invested in bank deposits and postal service deposits. When banks start to market mutual funds, this picture may drastically change. Also, important reforms were made to the mutual fund system. For instance, a company-type fund (which is popular in the U.S. but was not permitted in Japan) has become available (effective 1 December 1998). Also, private funds (funds marketed to a limited number of institutions) have been permitted (effective 1 December 1998). However, mutual funds have not become popular in Japan and since 1998 the percentage of individuals' financial assets invested in mutual funds has been decreasing.

7. Asset management by securities firms (effective 1 December 1998)

Securities firms are now permitted to offer asset management services, typically by offering a product known in the U.S. as a 'wrap account'.

8. Improvement in accounting (effective fiscal year 1999 and 2000)

Consolidated accounting and market-value accounting of financial assets were introduced in the fiscal years beginning April 1999 and April 2000 respectively. The new accounting rules are consistent with the International Accounting Standards.

9. Defragmentation among banking, securities, and insurance industries

This is an ongoing liberalization program of fragmented industry regulation in Japan. Liberalization measures include permitting mutual entry among the banking, insurance, and securities industries through subsidiary or holding company structures, and reducing firewall regulations among the banking, securities, and insurance industries. Implementation dates vary, but the majority of these liberalization measures were completed on 1 October 1999.

---

7 Partly effective December 1997 and fully effective 1 December 1998.

10. Securitization of loans, receivables, and real property

A special statute was passed in the Diet in June 1998 (effective 1 September 1998). This special legislation permits a low-cost method of securitizing financial assets so that financing in the capital markets will become more attractive. See below for further details.

III. Five Pieces of Legislation in 2000

A. Overview

In May 2000, five important pieces of legislation were passed in the Diet. Two of these provide insolvency procedures and a safety net for failed banks and insurance companies. Most of this reform is aimed at creating rules relating to the insolvency of banks and insurance companies after 1 April 2002, when the current government's promise of protection of entire deposits will expire and 'payoff' of banks may happen. The reforms, however, also include various measures until then; in particular, these include the injection of taxpayers' money into failed banks and/or insurance companies during the current 'emergency' period. The legislation also includes provisions that enable mutual-type insurance companies to change their form to for-profit companies.

The remaining three pieces of legislation concern further advancement of the Big Bang program with further deregulation of the financial sector. The first piece of legislation amended the Securities and Exchange Act (the 'SEA') and contained two matters. First, the disclosure system was changed to permit an electronic filing system, beginning 1 June 2001. Second, as of December 2000 stock exchanges may become for-profit organizations if they wish. The Osaka Securities Exchange became a stock company on 1 April 2001, and the Tokyo Stock Exchange became a stock company on 1 November 2001. The second piece of legislation drastically amended the Act of Securitizing Specified Assets by Specified Purpose Companies (the 'SPC' Act) and the Securities Investment Trusts Act. The reform regarding asset securitization will be discussed further below. The third piece of legislation is the Act for Marketing of Financial Products (effective on 1 April 2001). This new act has introduced a new form of consumer protection in the financial sector by imposing private law obligations on 'merchants' (including banks and securities companies) who attempt to sell any financial product to customers. The basis of the act is to impose on such merchants the 'duty to explain' the risk involved in the financial product being marketed to their customers. If the merchant fails to comply with the duty, it will be subject to damage liability under conditions that are easier to prove than in the case of general tort liability.

B. Short Analyses of Selected Items

1. Demutualization of Stock Exchanges

While permitting demutualization of stock and other exchanges is a global trend, it is interesting that Japan permitted it very quickly. The U.S., for example, has not yet permitted this. Generally there are two ways of accomplishing this: one is to permit an entire exchange to become a stock company, and the other is to separate functions between a self-regulatory organization and a body for operating trading markets and permit the latter to be in the stock company form. After extensive discussion, Japan took the first approach for stock exchanges and the second approach for over-the-counter markets. More specifically, a stock exchange and a futures exchange are permitted to become a stock company as a whole, but the Japan Securities Dealers' Association (JASD) cannot become a stock company; instead, it is permitted to set up a stock company separately to operate OTC (over-the-counter) markets. The JASD already took this path and today owns a stock company that operates OTC markets (known as 'JASDAQ' markets).

There was heated debate in the process of the regulatory change regarding how the 'public' nature of stock exchanges can be consistent with the for-profit nature of the organizational form of a stock company. This public/private interests concern must be reconsidered several years from now when stock company-form exchanges have more experience. Advocates for permitting demutualization point out the advantages of the stock company form in financing, expansion of activities, and corporate governance. Again, whether these advantages are real ones must await future evaluation several years from now.

2. Act for Marketing of Financial Products

This is quite a unique experience in Japan, because traditionally investor protection was pursued by regulation rather than private law, especially when the regulator prepared a bill for new legislation. This time the regulator prepared a bill with a private law nature; that is, the new law does not give any role to the FSA. Aggrieved investors must go to courts for damages if they think the brokers they dealt with breached the duty to explain. There was a great amount of court litigation in the past where investors sued brokers based on general principles of tort law. Such litigation cost time and money. This new law aims at saving such time and costs by providing concrete requirements and remedies. But here again, the value of this new law must be re-examined several years from now. The act became effective on 1 April 2001, but there has not yet been any case that was brought into a court under this act.

IV. Legal and Regulatory Infrastructure for Asset Securitization

A. Legal and Regulatory Change in 1998

Unfavorable economic conditions – pervasive after the 'bubble' burst in 1991 and the subsequent decrease in the power and competitiveness of the financial and real property sectors in Japan – drew attention to the need to expand the securitization market. Although the resulting legislation was not a magic cure-all that resolved bad loans and other problems in the financial and real estate markets (as proponents of the expansion of the securitization market sometimes mistakenly believe), it brought about improvements in the general structure of the relevant laws and regulations. There were four legal obstacles for securitization in Japan at the time: impractical methods of perfecting an asset transfer, high corporate law compliance costs, no practical way for a sponsor to cut its ownership interest in an SPV (special purpose vehicle), and the lack of a secondary market among institutions (together with complex general securities regulation). The first two obstacles were considerably (though not completely) resolved, and the fourth was partially addressed. The third problem, however, was not resolved in 1998.

First, based on a bill prepared by the Ministry of Justice, the Diet passed the Special Assignment Act, which introduced a special rule about perfecting an assignment of loans, receivables, and other claims. The new scheme permits perfection by commercial registration at a registry office, and this method is available for an assignment of any monetary claim by any incorporated entity.

Second, based on a bill prepared by the Ministry of Finance (the 'MOF'), the Diet passed the 'SPC Act'. This legislation adopted a stick-and-carrot strategy. The main purpose of this act was to reduce the cost of setting up a specified purpose company (an 'SPC' under the act). An SPC can be set up with a minimum capital of three million yen and can issue debt securities (including commercial papers) and preferred stock. These securities became included in the definition of 'securities' in the SEA, and dividends for such preferred stock are exempt from double taxation under certain conditions. The governance structure of an SPC is simpler than that of an ordinary joint-stock company: specifically, it only needs to have one director, although an auditor and an accountant are required. An SPC must be registered with the regulator and is subject to its supervision, mainly to ensure that the SPC does not engage in activities other than serving as a vehicle of securitization. There is no merit review, as is the case under the Specified Claims Act (the first statute in Japan for securitization of assets of credit and leasing companies in 1992), but various restrictions are imposed by the SPC Act itself. This scheme is available for the securitization of any type of monetary claims (including loans and receivables) as well as real property.

Finally, the problem of the lack of a secondary market among institutions (such as a Rule 144A market) was resolved in June 1998, when the administrative release which restricted the transfer of privately placed securities was removed. Thus, today privately placed securities are freely transferable among qualified institutions without registration under the SEA.

However there are still some problems with the SEA, in particular its narrow definition of 'securities', the practical effect of which is that there are many financial products for which investor protection is offered only through scattered pieces of statutes instead of the SEA.

B. Reform in 2000

Further legislative changes were made in 2000. First, the SPC Act was amended drastically. Second, the Securities Investment Trust and Securities Investment Company Act was also amended.

The SPC Act was extensively revised. First, the act was renamed the Act of Asset Securitization ('Securitization Act'). Second, the amount of regulation of SPCs was liberalized. For instance, the minimum capital requirement for an SPC was reduced to 100,000 yen. The registration system was replaced by a notice system, and a scheme using an SPC under the Securitization Act is only subject to a requirement of simple notice to the regulator. Under the original SPC Act, a securitization plan had to be part of the charter of an SPC, but this requirement was removed, and the plan can be specified at the time of closing the deal rather than at the time of setting up an SPC. Previously, a change in the securitization plan required the unanimous consent of the stockholders, but now it can be made by a majority vote. Prior to the amendments preferred stock could not be redeemed, but now it can be; and convertible securities were not permitted, but now they are. An SPC was formerly prohibited from borrowing, but as a result of the amendments, it may now do so under certain conditions. And finally, the assets that could be securitized under the SPC Act were previously limited to monetary claims and real property, but this restriction was removed, and any asset may now be securitized under the Securitization Act.

Third, the problem of cutting off the sponsor's ownership interest in an SPC was solved. In short, a special scheme, a Japanese version of a 'charitable trust', which is a very popular vehicle in the securitization practice outside Japan, was introduced for this purpose.

Fourth, a trust form was recognized as a new vehicle under the Securitization Act. It must be noted that trusts were already popularly used as SPVs for asset securitization not falling under the Securitization Act, and thus there had to be certain 'carrots' offered for the trust-form SPV falling under the Securitization Act. There are two primary benefits in using the trust form under the Securitization Act. One is that the act permits a special-purpose trust to issue negotiable instruments representing beneficial interests in the trust. This means that outside the Securitization Act, beneficial interests cannot be represented in negotiable instruments and thus lack transferability among investors (except where there are special statutes permitting such transferability). The second benefit is that the Securitization Act permits a majority vote of the beneficiaries to change provisions of the trust contract; outside the act such change requires unanimous approval.

The Securities Investment Trust and Securities Investment Company Act is the major piece of legislation which regulates pooled investment funds that primarily invest in securities, and this act also was substantially amended in 2000. The act now permits such funds to invest in anything, so that the name of the act has been changed to the Investment Trust and Investment Company Act. Also, the act recognizes both the trust form and the company form. In the trust form the managing company and the custodian were previously required to be separate, but the 2000 amendments introduced a new form in which the same trustee may serve as both manager and custodian. For asset securitization, these amendments permit a Japanese version of what is known in the U.S. as REITs (real estate investment trusts), where the manager has investment discretion over a pool of real property. While REITs may not be commonly considered securitization, this legal change is mentioned here because they sometimes are.

The remaining legal hurdles for asset securitization in Japan include the validity of a contract clause that prohibits an SPV from filing an insolvency petition. This type of clause is of particular concern to rating agencies, but is most likely to be invalid under current Japanese law. Also, except for schemes that fall within the Securitization Act, tax law is not favorable to a corporate-form entity. However, these factors are rather small, and after the recent changes that have came into force (30 November 2000), the securitization market in Japan is expected to grow. For example, in 2001 two public REITs were organized and listed on a Tokyo Stock Exchange in Japan.

V. Trends in 2001

We did not observe the same drastic reform trends in 2001 as those that occurred in 1998 and 2000, but a few developments may be worth mentioning. First, a large-scale reform of securities settlement systems has been underway since 2000, and the first set of legislation was made in June 2001. This legislation covered two issues One is that a new statute was made to permit dematerialization of commercial papers, a means of short-term financing in Japan. Commercial papers in Japan were introduced in 1987 but legally were characterized as promissory notes rather than debt securities to permit banks to offer intermediary services. Because promissory notes are thought to be unable to be dematerialized, a new statute was introduced. The new statute permits issuance of uncertificated short debts that are exempted from many strict regulations under company law regarding debt securities. It is also important that this new statute permits transfer of (dematerialized) debts by book entry only, a completely new direction in Japanese private law regarding the transfer of debts. The second aspect of the new legislation is that an amendment was made to permit a CSD (Centralized Securities Depository) for shares to become a stock company. Previously a non-profit organization, it now plans to become a stock company under this new legislation. The remaining part of the reform of securities settlement systems includes many important matters. For instance, a comprehensive legal and regulatory system for indirect holding situations where investors hold various securities through custodians in a multi-layer fashion has not yet been provided in Japan. Also, regulation of clearing organizations has not been provided. Another issue is that the rule of private international law regarding the situation of indirect holding of investment securities is uncertain. A comprehensive reform for dealing with these remaining issues is expected to be made in 2002.

Second, simplification of disclosure is currently being considered for mutual fund prospectus. The U.S. already made this simplification several years ago, and Japan is catching up in this area.

VI. Impact of the Recent Reforms

A. From a Bank-Centered System to a Capital Market-Centered System

In the past, bank lending dominated the financial sector in Japan. This infrastructure successfully helped Japan achieve high economic growth during the thirty years following World War II. Once the Japanese economy matured, however, the relatively high costs of the services of the bank-centered system began to affect the national economy. Today, other major countries, most notably the U.S., have well-developed capital markets, and the globalization of financial markets will inevitably require an increased role of capital markets in Japan. The Big Bang program thus encourages dramatic improvement of the Japanese capital markets. However, I do not think that Japan will become a completely capital market-based country. Banks and capital markets will coexist; therefore, the form regulations should take in this coexisting situation is the key issue for the coming decades.[8]

B. From Stability to Adaptability

As we have seen, Japan's system in the past emphasized stability, especially employment stability, and this policy made great contributions to Japan's economic growth. Stability, however, is not compatible with adaptability, and thus Japan was slow at adapting to rapidly changing environments in global financial (especially capital) markets. The U.S. system, in contrast, represents a system that emphasizes adaptability. The Big Bang program includes various measures to increase the adaptability of the financial system in Japan. The drawback may be some loss in stability. Here again the key

---

[8] See, for example, *F. Allen/D. Gale*, Comparative Financial Systems: A Survey, Wharton School FIC Working Paper No. 01-15 (2001); *H. Kanda*, Regulatory Differences in Bank and Capital Market Regulations: A Draft, available at the website of Wharton School FIC (2001).

policy issue is whether and how Japan can make stability and adaptability coexist.

C. Increased Choice for Consumers

Because the Big Bang program includes wide-reaching deregulation of the financial sector, it obviously will give Japanese consumers and investors more choice. However, more choice by itself is not always a good thing. It also opens up opportunities to brokers and other intermediaries for fraud and other misbehavior. The key policy issue is how ex-post remedies are prepared and enforced at low costs. The Act for Marketing Financial Products is an important effort in this sense. But it is too early today to make any judgment in this area, and one must wait several years to see how increased choice for consumers benefits Japan.

D. Increased Business Opportunities for Foreign Institutions

The Big Bang program will open more doors to foreign institutions. Some people have characterized the Big Bang program reforms as a 'Wimbledon'-style reform: although the Wimbledon Tennis Championship is located in the UK, most players are foreigners. Whether the Big Bang program will attract foreign companies in a similar manner will depend on language, business custom, and other cultural contingencies. In selected markets, foreign financial institutions will probably play a major, if not dominant, role.

VII. Conclusion

The reform efforts in the regulation of exchanges and investment services seem unending. While the driving forces are coming more from domestic situations than from outside pressure, the trend of the reforms in recent years in Japan is consistent with the global one: toward more free and transparent capital markets. Within this trend, however, the precise response in laws and regulations in Japan takes different forms from those in the U.S., as we see, for instance, in the fields of PTSs, asset securitization, and securities settlement systems. Thus, substantive regulations around the world in this area do not seem to be converging, although one could say that they are converging functionally.

Part 3:

REGULATION OF INSURANCE SERVICES

REGULATION OF INSURANCE SERVICES: THE EUROPEAN PERSPECTIVE

by Wulf-Henning Roth, Bonn

I. The Historical Background

With the adoption and transformation of the third generation of insurance directives in the 1990s, the single insurance market for undertakings has finally become reality.[1] It has taken more than thirty years to overcome the

---

1 *Müller*, Versicherungsbinnenmarkt (1995); *Merkin/Rodger*, EC Insurance Law (1997); *McGee*, The Single Market in Insurance (1998); *Rabe*, Liberalisierung und Deregulierung im Europäischen Binnenmarkt für Versicherungen (1997).

J. Basedow, H. Baum, K. Hopt, H. Kanda and T. Kono (eds.), Economic Regulation and Competition, (167-188)

impediments that were in the way on the road toward harmonization. By the end of 1969, the single insurance market should already have been effectuated,[2] but the difficulties turned out to be so great that the first piece of substantial legislation in the field of insurance was not adopted by the Council until 1973: the so-called First Non-Life Directive facilitating freedom of establishment.[3] And the follow-up directive in the field of non-life insurance, mainly devoted to facilitating the effective exercise of freedom to provide services, took another twelve years of consideration in the Council before it was finally adopted in 1988.[4] In the end, the driving impetus of the single market project ('1992') led to the adoption of the Third Non-Life Directive,[5] installing the regulatory system that will be discussed later on.[6] The story of the creation of the internal market for life assurance is a similar one: the relevant directives were adopted in 1979[7], 1990[8], and 1992[9], respectively.

One may wonder why the creation of the single insurance market has been such a time-consuming task. Though insurance services may be provided without being impeded by customs duties and border controls, a truly international market in insurance services has developed only in branches like reinsurance, maritime insurance, and the insurance of large risks (by means of coinsurance). Apart from these branches, insurance markets used to be – and indeed still are – national markets with respect to some member states. The explanation for this state of affairs is quite simple: a number of states – such as France[10], Germany[11], and Austria[12] – have been accustomed

2 A short overview on the work in progress in the 1960s and early 1970s is given by *Roth*, Internationales Versicherungsvertragsrecht (1985), pp. 675-689.

3 Directive 73/239/EEC: (1973) OJEC L 228/3.

4 Directive 88/357/EEC: (1988) OJEC L 172/1. For an account of the problems involved and for the development of the internal insurance market, see *Ellis*, European Integration and Insurance (Creating a Common Insurance Market) (1980); *Pool*, Will There Be a Single European Community Insurance Market After 1992?: (1989) 9 International Law & Business Review 525; *Pool*, The creation of the internal market in insurance (1990); *Ottow*, An Internal Insurance Market Before the Turn of the Century?: (1992) 29 C.M.L.Rev. 511.

5 Directive 92/49/EEC: (1992) OJEC L 228/1.

6 For an analysis of the regulatory system based on the third generation of directives, see, e.g., *Miersch*, Versicherungsaufsicht nach den Dritten Richtlinien (1996).

7 Directive 79/267/EEC: (1979) OJEC L 63/1.

8 Directive 90/619/EEC: (1990) OJEC L 330/50.

9 Directive 92/96/EEC: (1992) OJEC L 360/1.

10 For an overview, see *Hübner*, Rechtliche Rahmenbedingungen des Wettbewerbs in der Versicherungswirtschaft (1988), pp. 81-92; *Bigot/Moreau*, Traité de droit des cont. ...

to a regulatory scheme of more or less intense state supervision over the activities of insurance undertakings. In contrast, the United Kingdom[13] and the Netherlands traditionally have stood for a free market tradition with some degree of self-regulation.

In the words of a French author,[14] the creation of the single insurance market has led unavoidably to a clash of two cultures of insurance: on the one hand, the so-called 'maritime insurance' tradition, with a low level of regulation by the state, reliance on competition, and no developed policy of protection of the insured; on the other hand, the 'alpine insurance' tradition, with heavy governmental supervision that extends not only to the financial health of the undertaking (solvency control, minimum capital, guarantee fund, calculation of technical reserves, regulation of investment in assets), but also to the control of the calculation of premium tariffs and of insurance policies and conditions.[15] Protection of the insured against the danger of insolvency runs high as the primary regulatory goal, and this at the expense of competition between insurance undertakings. The somewhat restrained role that competition was meant to play in this regulatory framework is underlined by the special status that insurance was long attributed in antitrust law, e.g., in Germany. The so-called *special characteristics* of the insurance industry that traditionally were deemed to justify state regulation in this

---

assurances (1992), pp. 521. The classic text is *Picard/Besson*, Les assurances terrestres en droit francais, 2nd vol. (4th edn, 1977).

11 Cf. *Roth*, supra note 2, p. 65 et seq., p. 80 et seq.

12 *Reti*, Versicherungsaufsichtsrecht und Europäische Integration (1992), pp. 4-10.

13 For an analysis of the state of law (with some regulation of the life assurance business) before the implementation of EC law: *MacGillivray* (*-Browne*), Insurance Law Relating to All Risks other than Marine, vol. 1 (5th edn, 1961), p. 79 et seq.; *Ahlenstiel*, Die Staatsaufsicht über Versicherungsunternehmen in Großbritannien (1967); *Hübner*, supra note 10, p. 23 et seq.; *Lowry/Rawlings*, Insurance Law: Doctrines and Principles (1999), p. 349 et seq.

14 *Albert*, as cited by *Cousy*, The distribution of insurance services: Legal aspects, in: Stuyck/Abraham/Terryn (eds), Financial Services and Financial Markets in Europe: Changes and Adjustments (2000), p. 91 (92).

15 For a comparative overview of insurance supervision in the OECD member countries, see *Angerer*, Insurance Supervision in OECD Member Countries, in: OECD (ed.), Policy Issues in Insurance (1993), pp. 13-72.

field[16] were also taken as a reason to exempt insurance from the general rules of competition law.[17]

II. The Legal Background

A. *The Primary Regulatory Goal: The Creation of a Single Insurance Market*

At the outset, it is important to note that insurance regulation was not introduced on the European level in order to pursue a certain regulatory philosophy. The basic aim of European legislation has rather been the creation of a single insurance market. The harmonization efforts of the Community were primarily directed toward the facilitation of freedom of establishment and freedom to provide services. It is in this perspective that the regulatory infrastructure of the Community has evolved: harmonization of insurance law of the member states has meant the task of finding a compromise between the British and Dutch free market tradition on the one hand and the regulatory traditions of France and Germany on the other. In the end, this compromise has led to an increase of regulation in some member states, e.g., the United Kingdom[18] (and to a certain degree a shift from self-regulation to state regulation), and to a decrease of regulation in some other member states, the most prominent example being Germany, which had to give up its system of prior approval of policy conditions and tariff premiums.[19]

---

16 See *Roth*, European Competition Policy for the Insurance Market: (2000) Eur.C.L.Rev. 107 (107-108): capacity, premium calculation, transparency, financial security arguments; see further *Hootz*, in: Gemeinschaftskommentar, Gesetz gegen Wettbewerbsbeschränkungen und Europäisches Kartellrecht (4th edn, 1988), § 102 No. 2.

17 Cf. § 102 GWB a.F.

18 See *McGee*, supra note 1, p. 4; *Lowry/Rawlings*, Insurance Law: Doctrines and Principles (1999), p. 349 et seq.; *Rabe*, supra note 1, p. 55 et seq.

19 It should be noted, however, that, at the same time, an increase in regulation took place regarding obligatory information on ownership and qualifying holdings in an insurance undertaking (and of any proposed increase in a qualified holding passing certain thresholds of voting rights or capital). The authorities of the home member states have to check whether the proposed shareholder may prove to be unsuitable in

cont. ...

B. Traditional Instruments to Be Abolished

In order to facilitate freedom of establishment and freedom to provide services,[20] some member states had to give up a number of traditionally applicable regulatory instruments in relation to undertakings from other member states that had the effect of upholding the separation of national markets. Such instruments were the control of admission to the market on the basis of economic expediency (applying a 'need test'), posting deposits related to intrastate business, the requirement of an establishment as a prerequisite for the provision of interstate insurance services, license requirements for the provision of services and the setting-up of a branch or agency, the prohibition of cumul (to provide interstate services alongside an existing branch), and the abolition of state monopolies in certain insurance branches.

C. The Basic Choice: Host State or Home State Regulation and Control

The regulation of the single insurance market confronted the European Community with the choice between the principles of host state and home state regulation and control.[21] The history of Community regulation of insurance may be described as a process from complete host state regulation to a system that today is dominated by the principle of home state regulation and control.

Keeping up a system of *host state regulation* would have left the national insurance markets untouched, the member states retaining their sovereignty to determine their regulatory goals and the intensity with which they are enforced. Host state regulation and control preserves the traditional regulatory culture and, in terms of enforcement, the supervisory authorities are close to the undertakings to be supervised, unimpeded by any burden of unknown languages, an unknown legal environment, and unknown traditions.

Under the system of host state regulation and control, insurance undertakings located within the member state and in other member states would compete on the same conditions: the regulations of the host state. In such a

---

view of the need to ensure sound and prudent management; cf. Art. 15 of Directive 92/49/EEC: (1992) OJEC L 228/1.

[20] An overview of the implications of the freedoms for financial services is presented in: *Roth*, The Internal Market for Financial Services: Legal Aspects, in: Stuyck/Abraham/Terryn (eds), Financial Services and Financial Markets in Europe: Changes and Adjustments (2000), pp. 23-50.

[21] See, e.g., *McGee*, supra note 1, pp. 12-13.

system, the relevant freedoms (concerning establishment, services, and capital) guarantee a nondiscriminatory treatment of out-of-state undertakings, and thereby undistorted competition. Beyond that, the freedoms may be called upon to guarantee market access vis-à-vis unjustified restrictions of the host state, and they may serve as a check on unnecessary burdens for the interstate provision of services. However, a system of host state regulation would unavoidably imply an extra burden for out-of-state undertakings: prudential supervision by the host state leads to potentially conflicting regulatory standards and necessitates enforcement instruments that create extra costs for the transaction of interstate insurance business: insurance undertakings are confronted with fifteen varying legal orders and fifteen supervisory authorities to deal with.

A system built on *home state regulation and control* attempts to evade these disadvantages of host state regulation: the insurance undertakings underlie (ideally) only one set of legal rules; they are under the supervision of and answerable to only one supervisory authority. Compared to a system of host state regulation, transaction costs are heavily reduced and competition on a transnational level is strengthened. Home state control offers the advantage of administrative simplicity, but it goes without saying that a price has to be paid as well: undertakings from different member states that are competing with one another underlie varying regulatory systems and enforcement strategies. Such regulatory competition may create problems of fairness concerning insurance companies and problems of information for consumers who may not be able to judge the varying regulations and enforcement strategies in the relevant home states. It goes without saying that such a system of home state control will be acceptable for the member states only if it goes hand-in-hand with some sort of safety net which prevents the obvious disadvantages of this system.

III. European Insurance Regulation: The Framework

In the last decades, the Community has developed a regulatory scheme for insurance services that is strongly directed toward the system of *home state* regulation. Six well-known elements are characteristic for this regulatory framework.[22]

---

[22] See *Royla*, Grenzüberschreitende Finanzmarktaufsicht in der EG (2000), p. 38 et seq.; *Roth*, supra note 20, pp. 44-46.

A. Supervision by National Authorities

The regulatory scheme is based on the premise that supervision of the activities of insurance undertakings should be entrusted to the authorities of the *member states*. There is no Community supervisory agency (comparable to the Commission in competition matters) nor is the Commission directly involved in the task of supervision.[23] From the very beginning of the EEC, debate has arisen as to whether business activities that are designed to take place on the European level can be adequately and effectively supervised on the national level by a multitude of national agencies.[24] Up until today, the EC regulatory scheme is based on the assumption that *cooperation* between the competent national authorities will suffice, at least if tight cooperation is ensured. For a long time, there seemed to be no realistic political alternative to supervision on the national level by national authorities. Recent developments indicate that not only has a fusion of insurance and banking supervision become a 'topic',[25] but some day Community-wide supervision by a Community institution may also become reality.[26]

B. Single License

The European regulatory model has introduced the *single license* system. Such a 'European license' is issued whenever the competent national authority authorizes an undertaking to transact business in another member state. Accordingly, the *host* member state may no longer demand an authori-

---

[23] The Commission is attributed only certain minor functions related to the regulation of supervision, e.g., the clarification of definitions in order to ensure their uniform application; Art. 47 sec. 1 Directive 92/96/EEC: (1992) OJEC L 360/1. The Commission is assisted by the Advisory Insurance Committee; Directive 91/675/EEC: (1991) OJEC L 374/32.

[24] Cf., e.g., *Kimball*, Versicherungsaufsicht in föderativen Staatensystemen insbesondere im Hinblick auf Allgemeine Versicherungsbedingungen: (1964) ZVersWiss 233.

[25] See the Commission's proposal of a directive concerning the additional supervision of a financial conglomerate, Doc 501PC0213; *Visnovsky*, La réglementation des conglomérats financiers: (2000) 60 Revue d'économie financière 161.

[26] *Andenas/Gebhardt*, Financial market regulation in Europe – Some institutional aspects, in: Hummel/Breuer (eds), Handbuch Europäischer Kapitalmarkt (2001), p. 151; *Couppey-Soubeyran*, Pour une autorité de supervision financière européenne: (2000) 60 Revue d'économie financière 143.

zation of its own, but it has to recognize the authorization of the competent authority of the *home* member state as sufficient for doing business in the territory of the host state.[27] From a legal point of view, the European passport is *not* a Community license.[28] Rather, the license being issued by a national authority is a national license that is attributed extraterritorial reach by the obligation of the other member states to recognize it; the principle of *mutual recognition* is at the very basis of the European license.

The single license principle facilitates freedom to provide services, freedom of establishment, and freedom of capital movement as well. The relevant undertaking needs only *one* authorization instead of fifteen. However, this facilitating effect is not an absolute one. An authorization issued by the competent authorities of the host state does *not* empower the undertaking to do business in the host state without any precondition. Concerning the provision of services, the authorization requirement has been replaced by an obligation of the undertaking to notify the competent authority of the home state, accompanied by information on the activities to be carried out. This notification will then be transmitted to the competent authority of the host member state.[29] Regarding the setting up of a branch, the competence of the host state to require an authorization has been replaced by the supervisory competence of the home state to which a notification shall be addressed. The home state authorities have to check whether the administrative structure of the undertaking – including the organizational set-up of a branch and the financial situation – are adequate. The directives envisage a consultation and cooperation procedure with the competent authorities of the host states.[30]

C. Home Country Regulation and Control

The single license principle goes hand-in-hand with the concept of home country control regarding the ongoing business: an insurance undertaking is subject to the supervision of the authorities of the home state, which is attributed *exclusive competence in prudential matters* (concerning the finan-

---

27 Art. 5 Directive 92/49/EEC: (1992) OJEC L 228/1; Art. 4 Directive 92/96/EEC: (1992) OJEC L 360/1.

28 See *Royla*, supra note 22. p. 49 et seq.

29 Art. 34 and 35 Directive 92/49/EEC: (1992) OJEC L 228/1; Art. 34 and 35 Directive 92/96/EEC: (1992) OJEC L 360/1.

30 Art. 32 Directive 92/49/EEC: (1992) OJEC L 228/1; Art. 32 Directive 92/96/ EEC: (1992) OJEC L 360/1; see *Royla*, supra note 22, p. 111 et seq.

cial 'health' of the undertaking). In essence, this principle of home country control amounts to a *fundamental change* in the traditional system of regulatory jurisdiction of the EU states, shifting the competence from the host state to the home state of the undertaking. The facilitating effect for the relevant freedoms is obvious: the undertakings have to deal only with 'their' national authorities (instead of the authorities of all states in which they transact business), and they underlie only one set of rules, regulations, etc., for prudential matters.

D. Harmonization

The principle of home country control for prudential matters goes together with a harmonization of rules on the institutional set-up of the insurance undertakings, on capital adequacy (minimum capital; solvency ratio; calculation of technical reserves; regulations concerning matching assets), on qualifications concerning the management personnel, the existence of adequate administrative and internal controls, on shareholder suitability, and on commercial holdings. Such (mostly minimum) harmonization is a precondition for the principle of home country control in prudential matters and the mutual recognition of this control among the member states.

Harmonization also touches on business activities. The third generation of insurance directives prescribe the *abolition* of any prior approval requirement concerning insurance policies and tariffs. Again, the effect of the latter measure in facilitating the freedoms for insurance undertakings is all too obvious.

E. Mutual Recognition

The system of home country control goes hand-in-hand with the principle of *mutual recognition*. The *single passport* is a license which has to be recognized by all other member states, even if the conditions for admission to the insurance business are different (and stricter) in the member state of risk. The same goes for the supervision of management and for the supervision of the ongoing business.

F. Host Country Regulation and Control

The principle of home country regulation is not completely carried through as far as the regulation of *business behavior* is concerned. The host states have retained some of their *legislative* jurisdiction for the regulation of insurance products and business behavior that shall, however, be exercised under the control of the freedoms. The Second Life[31] and the Second Non-Life Directive[32] proceed on the assumption that the host member states, i.e., the member states where the relevant risk is located, are competent to apply their substantive insurance contract law if they wish. Moreover, they are still competent to regulate advertising for interstate activities (as it appears from Art. 41 Third Non-Life Directive[33] and Art. 41 Third Life Directive[34]). Finally, both Art. 28 Third Non-Life Directive and Art. 28 Third Life Directive[35] presuppose the legislative and enforcement jurisdiction of the member state of risk when they state that a policyholder may not be hindered from taking out a contract under the law of the state of origin, provided that such a contract would not contradict regulations of the state of risk justified by the general good.[36]

The *home* country authorities are *primarily* competent to supervise the business behavior of undertakings they have licensed. This competence, which amounts to an *obligation* to supervise as well, extends not only to intrastate business, but to the out-of-state business of insurance undertakings

---

31 Art. 4 Directive 90/619/EEC: (1990) OJEC L 330/50.

32 Art. 7 Directive 88/357/EEC: (1988) OJEC L 172/1.

33 Directive 92/49/EEC: (1992) OJEC L 228/1.

34 Directive 92/96/EEC: (1992) OJEC L 360/1.

35 Art. 28 reads: 'The Member State of the commitment shall not prevent a policyholder from concluding a contract with an assurance undertaking authorized under the conditions of Article 6 of Directive 79/267/EEC, as long as that does not conflict with legal provisions protecting the general good in the Member State of the commitment'.

36 It is not clear what kind of regulations Art. 28 of both directives have in mind; see *Wördemann*, International zwingende Normen im Internationalen Privatrecht des europäischen Versicherungsvertrages (1997), p. 300 et seq.; *Roth*, Dienstleistungsfreiheit und Allgemeininteresse im europäischen internationalen Versicherungsvertragsrecht, in: Reichert-Facilides (ed.), Aspekte des internationalen Versicherungsvertragsrechts im Europäischen Wirtschaftsraum (1994), p. 1 (4 et seq.); *Fallon*, The Law Applicable to Compulsory Insurance and Life Assurance: Some Peculiarities, in: Reichert-Facilides/Jessurun d'Oliveira (eds), International Insurance Contract Law in the EC (1993), p. 113 (118 et seq.).

transacted in other member states as well. As far as the host member states have retained their jurisdiction to legislate, this obligation to supervise implies that national authorities of the home state are in a position to take note of the standards set by the host states and to enforce them in an effective manner. It is obvious that at this point a *close cooperation* between the national authorities (as provided for by the directives) will become a matter of necessity. Lacking any empirical research on that topic, it is hard to evaluate whether this presupposed cooperation on the national level is in fact working in an effective manner. It should be mentioned in passing that the host states have retained a residual supervisory competence, notably for cases of emergency.

IV. The Regulatory Philosophy

A. Regulatory Competition

Harmonization as to prudential matters is for the most part devised as *minimum* harmonization, leaving it to the member states in their respective roles to impose more stringent standards on insurance undertakings as a prerequisite for obtaining or keeping up a license. Minimum harmonization is, of course, the safety net that goes together with the system of home country regulation, and is generally regarded as a prerequisite for the functioning of this system.

This strategy of minimum harmonization – at least to some extent – may be regarded as a regulatory philosophy devoted to the concept of 'competition between legal orders':[37] beyond the minimum standard, member states shall be free to decide on the appropriate level of regulation and enforcement. It is well recognized that such a concept of minimum harmonization leads to a potential (reverse) discrimination for undertakings seated in member states with intense regulation. Though the Community is bound by and to the principle of undistorted competition (Art. 3 sec. 1 lit. g EC), there

[37] See generally *Baldwin/Cave*, Understanding Regulation (1999), p. 180 et seq. For an analysis with regard to banking law, see *Köndgen*, Mindestharmonisierung im europäischen Bankrecht – konzeptionelle Grundlagen, in: Everling/ Roth (eds), Mindestharmonisierung im Europäischen Binnenmarkt (1997), p. 111 et seq.; *Wörner*, Europäische Bankenregulierung im Spannungsverhältnis zwischen Regulierungswettbewerb und Harmonisierungsbemühungen (2000).

is probably no conflict with that principle, because the distortive effect is a consequence of member state regulation rather than Community action.[38]

Assuming that the concept of minimum harmonization may have the consequence of distortive effects on competition between insurance undertakings seated in different member states, one may expect the insurance industry to react to this phenomenon by setting up new companies (subsidiaries) in member states with the lowest standards of regulation in order to pursue business from there in member states with higher enforcement standards. However, such a regulatory *arbitrage* has not yet taken place in the insurance sector. This may be derived from the fact that, to a certain extent, Community law takes care of the problem. The Second Banking Directive[39] has, for the first time, dealt with the problem of regulatory arbitrage: in the eighth recital of the preamble, the directive provides that the competent authorities may not grant, or must withdraw, an authorization in a case where the incorporation of a credit institution in a member state of lower standards serves the purpose of evading the application of the stricter standards of some other member states. This line of thinking is borne out in the seventh recital of Directive 95/26/EEC relating to life and non-life insurance,[40] and again in the proposal of a consolidating directive concerning life assurance (recital 12)[41] as well.

It is noteworthy that the concept of evasion is relevant in this setting not as a concept relating to the competence of the member states to apply *their own law*, but – to the contrary – for establishing an obligation to prevent the circumvention of the law of some other member state. Because the system of

---

38 One may nevertheless argue that the Community is obliged to pursue the policy of undistorted competition in relation to member state action, as long as the undertakings cannot escape the disadvantages of reverse discrimination by moving their seat to some other member state.

39 Directive 89/646/EEC: (1989) OJEC L 386/1.

40 Directive 95/26/EEC: (1995) OJEC L 168/7; for a comment, see *Callies*, Heimatstaatprinzip und Europa-Pass (single license principle) im europäischen Finanzmarktrecht: Wettbewerb der Finanzdienstleister oder der Finanzplätze?: (2000) EWS 432 (436 et seq.).

41 'The principles of mutual recognition and of home Member State supervision require that Member States' competent authorities should not grant or should withdraw authorisation where factors such as the content of programmes of operations, the geographical distribution of the activities actually carries on indicate clearly that an assurance undertaking has opted for the legal system of one Member State for the purpose of evading the stricter standards in force in another Member State within whose territory it carries on or intends to carry on the greater part of its activities'.

home country control, as set forth by the third generation of directives, has led to a transfer of regulatory competence from the host member state to the home member state, such a transfer has to be supported by an obligation of the home member state to take care of the legitimate interests of the host member state that are reflected in its legislation exceeding the minimum level of regulation set forth by Community law. In passing, it should be mentioned that Art. 3 Directive 95/26/EEC sets up the requirement that member states have to demand that an insurance undertaking's head office always be situated in its home member state where it has its registered seat and where it has received its license to do business. We may assume that within this regulatory scheme the perceived problem of evasion of higher and more burdensome standards has – to some degree – been forestalled.

B. Regulatory Goals

1. European Competition Law

Before analyzing the regulatory goals of the relevant Community legislation, it is worth noting that European competition law – as opposed to its traditional German counterpart – applies *without exception* to the insurance industry.[42] The arguments related to the so-called 'special characteristics' of the industry have not led to an exemption to the general applicability of competition rules.[43] To some extent, the problems (e.g., the capacity and security arguments) may be regarded as being taken care of by insurance supervision; moreover, insurance undertakings may cooperate under the Block exemption Regulation No. 3932/92[44], e.g., developing non-binding model conditions or gathering statistical material and calculating the average cost of the risk cover.[45]

---

42 ECJ 27 January 1987, case 45/85, *Verband der Sachversicherer*: (1987) ECR 405.

43 In the monograph by *Fitzsimmons*, Insurance Competition Law (1994), they are not even mentioned.

44 (1992) OJEC L 398/7.

45 Cf. *Roth*: (2000) Eur.C.L.Rev. 107.

2. Policyholder Protection

The directives are not very illuminating when it comes to an analysis of the relevant *regulatory* goals pursued. As the major aim of the directives lies with the facilitation of freedom of establishment and freedom to provide services, the directives explain that and why harmonization is necessary in this respect, whereas the regulatory philosophy stays in the background.

The major purpose of the directives undisputedly relates to *policyholder protection*: Recital 2 of the First Non-Life Directive of 1973 refers to the 'adequate protection' for insured and third parties which calls for the control of the *financial soundness* of the companies. With this aim in mind, Community legislation has established rules that attempt to guarantee that the insurance companies are financially strong enough to meet their liabilities in relation to their policyholders. Instruments to reach this aim encompass the installment of a solvency margin and a guarantee fund, the definition of technical reserves, common actuarial principles governing their calculation and limits, and rules concerning the admissibility and the diversification of investment in assets.

In contrast to the traditional German system of *materielle Staatsaufsicht* (substantive supervision) regarding the insurance product, encompassing ex ante approval and control of policy conditions and tariff premiums, the European regulator has opted for a far more liberal and *pro-competitive model*. Except for the branches of obligatory insurance and permanent health insurance, member states may no longer practice ex ante control. Premium control has simply become a matter of prudential supervision, exercised exclusively by the home country authorities, whereas the control of the policy conditions is reduced to an ex post control, based on the standards of the directive on unfair terms[46] and the relevant general good considerations of the member state concerned.

National requirements as to prior approval of policy conditions have worked as a powerful obstacle to cross-frontier business. The removal of such obstacles has gone hand-in-hand with a dramatic change in the perception of the *role of the policyholder* as contract partner: the policyholder as contract partner is meant to play an *active role*, choosing among products from different member states[47] at the most competitive prices. It is the concept of the *active and reasonably informed consumer* that lurks in the back-

[46] Directive 93/13/EEC: (1993) OJEC L 95/29.
[47] Cf. recital 19 of Directive 92/49/EEC: (1992) OJEC L 228/1.

ground.[48] This concept presupposes the existence of market transparency, and it is built on the premise that the insured will have received substantial information before concluding the contract – a premise which the Third Life Directive attempts to fulfill with its far-reaching information requirements (Art. 31 sec. 1 and 2), whereas the Third Non-Life Directive falls short of nearly any information requirements. With regard to life assurance, the right to revoke the contract within a cooling-off period of 24 to 30 days may be regarded as part of this concept;[49] the same holds true for the endeavor of the Community to transform the insurance intermediary into a more active and sophisticated player in the market to whom the person seeking out insurance may turn with confidence.[50]

In passing, it should be mentioned that the prevailing European regulatory philosophy, though tending toward 'consumer sovereignty' as an ideal, is still very realistic when it comes to the *law applicable to insurance contracts*. Regarding the insurance of large risks, the partners of an insurance contract enjoy party autonomy (at least to a large extent).[51] The potential buyer of such insurance is regarded as sophisticated enough to judge the consequences of the application of a foreign, potentially unknown legal system; he or she is therefore in a position to shop around in the Community and to look for the best and cheapest insurance coverage available. In contrast, for all mass risk insurance, the applicable law will be the one where the risk is located, unless this member state opts for party autonomy.[52] The relevant consideration is, of course, that the costs and problems involved in the application of a foreign legal systems shall be borne not by the insured but by the insurance company, which can deal with them in a more efficient manner.

---

[48] *Hübner/Matusche-Beckmann*, Auswirkungen des Gemeinschaftsrechts auf das Versicherungsrecht: (1995) EuZW 263 (270).

[49] Art. 15 sec. 1 Directive 90/619/EEC: (1990) OJEC L 330/50.

[50] See Recommendation 92/48/EEC: (1992) OJEC L 19/32; proposal of a directive concerning insurance intermediaries: (2000) COM 511.

[51] Art. 7 sec. 1 lit. c)-f) Directive 88/357/EEC: (1988) OJEC L 172/1; Art. 27 Directive 92/49/EEC: (1992) OJEC L 228/1.

[52] Art. 7 sec. 1 lit. a) Directive 88/357/EEC: (1988) OJEC L 172/1.

3. Insurance Market and Competitive Process

The opening up of national insurance markets and the abolition of prior approval of conditions and of tariff premiums not only give the individual policyholder the chance to serve his interest in an optimal manner, but also tend to invigorate *competition* both with price and product on a Community scale, thereby ultimately serving the consuming public as a whole. In a comparable macroeconomic perspective, regulations on the financial status and control are meant to create *policyholder confidence* in the products on offer,[53] policyholder confidence being an important precondition for the existence of a viable insurance market.[54]

C. *The Case for Insurance Regulation*

The legislative acts of European insurance regulation do not expressly refer to theoretical insights of regulation theory. As already mentioned, the third generation of insurance directives proceeds on the assumption that it is in the (well-understood) interest of the (potential) policyholder to have access to a broad palette of insurance products from all member states.[55] Whether and to what extent unsophisticated policyholders are in a position to gain the necessary information in order to make rational decisions concerning the insurance product and the alternatives available on the (European) market is not really touched upon. The instruments of European insurance regulation, however, do reflect the insight that information deficits on the side of the insured are typical for insurance markets, at least as far as mass insurance is concerned.[56]

---

53 *Brittan*, Financial Solvency and Liberalisation of the Insurance Industry before the 21st Century: (1992) VW 671 (672); discussing the importance of consumer confidence to the U.S. experience in the 1980s: *Gart*, Regulation, Deregulation, Reregulation (1994), p. 187 et seq.

54 Finally, it is the *competitiveness* of the European insurance industry that is at the basis of the latest proposal of a directive concerning the supervision of financial conglomerates. Cf. the introductory remarks to the proposal referring to the fact that an integrated financial market will tend to reduce the capital costs for small and middle-sized business and will thereby support the competitiveness of the European economy; Document 501PC0213.

55 Recital 19 Directive 92/49/EEC: (1992) OJEC L 228/1; recital 20 Directive 92/96/EEC: (1992) OJEC L 360/1.

56 *Rabe*, supra note 1, pp. 35, 91, 97.

The insurance market is characterized by *information deficits* on the side of the consumers in more than one direction.[57] Insurance products may be regarded as an experience or a credence good:[58] the quality of the product 'insurance' can be evaluated by the insured only a long time after the conclusion of the contract, if at all. The quality of the product will heavily depend on the financial status (soundness) of the insurance undertaking. The potential policyholder will normally not be in a position to rationally judge the financial status of an undertaking at the time of the conclusion of the insurance contract, even if the companies are under the obligation to disclose essential information regarding their financial status.[59] The policyholder is heavily dependent on expert advice in this regard. Moreover, the financial status of the undertaking may change after the conclusion of the contract; with regard to long-term contracts (life insurance and health insurance), even perfect information on the financial status, if properly made known and analyzed, cannot prevent the policyholder from suffering severe losses.[60]

Prudential regulation in European insurance law has to be regarded as the answer to the financial security problem: the requirement of a license, minimum capital requirements, a guarantee fund, the solvency ratio, the calculation of the so-called technical reserves, and their coverage by assets are all meant to counterbalance the above-described information deficits of policyholders.[61] Moreover, these instruments are meant to serve the protection of policyholder confidence and thereby form a basis for a viable European insurance market.

The problem of asymmetric information appears also with regard to the *insurance cover*: insurance is a *legal product*, which is constituted by the applicable contract law and the policy conditions formulated by the insur-

57 *Ogus* , Regulation (1994), pp. 38-41; *Breyer*, Regulation and its Reform (1982), pp. 26-28; *Cartwright*, Consumer Protection in Financial Services: Putting the Law in Context, in: Cartwright (ed.), Consumer Protection in Financial Services (1999), p. 1 (10-12).

58 See for this notion, e.g., *Ogus*, supra note 57, p. 133 et seq.

59 To a certain extent, uninformed policyholders may (indirectly) profit from control activities of buyers of large risk insurance.

60 An account of the problems appearing in the U.S. in the 1980s is given by *Gart*, supra note 53, p. 181 et seq.

61 For an overview of the instruments of prudential supervision, see *Schmidt*, Die Finanzaufsicht über Versicherungsunternehmen unter besonderer Berücksichtigung der für den Versicherungsbetrieb erforderlichen Finanzmittel: (1990) ZVersWiss 479. For a critique of prudential supervision concerning credit institutions, see *Knorr*, Staatliche Bankenaufsicht – eine effiziente Institution?: (1999) 50 ORDO 345.

ance company. It is an open secret that the insurance conditions are sometimes of a highly complex structure, using technical terms that are often not comprehensible for even the sophisticated policyholder. Though courts may interpret policy conditions in the light of (legitimate) expectations of the policyholders[62] and control the conditions as to their fairness in relation to the insured, such an approach will not solve the problem: product and market intransparency will still remain a vital issue. Given the low level of information on the product and the reduced capability to process available information, it cannot be expected that the policyholder is in a position to make a rational choice, maximizing his (or her) expected utility.

Faced with these information deficits, the policy decision taken on the European level has nevertheless been to side with the 'information model': ex ante approval of the policy conditions has been replaced by ex post control on the basis of the Unfair Terms Directive[63] by the courts, and potential policyholders are expected to seek informed and reliable advice from specialized and professionally working intermediaries.[64] The Recommendation of 1992[65] and the proposal of a directive concerning insurance intermediaries[66] call for higher standards that intermediaries have to stand up to. It remains to be seen whether a viable and efficient market for information on insurance products will develop in the future, including the sector of mass market insurance products. It is submitted that the danger remains that potential policyholders may misjudge the importance and value of information available from highly qualified intermediaries, and that policyholders may not be in a position to judge on the quality of those intermediaries either.[67]

---

62 Cf. Prölss (-*Prölss*), Versicherungsvertragsgesetz (26th edn, 1998), Vorbem. III para. 1-20; for the U.S. adjudication (in a critical perspective), see *Abraham*, Distributing Risk (1986), p. 101 et seq.

63 Directive 93/13/EEC: (1993) OJEC L 95/29.

64 For a critical description of the British setting (which has been praised by some as a role model for the internal insurance market), see *Clarke*, Policies and Perceptions of Insurance (1997), p. 66.

65 (1992) OJEC L 19/32.

66 (2000) KOM 511, (2001) OJEC C 29E/245.

67 Cf. *Clarke*, supra note 64, p. 66.

V. Unfinished Tasks

Though the internal market for insurance undertakings was meant to come true with the third generation of directives, the European regulatory system has since been supplemented by some more bits and pieces: Directive 95/26/EEC[68] intends to harmonize and to improve the tools of national supervisory authorities in the financial sector, whereas Directive 98/78/EC[69] concerns the consolidated supervision over groups of insurance undertakings. Directive 2001/17/EC[70] addresses the issue of restructuring and liquidation of insurance undertakings, and a proposal of a directive of 25 June 2001, concerns the additional supervision of financial conglomerates.[71] Proposals dealing with a new calculation of the solvency ratio for life assurance undertakings[72] and non-life insurance undertakings[73] are in the process of consideration. The development of a market of insurance information services is still a task to be fulfilled.

One problem for which a solution will not be easy to achieve concerns insurance as a legal product. The European information model is still characterized by a compromise. As has been mentioned, the rules on the law applicable to insurance contracts provide that in the field of mass insurance, the law where the risk is situated shall apply to the contract. It is left to the member state of the risk to grant party autonomy and thereby to advance policyholder choice. The consequences for the internal market for insurance products are obvious: the insurance companies have to adapt their policy conditions even after the abolition of the prior approval requirement to the contract law of the member state of risk. An insurance undertaking doing business all over the internal market will not just sell one contract type, but ten or fifteen varying products, taking care of the national contract law of the state of risk. Are there ways out of this?

It is submitted that with regard to insurance contracts as a *mass phenomenon,* there is no way out. To be sure, in some cases a burden set up for the interstate provision of insurances services by mandatory contract law

68 (1995) OJEC L 168/7.
69 (1998) OJEC L 330/1.
70 (2001) OJEC L 110/28.
71 Document 501PC0213.
72 Document 500PC0617 (dated 17 April 2001).
73 Document 500PC0634 (dated 2 July 2001).

may be regarded as being prohibited by freedom to provide services.[74] But by and large, mandatory contract law pursuing the protection of the insured will have to be regarded as justified by the 'general good' of the relevant member state.[75] And even if a far-reaching harmonization of insurance contract law will be achieved some day, establishing an equivalent level of policyholder protection by mandatory rules in the national laws of the member states, the application of the law where the risk is located (mostly the law where the policyholder resides) will remain a necessity for quite a simple reason: insurance contracts will have to be interpreted and supplemented by national law. After the conclusion of the contract, the policyholder will need advice concerning his or her rights and obligations under the contract. If a foreign law is to be applied to the contract, the policyholder will not get satisfactory advice by legal counsel in his or her state of residence, potentially leading to a loss of contractual rights. Moreover, in case legal proceedings ensue, these proceedings will mostly be carried out before the courts where the policyholder resides.[76] Application of foreign and mostly unknown insurance contract law will be a time-consuming and risky task for at least one party and the courts alike, augmenting transaction costs and putting the goal of policyholder protection into question. In the sector of mass insurance, it seems to be a more efficient solution to apply the law of the state of risk; no concept of 'mutual recognition' can overcome or solve this problem.

One reservation has to be made, however: the interstate provision of services could be facilitated – not on a mass scale, but in the individual case – if *party autonomy* were also admitted for consumer/policyholders on the basis of an express and not prefabricated choice of law agreement by the parties.[77] Such an approach would be devoted to the concept of the 'active' policyholder. And such an approach is called for by freedom to provide

---

74 For a discussion of some examples, see the Communication of the Commission dealing with freedom to provide services and the general good: (2000) OJEC C 43/5.

75 As for the notion of 'general good', see the Communication of the Commission, supra note 74; *Van Schoubroeck*, The Concept of the General Good, in: McGee/Heusel (eds), The Law and Practice of Insurance in the Single European Market (1995), p. 149.

76 Cf. Art. 7-12 Bruxelles Convention and the newly promulgated 'Bruxelles I' regulation.

77 Cf. the discussion by the present author in *Roth*, Internationales Versicherungsvertragsrecht (1985), p. 747, with reference to a Commission proposal dating back to 1967.

services, because this freedom covers also the right of the recipient of a service to shop around in the internal market. A *total exclusion* of party autonomy by the law of a member state appears to be a disproportionate intrusion into that freedom.[78] It probably will need some minimum harmonization of mandatory contract law in order to exclude the ordre public exception and to support the confidence of the policyholder who chooses a product governed by foreign law.

Party autonomy could be strengthened by a requirement (perhaps to be set forth by Community law) that a choice-of-law agreement should be supplemented by *information* provided by the insurance company on the applicable law as far as it is relevant for the policyholder. Such an obligation should be fulfilled before the contract is concluded. Its goal would be the same as served by the information materials required for the distribution of pharmaceuticals: to put the buyer on alert when he or she acquires a product that is unknown and therefore potentially dangerous – an insurance contract governed by foreign law.

[78] This has been argued by the present author in: *Roth*, Article 59 EEC-Treaty and its Implications for Conflicts Law in the Field of Insurance Contracts, in: Reichert-Facilides/Jessuran d'Oliveira (eds), International Insurance Contract Law in the EC (1993), p. 59 (70 et seq.); to the same result (however based on Art. 28 of the 3rd Life and Non-Life Directives): *Ellis*, Policyholder Protection in the Single European Market, in: McGee/Heusel, supra note 75, p. 41 (50).

REGULATION OF INSURANCE SERVICES: THE JAPANESE PERSPECTIVE

by Kôji Kinoshita, Osaka

I. Introduction

The Japanese insurance business is primarily regulated by the Insurance Business Law[1] of 1995 (hereafter IBL). The IBL was first enacted in 1901,

[1] Hoken gyôhô, Law No. 105/1995, last amended by Law No. 150/2001.

J. Basedow, H. Baum, K. Hopt, H. Kanda and T. Kono (eds.), Economic Regulation and Competition, (189-210)

and from 1939 through 1995 it was never revised from its own perspective. Since the 1990s, however, we have experienced days of great upheaval in the Japanese insurance market. In the face of such a difficult situation, both the international regulatory circumstances and the purely domestic problems have forced legislators to revise the IBL and its subordinate regulations from time to time.

It is needless to say that the globalized economy and the trend toward deregulation exercised strong influence on the legislators to review the regulatory scheme. Deregulation on the insurers' scope of business, their distribution channels, and their use of financial derivatives now enable insurers to enjoy much more freedom than before in flexibly innovating their products. In this aspect, I believe that the regulations of the Japanese insurance business have been updated to fit these international circumstances.

It should be emphasized, however, that the negative impacts on the Japanese domestic economy of the violent swung from the overheated 'bubble economy' to the nightmarish recession afterward is much more important. In 1990, the assumed interest rate of the whole life and endowment life products amounted to around 5.5 percent. The assumed interest rate itself never consists of the terms of contract, but premiums are calculated based on that rate. Under those contracts, it is the life insurer's obligation to increase the value of investment assets above such a high interest rate throughout the contract term. Soon after, however, the stock prices slumped. Since then the extremely low official discount rate has been sustained by the government and the central bank. Life insurers suffered from the gap between their promises of high return to their policyholders and the actual low return or even the loss in investment.

On 25 April 1996, the Ministry of Finance ordered Nissan Life Insurance Mutual Company to suspend its business. This was the first case of an insurance company's insolvency since the Japanese economy revived in the 1960s. In the last six years, six more life and two non-life insurers in Japan have gone bankrupt. The number of failed insurers is very serious because the Japanese insurance market has been highly concentrated. Until the late 1980s, the number of domestic direct insurers amounted to only around twenty life and twenty non-life insurers.

In this paper, we shall examine three main aspects of the insurance business regulation in Japan. The first aspect is the deregulation and liberalization of market entry. We would like to see how widely our domestic markets are open to outside players. Market access from overseas was one of the most vigorously discussed issues in the U.S.-Japanese trade negotiations, but it should be noted that the laws on foreign insurers were not the central issue in that negotiation. Secondly, we will look at measures for life insurers to maintain and improve financial soundness and to rehabilitate in case of insolvency. Finally, we will examine the relationship between the regulatory authority, now the Financial Services Agency of Japan[2] (hereafter FSA), and insurers regarding policyholder protection.

II. Overview of Regulatory Schemes

A. Legislation of the Insurance Business Law of 1995

Soon after the bubble economy turned into the slowdown of the domestic economy, we started to review and improve the IBL. On 17 June 1992, the Insurance Council[3] submitted a consultation paper, 'The New Ideal Way of Insurance Business',[4] to the Minister of Finance, the minister responsible for the regulation of insurance business at the time. This 1992 consultation paper pointed out that in the operating insurance business, the insurers were expected to ensure fairness and soundness, to promote adequate competition under the principle of self-responsibility, and to seek efficiency. In order to achieve these goals, the paper proposed that the relevant regulations be deregulated, and supervision of insurance be operated in a fair and transparent manner.[5]

On 24 June 1994, the Insurance Council published a more specified amendment proposal[6] which led to the new IBL 1995. On that occasion, two other relevant laws – namely, the Foreign Insurers Law of 1949[7] and the Insurance Solicitation Control Law of 1948[8] – were consolidated into the IBL.[9]

---

2 Kinyûchô.

3 Hoken Shingi-kai. The Insurance Council is now integrated into the Financial System Council (Kinyû Shingi-kai).

4 Reprinted in: Hoken gyôhô nado no kaisei ni tsuite [On the Revision of Insurance Business Law etc.] (1994), pp. 89-205.

5 Supra note 4, p. 111.

6 Supra note 4, pp. 13-87.

7 Gaikoku hoken jigyô-sha ni kansuru hôritsu, Law No. 184/1949.

8 Hoken boshû no torishimari ni kansuru hôritsu, Law No. 171/1948.

9 The regulation on foreign insurers can be found in Artt. 185-240 IBL 1995, and the regulation on insurance solicitation can be found in Artt. 275-308 IBL 1995.

B. Self-Regulation by Business Associations

Among the Insurance Council's proposals in 1994, one proposal was exceptionally not adopted. Business associations were not recognized as self-regulatory organizations under the IBL. Both the Marine and Fire Insurance Association of Japan[10] and the Life Insurance Association of Japan[11] have long experience with (a) training and examination for insurance sales forces. They also recently established (b) contract data filing systems to detect insurance fraud in the field of personal insurance, and issued a series of guidelines (c) for personal data protection and (d) for good compliance of the insurers' duty to explain the economic risks of their products under the Financial Products Sales Law of 2000.[12] Of course, we may presume that these associations keep good communication with the FSA, but there is no explicit statutory ground for the authority to watch over the associations' activities.

C. Regulatory Objectives

Art. 1 of the new IBL 1995 prescribes the following regulatory objective: to secure, in view of the significance of insurance business to the public, the sound and proper operation of activities by insurance companies, as well as the fairness in insurance solicitation in order to protect policyholders, insureds, and beneficiaries and thereby contribute to the stability of people's lives and to the sound development of the national economy. Some commentators stress that insurance contributes to the development of the national economy.[13] Others see policyholder protection as the primary objective of

---

10 Nihon Songai Hoken Kyôkai. Information on its activities and an outline of the Japanese non-life insurance industry can be found in: Non-Life Insurance in Japan Fact Book 1999-2000, <www.sonpo.or.jp/english/publication/e_fact/fact2000e.html>.

11 Seimei Hoken Kyôkai. Information on its activities and an outline of the Japanese life insurance industry can be found at <www.seiho.or.jp/english/index. html>.

12 *Kôji Kinoshita*, Kinyû shôhin no hanbai [Sales of Financial Products]: (2001) 255 Hôgaku Kyôshitsu [Law Class] 104; Financial Products Sales Law in Japan – A 'Minimum' Overreaching Regulation on the Japanese Financial Services, to be published in Zeitschrift für Japanisches Recht No. 13 (2002).

13 *Shinsaku Iwahara*, Hoken kantoku shohô no kaisei [Revision of Insurance Supervision Laws]: (1994) 1363 Shôji Hômu [Business Journal] 34, 35; *Hoken* cont. ...

the IBL, and the sound development of the national economy should be regarded as the result achieved by ensuring policyholder protection.[14] From the latter's standpoint, it is not justifiable to introduce strong regulatory measures beyond the minimum requirement by just referring to the national economy development. More efforts should be made to develop a more precise dogmatic philosophy and principles of insurance regulation to fit the current circumstances in Japan, and to clarify the correlation between those regulatory principles.

D. Chronological Overview of Recent Regulatory Rule-Making

The substantively relevant amendments or establishments of new rules in the Japanese insurance business through January 2002 are listed as follows:

- Enactment of the Law Concerning Reorganization Proceedings of Financial Institutions,[15] effective 21 June 1996: rationalizing the demutualization procedure;
- Amendments of IBL, effective 11 March 1998: removal of prohibition against the incorporation of holding companies;
- Guidelines for Supervision of Financial Institutions, Book 2 for Insurance Companies, effective 8 June 1998: consolidation of circular letters and informal administrative guidance;
- Order Concerning Special Measures for Policyholder Protection, effective 4 November 1998: amendment of the renamed 'Ordinance Concerning Policyholder Protection Organizations';
- Overall amendments of the IBL and the Non-Life Insurance Rating Organization Law[16] (hereafter NIROL), effective 1 December 1998: so-called 'Financial System Reform Law 1998';

Kenkyû-kai [Insurance Study Group] (ed.), Saishin hoken gyôhô no kaisetsu [Updated Commentary on IBL] (1996), p. 10.

14 *Tomonobu Yamashita*, in: Tokyo Marine and Fire Insurance Co. (ed.), Songai hoken jitsumu kôza hokan, hoken gyôhô [Practical Guide Series on Non-life Insurance, Supplementary Volume on the IBL 1995] (1997), pp. 10, 11; *Masatoshi Furuse*, Commentary on Article 1 IBL: (1998) 125 Bunken Ronshû [Bunken Journal] 186-193.

15 Kinyû kikan-tô no saisei tetsuzuki no tokurei-tô ni kansuru hôritsu, Law No. 95/1996.

16 Songai hoken ryôritsu sanshutsu dantai ni kansuru hôritsu, Law No. 193/1948.

- Amendment of the Enforcement Ordinance of the IBL[17] (hereafter EO-IBL), effective 26 May 2000: improvement of rules on the standard underwriting reserve and the solvency margin ratio;
- Order to Prescribe Classifications for Implementing the Early Warning Measures under Art. 132 para. 2 IBL, effective 29 June 2000;
- Manual for Insurance Companies Inspection, effective 1 July 2000;
- Amendments of the EO-IBL, effective 31 March 2001: enabling cross-market access into the 'third category' (accident and private health) insurance, disclosure of fundamental profit index in life insurance, and improvement of rules on the solvency margin ratio;
- Enactment of the Financial Products Sales Law of 2000, effective 1 April 2001;[18]
- Amendments of the EO-IBL, effective 1 April 2001: lifting the ban on the sales of insurance at bank counters;
- Further amendments of the EO-IBL, effective in 2002.

Following the interim report issued by the Second Subcommittee of the Financial System Council concerning the overall revision of the life insurance business,[19] the FSA recently amended the EO-IBL, effective 2002.[20] In the following part of this paper, these papers shall also be examined.

III. Market Entry and Deregulation

A. Business License

In Japan, nobody may carry on any insurance business unless authorized to do so (Art. 3 para. 1 IBL 1995). The business license can be one of two kinds: for the life insurance business (Art. 3 para. 4 IBL) or for non-life insurance business (Art. 3 para. 5 IBL). No insurance office shall be authorized cumulatively for both kinds of businesses (Art. 3 para. 3 IBL). Life

---

17 Hoken gyôhô shikô kisoku, Ordinance No. 5/1996.

18 Kinyû shôhin no hanbai-tô ni kansuru hôritsu, Law No. 101/2000.

19 *The Second Subcommittee of the Financial System Council*, Seimei hoken wo meguru sôgô-teki na kentô ni kansuru chûkan hôkoku [Interim Report on the Overall Revision of Life Insurance Regulation], 26 June 2001, <www.fsa.go.jp/singi/singi_kinyu/tosin/f-20010626-2.pdf>.

20 *The Second Subcommittee of the Financial System Council*, Seimei hoken wo meguru taiô saku [Solutions on the Life Insurance Regulation], 25 January 2002, <www.fsa.go.jp/singi/singi_kinyu/siryou/kinyu/dai2/f-20020125/a. pdf>.

insurers' access to the non-life market and non-life insurers' access to the life market may be authorized only if such market access is sought through their subsidiaries (Art. 106 IBL). An insurance holding company is also available (Art. 271-3 IBL) for insurers wishing to offer a broader range of products under highly integrated management.

Accident insurance or the private health insurance business (the so-called 'third category' insurance) may be either authorized under the non-life business license – even though such undertakings are made to pay a specific sum insured – or under the life business license – even though they are to indemnify any loss (Art. 3 para. 4 no. 2 and para. 5 no. 2).[21] The business license for the third category may not be obtained independently without operating other sorts of life or non-life business.

B. Market Access from Outside the Industry

As Japan has never experienced the kind of market integration that can be observed in the EU, the foreign insurers' regulation in Japan is still rather restrictive and old-fashioned. There is no freedom of establishment (Art. 185 para. 1 IBL) and, except for some commercial line products, providing insurance services without establishment is banned (Art. 186) and, in principle, regarded as a criminal offense (Art. 316). A deposit is required to ensure that a sufficient amount of assets is located in Japan (Art. 190). In other respects, foreign insurers are subject to host state substantive supervision which is equivalent to that covering domestic insurers (Artt. 200-207).

Sale of insurance at the bank counter might have a deep impact on the insurance industry. Banks are prohibited from operating any business unless specified in Artt. 10 and 11 of the Banking Law[22] (Art. 12 Banking Law 1981). Following the deregulation on the sale of investment trust at bank counters permitted in 1998, sales of insurance at bank counters was also generally permitted under Art. 275 para. 2 IBL in April 2001. For the moment, the range of products is still restricted to those closely related to the banks' intrinsic business, such as sales of fire insurance or credit life insurance coupled with a mortgage loan (Art. 211 EO-IBL).

---

21 The only exception is the health insurance business under the non-life insurance license which covers the death of the insured resulting from disease (Art. 3 para. 4 item d).

22 Ginkô-hô, Law No. 59/1941, last amended by Law No. 129/2001.

The sale of insurance at bank counters is not subject to the FSA's prior approval under the Banking Law (banks are not required to submit any statement on the scope of their business in the business license application[23]). Banks and bankers in charge of insurance sales are required to be registered as insurance agents (Art. 275 IBL). Another condition banks must comply with is to introduce adequate measures to make sure that their customers' confidential personal data shall not be used without obtaining the customers' prior consent (Art. 211 para. 1 no.2 EO-IBL amended in 2000).

Even though the unfair outflow of customer information is prohibited, there might still remain another issue. Information on the cash flow of the customers' accounts, such as the pattern of their income and consumption, are kept by the banks. Under such an advantageous situation, only banks would control the customers' money flow by giving them investment advice. They might dissuade their customers from buying life insurance and recommend an investment trust instead. There is no evidence that bankers are more qualified than insurance agents in giving advice to their customers. The new legislation of the Financial Products Sales Law of 2000, being applicable to a wide range of financial products, does not cover a seller's duty of giving advice to his or her customers. Therefore, even though banks must comply with the market conduct rules in the IBL (Art. 300 para. 1 no.1 IBL) and the Financial Products Sales Law, the impartiality of advice is not guaranteed.

One may argue that life insurers would also benefit by allowing bankers to sell insurance because bankers would sell insurance more efficiently than the insurers' own sales forces. This might mean insurers would outsource the training and monitoring cost of sales forces to the banks. It would enable customers to choose financial products from a wider range of products at the 'one-stop shopping mall'. This could be more convenient for all the parties. Nevertheless, customers may not be able to enjoy this much broader range of choices at the bank counter as long as banks play their roles as tied agents of an insurer with a close relationship.

Furthermore, there is no prospect that insurance sales at bank counters would contribute to the reduction of premiums. Banks cannot discount insurance premiums at their own disposal because any alteration of premiums is subject to the FSA's prior approval (Art. 123 para. 1 IBL). It is prohibited for insurers and insurance intermediaries (banks in this case) to make a

---

23 Art. 4 and 12 Banking Law and Art. 1-3 Enforcement Ordinance of the Banking Law (Ginkô-hô shikô kisoku, Ordinance No. 10/1982, last amended by Ordinance No. 1/2002).

commitment for a discount or a rebate on an insurance premium (Art. 300 para. 1 no.5 IBL). Regarding the banks' dominant position in obtaining customers' information, there is little economic incentive for insurers who have already been equipped with distribution channels to set a discount rate in their tariff for those products sold by banks.

In addition to all these anxieties, the manner in formulating Art. 211 para. 1 EO-IBL reveals another dogmatic issues. The latter shall be discussed again later in this paper (see IV.2.).

C. Premium Calculation and Rating Organizations

The methods of premium calculation and any of their alterations shall be subject to the regulatory authority's prior approval (Art. 4, Art. 5 para. 1 item 4, Art. 123 para. 1 IBL 1995). In life insurance and the large risk sector of non-life insurance, there have never been any obligatory or standard premium rates with any specific statutory background. In the mass risk sector of non-life insurance – namely, automobile insurance, house fire insurance, earthquake insurance, and personal accident insurance – the premiums had long been calculated by the rating organizations (hereafter RO).[24] Non-life insurers were obliged to employ these RO premium rates for their own products until 1998 (Art. 10-5 para. 1 Non-life Insurance Rating Organization Law, hereafter NIROL).

The current NIROL, revised by the Financial System Reform Law in 1998 and again in 2000, abolished the insurers' duty to employ the ROs' premium rates. The ROs must now calculate non-obligatory 'reference loss cost rate' and 'standard full rate'. Reference loss cost rate is applicable as the basis for calculation of premium rates by its members to the extent that the filing and authority's examination procedures (Art. 9-2 NIROL) required under NIROL have been duly fulfilled (Art. 2 para. 5 NIROL). Standard full rate is provided for use by its members, and it will be deemed to have been approved or filed under the stipulations of the IBL[25] if the filing, examination, and objection procedures (Art. 9-3 et seq. NIROL) required under NIROL have been duly completed (Art. 2 para. 6 NIROL). By adopting

---

24 There are two ROs under NIROL: Property and Casualty Insurance Rating Organization of Japan (PCIRO, <www.sonsan.or.jp/>) and Automobile Insurance Rating Organization of Japan (AIRO, <www.airo.or.jp/>).

25 Art. 123 para. 1 with regard to Art. 4 para. 2 no. 4 IBL: prior approval of alteration of statement on premium calculation methods.

either of these RO's rates, insurers shall be able to depend on the appropriateness of the RO's premium rate and to omit detailed explanation and justification to the regulatory authority.[26]

In addition to calculating the reference loss cost rates and standard full rates for use by their members, ROs also produce model standard policy conditions as their incidental business (Art. 7-2 para. 2 no. 3 NIROL). The ROs' policy conditions have also long been adopted by most of the domestic insurers, and thus in the Japanese non-life mass risk market the de facto uniformity of the policy conditions was achieved by 1998. In the field of fire insurance, the situation has changed little. In contrast, in automobile insurance, some foreign direct-sales insurers and other newcomers started to offer 'differentiated risk estimate' automobile insurance with a premium discount and wider range of services (settlement support, rescue service in accidents, prompt indemnity, and so on). The automobile insurance market is now becoming much more competitive than ever before. From a regulatory point of view, we must watch over the current situation carefully so that the transparency of products will not be spoiled. At present, the prior control on products seems to be striking a good balance between the diversity and transparency in products, and no serious irregularities, such as excessive discount sales, can be observed.

IV. Financial Soundness and Rehabilitation of Life Insurers

A. Diagnosis

To secure the financial soundness of life insurers is absolutely the most serious concern in the current Japanese insurance regulation. The FSA is equipped with three criteria to test the insurers' financial soundness under the IBL 1995.

The first test is the solvency margin ratio (Art. 130 IBL). For the determination of the adequacy of insurers' solvency to meet insurance claims, the proportion of the total amount of capital (including foundation fund and reserves) is compared with the estimated amount of risks of suffering from loss which would exceed those ordinarily expected. The solvency margin ratio is to test the insurers' instantaneous resistivity against unforeseeable

[26] *AIRO*, Ryôdan-hô no kaisei to Jisan-kai no atarashii yakuwari [The Reform of the NIROL and the New Role of the AIRO]: (1999) 1 Jidôsha Hoken Kenkyû [Automobile Insurance Journal] 57, at 61 et seq.

risk at a certain point of time by presuming their business will continue. This test is connected with early warning measure (Art. 132 IBL).[27] The solvency margin test was expected to be a deterrent from risky or careless operation of business, but not to tell us future trends. What actually happened was that life insurers whose solvency margin ratio showed above 200 went insolvent.[28] Accordingly, the details of risk evaluation ratio should be revised from time to time so that the solvency margin ratio can represent the insurers' financial soundness more precisely.

The second test, liquidation value criterion, is an exceptional criterion of the solvency margin ratio under an early warning regime. Even when the solvency margin ratio shows above 0 percent (second grade), if the amount of the assets in the balance sheet will be insufficient to cover the amount of the debts, the FSA must order the insurer to cease its business activities (Art. 3 para. 3 Order to Prescribe Classifications under Art. 132 para. 2 IBL 2000). In this case, the assets will be estimated as if the company would be liquidated.[29]

The third test is a future profit prospect report submitted by the insurer's appointed actuary to the board of directors and the FSA (Art. 121 IBL in connection with Artt. 79-2 and 80 EO-IBL). In the future profit prospect, the actuary is to ascertain, given the analysis on the future profit from the actuarial point of view, whether or not the insurer would find any difficulty in its continuation of business (Art. 79-2 EO-IBL). The criterion is whether at a certain point the reasonably foreseeable amount of assets would be sufficient to cover the reasonably foreseeable amounts of debts in the light of continuation of business (Art. 80 no.3 EO-IBL). In this prospect, reasonably foreseeable tendency of cash flows – e.g., increase of premium income, cancellation of contracts, or investment return – must be taken into consideration.

---

27 When the ratio shows below 200%, the FSA will order the insurer to submit a statement of business improvement plan (100-200%: the first grade), to take certain actions to improve its solvency (0-100%: the second grade), or to cease the whole or a part of its business activities (below 0%: the third grade).

28 In the cases of Chiyôda Life (221%) and Kyôei Life (203%).

29 *Masatoshi Furuse*, Kinyû shisutemu kaikaku ni tomonau hoken seido kaikaku [Insurance System Reform in the Financial Systems Reform]: (2001) 135 Jili Journal 17, at 36.

B. Preventive Measure

Insurance companies must establish underwriting reserves at the end of each accounting period to provide for the fulfillment of future obligations under insurance contracts (Art. 116 para. 1 IBL 1995).[30] With regard to long-term insurance contracts, unless specified in Art. 68 EO-IBL,[31] the authority lays down rules on the standard requirement in calculating the amount of underwriting reserves (Art. 116 para. 2 IBL 1995). The standard underwriting reserve shall be established, in principle, not by following Zillmer's method but by following the calculation method of net level premium (Art. 69 para. 4 EO-IBL). In case the established underwriting reserve is likely to be insufficient to fulfill the insurer's future obligation, insurers must alter the statement of methods of calculating underwriting reserves (which is subject to the FSA's prior approval: Art. 123 para. 1) and establish additional underwriting reserves (Art. 69 para. 5 EO-IBL).

This standard underwriting reserve is not a regime to set a strict minimum requirement. As long as the value of assets and nature of risks permit, in theory, insurers are free to deviate from the 'standard' assumed rate of interest and set a higher assumed rate of interest[32] by obtaining the FSA's prior approval. The appropriateness of calculation in establishing an underwriting reserve and the compliance to the standard underwriting reserve requirement are to be assessed by an appointed actuary (Art. 121 para. 1 IBL in connection with Art. 80 no.1 EO-IBL). The actuary must submit a report on it annually to the insurer's board of directors and to the FSA. Then the FSA shall also monitor the appropriateness of the calculation from the supervisory standpoint. If the underwriting reserve proves to be insufficient in the light of the standard underwriting reserve requirement, life insurers will be

---

30 Methods of calculating underwriting reserves and any of their alterations shall be subject to the regulatory authority's prior approval (Art. 4, Art. 5 para. 1 item 4, Art. 123 para. 1 IBL).

31 The following types of life insurance are excluded from the standard underwriting reserve scheme: 1) fund-link life insurance, 2) those insurances under which a premium reserve need not be established, 3) those life insurances under which the insurer's right to alter the premium calculation bases is reserved, and 4) those insurances not suitable for fixing the calculation basis for the underwriting reserve.

32 *Masatoshi Furuse*, Wagakuni no shin-hoken gyôhô ni okeru hyôjun sekinin junbi-kin no kangaekata [Ideas of Standard Underwriting Reserve under the Japanese New IBL], *Kôichi Hiroumi/Isao Shimowada* (eds), Gendai shakai to hoken [Modern Society and Insurance] (1996), p. 131 at 138 et seq.

requested to alter their calculation bases of the underwriting reserve and cover the deficit, probably by their distributable profit.

Under the IBL, the FSA's prior approval requirement on the calculation bases of the underwriting reserve (Art. 4 para. 2 no.4) is not expected to be abolished. The regulation on the underwriting reserve in Japan is unique compared with those in other jurisdictions in the sense that both the supervisory authority and actuary are expected to examine its calculation bases.[33] Our experiences of insolvency cases showed that even such cumulative actuarial and supervisory monitoring might be unsatisfactory.

C. *Rehabilitation and Cure*

As of April 2001, the FSA is allowed to order those insurers who find difficulty in continuing business to cease their activities before the insurers go insolvent (Art. 1-2 Order Concerning Special Measures for Policyholder Protection 1998). An insurer whose actuary reports a negatively estimated future profit prospect may apply for a rehabilitation procedure. In the rehabilitation procedure, the FSA may order the insurance company to suspend its activities, to have consultations regarding the transfer of an insurance portfolio or merger, or to order the insolvent insurer to have an insurance administrator administer the insolvent insurer's activities and assets (Art. 241 IBL). An insurance administrator is to be appointed by the FSA (Art. 242 IBL).

A policyholders' protection organization (Art. 259 IBL) is to provide financial assistance either as insurance administrator (Art. 242 IBL) or as financial sponsor to a rescue insurance company for the purpose of smoothly carrying out an insurance portfolio transfer, a merger, or an acquisition. In the absence of any prospective rescue insurance company, the policyholders' protection organization is entitled to receive the transfer of an insurance portfolio of an insurance company in difficulties (Art. 259, 265-28 IBL). In the rehabilitation process, the insurer in difficulties is entitled to alter or reduce the sum insured and to adjust other policy conditions in the existing insurance contracts (Art. 250 IBL).

Those insurers who made every effort to improve their financial soundness but failed are obliged to seek rehabilitation. The problem is what can be

---

33 *Masatoshi Furuse*, Hoken keiri-nin no yakuwari ni tsuite [On the Role of Actuaries]: (1993) 104 Bunken Ronshû 71 at 72, 98.

done before giving up the company's restoration through its own efforts. The latest amendments of the EO-IBL, to be made effective in 2002, will implement some of the proposals in the Interim Report of 2001 to assist life insurers' efforts to recover their policyholders' and markets' confidence in them. The Interim Report proposed these measures as listed below:

1. to loosen the regulation on the minimum ratio of the surplus dividend, 80 percent of the total surplus,[34] up to 20 percent and to leave room for each insurance company's autonomous decision (implemented in Art. 29 EO-IBL amended in 2002);
2. to promote the establishment of underwriting reserve in the criterion of net level premium and application of the standard underwriting reserve requirement for a wider range of products;
3. to promote demutualization so that insurers can more easily reorganize their business through mergers or raising capital through direct financing; and
4. to introduce authorized capital rule[35] into the law of the mutual company so that mutual companies may raise their foundation funds in a flexible way.

The deregulation of the minimum requirement on the distribution of surplus dividend might be regarded as making light of the policyholders' right to receive the investment return, which would make it an inappropriate measure to adopt. It should be noted, however, that in ordinary life insurance with a guarantee of the sum insured – in contrast to the unit-linked policies with no guarantee of the sum insured – the saving premium is collected for a very specified purpose, not for pure investment. It is collected in order to establish enough reserve funds for each policyholder to cover the increase of risk premium at the later stage. The insurers' primary contractual obligation is not to distribute the surplus, but to guarantee the agreed sum insured throughout the contract term. There is good reason under the current circumstances for the Japanese life insurers to be entitled to give priority to cover the (potential) deficit of the underwriting reserve over the distribution of the surplus.

Although in some aspects the procedure has already been simplified, demutualization is still a very costly task for insurers. In order to raise foundation funds or capital through issuing subordinated debts, insurers must

---

[34] Art. 29 no. 1 EO-IBL.

[35] Cf. Art. 166 para. 1 no. 3 Japanese Commercial Code (Shôhô, Law No. 48/1899, last amended by Law No. 149/2001).

recover trust from the financial market. For this purpose, they must disclose more details of their financial states. The Interim Report also proposed the improvement of insurers' disclosure on the details of the underwriting reserves, calculation bases of solvency margin, and the precise amount and calculation bases of the negative spread,[36] and these proposals were implemented in 2002 (Artt. 16 and 59-2 EO-IBL).

It should be noted, however, that one of the major triggers leading to life insurers' insolvency was the increase of cancellations in response to negative reports by journalists. In insolvency cases, insurance administrators are entitled to retain policyholders' policies when they cancel them, a step that actually gives policyholders' policies much more value. Nevertheless, more than a few policyholders tend to cancel their policies in the belief that they would lose much more money by retaining their policies. It would be the role of the supervisory authority to adopt adequate measures to make sure that the change of regulatory rules does not invite confusion in the market, and economic loss for the majority of policyholders must not caused by such regulatory reforms.

V. Relationship between the Regulatory Authority and Insurers

A. Compliance Monitoring and Inspection

When the FSA deems it necessary for the purpose of securing the sound and proper operation of activities of an insurance company and for the protection of policyholders, it may require an insurance company to submit a report or materials (Art. 128 IBL), or it may direct authorized public officials to enter an insurance company's place of business, make inquiries as to the state of its activities or assets, or examine books and other property (Art. 129 IBL). In order to improve the inspection and enhance transparency in the FSA's administration, the FSA published a series of 'Financial Inspection Manuals' in 1999.[37] According to the manual, its basic principle is that financial institutions should be run on the principle of self-responsibility (of the financial institutions), with financial inspection serving a means of supplementing this. The external inspection should focus on the process examination to

[36] Financial System Council, Interim Report 2001, supra note 19, pp. 7, 8.
[37] The Japanese text can be browsed at the FSA's website: <www.fsa.go.jp/manual/manualj/hoken.pdf>.

verify the appropriateness of each company's internal control and external auditing.[38]

Based on this understanding, the FSA changed the manner of formulating some sorts of regulatory rules in the statutes or ordinances. A good example is the prohibition on banks from making use of customers' personal data, which we have seen above. Here, the rule specifies not only the prohibition of using personal data, it also requires banks to introduce adequate measures to make sure that such irregularities shall not take place. Let us further examine questions this may cause by taking another example on a product disclosure rule.

B. Rule-Making on Market Conduct

In Japan, there is no statutory requirement on the disclosure of policy conditions to the customer. This does not mean there have never been any irregularities of misrepresentation or non-disclosure of products. During the 20th century, non-disclosure and misrepresentation of products often caused disputes between insurers and policyholders, and it is recognized as one of the major misconducts of intermediaries.[39] The first legislative resolution with criminal sanctions was adopted in 1948 (Art. 16 para. 1 no.1 Insurance Solicitation Control Law). This provision still survives in the Art. 300 para. 1 no.1 IBL.[40]

After the bubble economy boom, many life offices suffered from a number of litigations claiming that life insurance solicitors made false or misleading statements on the main features of the unit-linked policy, that is, its investment risk. Many private customers who purchased this type of product between 1989 and 1992 suffered from loss of value on their contracts.[41] In 1999, another scandal took place concerning the life policy con-

38 FSA, Outline of the 'Final Report' of the Working Group on Financial Inspection Manuals, 8 April 1998, <www.fsa.go.jp/p_fsa/news/newse/ne_023/01.pdf>.

39 Kôji Kinoshita, Hoken boshû kisei no tenkai [The Historical Development of Regulations on Insurance Solicitation], in: Okushima / Kurasawa (eds), Shôwa shôhô gakushi [History on the Study of Commercial Law in the Showa Era] (1996), p. 647 at 648.

40 Art. 300 para. 1 no.1 IBL prescribes that no insurance company and insurance solicitors may make a false representation to a policyholder or fail to represent to him any matters of importance regarding the contractual terms of insurance contracts.

41 At that time, land prices in urban areas soared extremely and inheritance tax became one of the main concerns for aged family with property. Life offices and retail

cont. ...

version.[42] In these cases the breach of Art. 300 para. 1 no.1 was in question, but this provision was deemed inconvenient because criminal sanction is connected to the least-clearly formulated text. The regulatory authority of the time had to issue circular letters or informal guidance with more specified requirements.

In 1998, the Financial System Reform Law introduced a new rule on product disclosure into the IBL. An insurance company must, as specified by the EO-IBL, adopt measures to ensure that its activities are conducted in a sound and appropriate manner, including measures for explanations regarding matters of importance to be provided to clients (Art. 100-2 IBL). Under this article, the FSA is authorized to consolidate and introduce the specified rules on product disclosure by its ordinance. At the same time, this article adopted the above-mentioned new style of formulating text.

Consequently, the text of the ordinance requires insurers to adopt appropriate measures, but it often does not mention what the appropriate measures could be. The rule primarily focuses on the organizational negligence of the insufficient measures adopted internally, purely from the regulatory point of view. The FSA only has to specify what sort of business activities should be

---

bankers teamed up with each other and recommended that such families should purchase unit-linked policies by mortgaging their accommodations. By doing so, policyholders could have reduced their taxable value of asset, accordingly their inheritance tax, and at the same time they could prepare for that tax with that policy, but it turned out to be just the opposite.

As to the analyses of cases of the mis-selling of unit-linked life policies, see *Shôken Torihiki-hô Kenkyû-kai* [Study Group on the Securities Exchange Law], Shôken torihiki-hô ni kansuru saikin no hanrei no dôkô (4)(5) [The Latest Trends on the Cases on the Securities Exchange Law (4)(5)]: (1999) 49 Inbesutomento [Investment] No. 5, p. 53; (1997) 50 Inbestumento No. 1, p. 60; *Toshihiko Shimizu*, Tôshi kanyû to fuhô kôi [Investment Solicitation and Tort] (1999); *Akira Morita*, Kinyû sâbisu-hô no riron [Theories on the Law of Financial Services] (2001), pp. 156-211; *Yoshio Shiomi*, Tôshi torihiki to minpô riron [Investment Transactions and Civil Law Theories]: (1999) Minshôhô Zasshi Vol. 117 No. 6 p. 807, Vol. 118 No. 1 p. 1, No. 2 p. 161, No. 3 p. 363.

42 The life policy conversion scandal was reported only by the press and consumer organizations. No case has been reported yet. Life offices were said to have obstinately approached their policyholders whose policies were based on the high assumed interest rate, and recommended that they convert their policy to the new product with improved health insurance riders; but the main product's (whole-life or endowment) premiums were disadvantageous. The increase of premiums was likely to be camouflaged by extending the period during which premiums must be paid, and only this deviation was not highlighted in the written recommendation.

improved, but often without any indication of what should be done by the individual intermediaries. The FSA justifies this by explaining that the deregulation trend should be taken into consideration. By doing so, the FSA may evade the risk of both under- and over-regulation. More specified minimum requirements of market conduct rules, however, are unlikely to be crystallized under such supervisory practices. In my view, this reflects the FSA's detached and daunted attitude toward delicate issues, which may cause political pressure and impairment of the people's trust in the FSA.[43]

C. *Adjustment of Life Premium*

One of the most urgent and vitally discussed issues before this September was the possibility of life insurers' adjustment of premium in the existing contracts. As stated above, the assumed interest rate, which is meant to reflect the estimated investment return of the life offices and constitutes the major part of their profits, was 5.5 percent per year. Now it is around 2 percent or less. Though this interest rate itself never constitutes the content of an insurance contract, it is technically incorporated into the premiums calculation. The methods of calculating insurance premiums and any alteration must be submitted to and approved by the regulatory authority (until 1995 Art. 10 para. 1 IBL 1939, now Art. 123 para. 1 IBL 1995). Until very recently, the assumed interest rate has been fixed in the statement of the methods of premiums calculation. No insurer's right to adjust this rate has ever been reserved in the standard policy conditions.[44]

---

43 This attitude reflects the discussion in the Financial System Council, where business conduct rules are classified into three categories. The first is the 'transaction rule', which governs the private law relationship between financial services providers and their customers. The second is the internal 'business rule', which is applicable to the internal business processes in a technical manner and each business entity should be responsible for their compliance. The last one is the 'market rule', regarded as a more fundamental rule to maintain the market confidence and in principle actionable for any breach. Financial System Council, Wholesale and Retail Working Group Report, 6 July 1999, <www.fsa.go. jp/p_mof/singikai/kinyusin/tosin/kin003b.pdf>.

44 Nowadays things are changing. Some life insurers (Sumitomo Life and Meiji Life) apply a floating rate (but with a minimum rate guaranteed) as an assumed interest rate in the premium account, where the premium will be saved for the purchase of life insurance products in the future. This condition, including the application of the floating rate, is explicitly prescribed in their policy conditions. In Japan, the nature of whole-life and endowment life insurance with a saving element has not been so

cont. ...

Until 1995, the IBL 1939 left insurers two measures for premium adjustment. The first method was the retroactive alteration of the business plan by an adminisitrative order of the competent minister (Art. 10 para. 3 IBL 1939). The second was the reduction of sum insured subject to the provisions in the company's articles of incorporation[45] (Art. 46 IBL 1939). The competent minister (the Minister of Finance) may, in giving the approval of the alteration in the business plan, impose the condition that such alteration shall also apply for the future to any existing insurance if he considers that such a condition is especially necessary for the protection of the interests of the policyholders, the insureds, or the beneficiaries of the existing insurance.

Art. 10 para. 3 IBL 1939 was abolished because it was deemed to be exceptional, and therefore there is some doubt about the conformity with the constitution in that the regulatory authority is entitled to issue an administrative order which enables a private party to be exempted from his contractual obligation.[46] Art. 46 IBL 1939 was abolished in order to guarantee a similar level of policyholder protection and provide a plain field of competition between insurance mutual companies and insurance stock companies.[47] Even though Art. 46 was not abolished, it could not work in the present situation because under the articles of incorporation, mutual insurers must appropriate all the relevant reserves before proposing to reduce the sum insured.

The Financial System Council Interim Report of 2001 proposed an idea of rules on the condition alteration procedure.[48] According to this, conditions of the alteration shall be carried out by the following steps shown below:

---

vigorously discussed as in Germany (cf. *Walter Karten/ManfredWerber/Gerrit Winter* (eds), Lebensversicherung und Geschäftsbesorgung, 1998), but we must carefully find the nature of life insurance with such accounts.

45 For example, Nihon Life Insurance Company provided in its articles of incorporation until 1995 as follows:
Art. 41 para. 1: In case of deficit in the settlement of account, special reserve, retirement allowances reserve, policyholder dividend reserve, loss compensation reserve, and foundation fund reserve shall be used in order to compensate this deficit, and should there still remain deficit, the sum insured may be reduced by the assembly of members' representatives.

46 *Masaaki Nakanishi*, Jigyô no kantoku [Supervision of Business], in: Akio Takeuchi (ed.), Hoken gyôhô no arikata [The Ideal Way of Insurance Business Law] Vol. 2 (1992), pp. 113-125.

47 *Hoken Kenkyû-kai*, supra note 13, pp. 41, 42.

48 *Financial System Council*, supra note 19, pp. 14-17.

First, (1) the alteration procedure shall be commenced by a resolution of the board of directors. As soon as the resolution is made, (2) the rough ideas of the original alteration plan shall be disclosed to the policyholders (reason for the necessity of the adjustment; scope of the adjustment; expected assumed interest rate; capital enhancement plan; liability of the existing management; treatment of equity capital; and restoration strategy, for example, de-mutualization or cooperation with sponsors). Then, (3) the alteration plan shall be examined by experts[49] (appropriateness of alteration, disclosure on the individual sources of profit,[50] liability of existing management, treatment of equity capital, prospect on future profit, and policyholder dividend policy, etc.). (4) The alteration plan must be approved by the corporate organ, e.g., at the shareholders' general meeting or the assembly of members' representatives. (5) The result and contents of the resolution on the alteration plan shall be communicated to the individual policyholders (details of general alteration plan and expected amount of premium/sum insured in individual contracts). (6) Collective consent must be given to the alteration plan at the policyholders' assembly. (A qualified majority is required.[51] Procedural fairness shall be monitored by experts.) Finally, (7) the alteration plan shall be announced to the public, and policyholders are given an opportunity to express their opposition. More than a certain ratio of objections would frustrate the whole plan. After the expiration of the objection period, the alteration shall finally take effect.

It is certainly the insurers' responsibility to obtain the policyholders' consent to the alteration. Nevertheless, the proposal obviously requires a too burdensome procedure in obtaining their consent. Furthermore, it requests insurers to make a successful effort in persuading the policyholders to strengthen the insurer's financial soundness, and at the same time expects the majority of policyholders to give consent to the alteration if they are satisfied with the announced financial improvement plan. These two things might be in conflict with each other. If policyholders would be satisfied with the announced improvement plan, they might wonder why then the conditions alteration is still necessary to overcome the insurers' financial crisis. If policyholders should believe that the alteration were inevitable, why could they be satisfied with the temporary solution of capital reinforcement?

---

[49] Attorneys, accountants, or independent actuaries.

[50] Investment profit, expenses profit, and profit from risk taking.

[51] Artt. 70, 137, 166, and 173-4 also provide for the objection procedure.

On this issue, one commentator bases the possibility of allowing premium adjustment on the grounds that the long recession and extreme low interest rate were not foreseeable to the parties.[52] Another claims that the Interim Report makes light of the nature of a mutual company and should seek a possibility to allow the autonomous decision of premium adjustments by improving the once-abolished Art. 46 IBL 1939.[53] Another suggests that there could be a new approach by emphasizing the important role of the life insurance industry in the financial market.[54]

It would be realistic to presume in Japan that the disclosure of negative information might cause cancellation of not a few policyholders, even though, reasonably considered, by canceling policies they might suffer from much more serious economic loss than if they were to maintain them. In order to stop such an increase of cancellation, it would be inevitable to intervene in the alteration and prohibit the policyholders' cancellation for a while. In case of rehabilitation, the cancellation may be suspended by the FSA's suspension order of insurer's activities. Similarly, in the case of a condition alteration, without any restriction on cancellation there would be no successful premium adjustment. The FSA should take the initiative to control the whole alteration procedure, but the proposal never mentioned the FSA's positive commitment. Again, this proposal reflects the FSA's risk-evasive attitude. It is quite natural that the proposal did not obtain nationwide support and was abandoned by the FSA.[55]

The restriction of cancellation could not be achieved by the supervisory authority's appropriate intervention against the policyholders' contractual right. Can it be really unjustifiable purely from the contractual right approach by rationally assessing the actual cost and the expected benefit for the individual policyholders?

---

52 *Hideaki Ôtsuka*, Yotei riritsu no hikisage mondai towa [What Is the Reduction of the Assumed Interest Rate?]: (2001) 1206 Jurisuto [Jurist] 2 at 4.

53 *Tsutomu Chano*, Yotei riritsu hikisage mondai to seihô-gyô no shôrai [The Issue of the Assumed Interest Rate Reduction and Future of Life Insurance Business] (2002), pp. 41-43.

54 *Makoto Munezane*, Kinyû Shingi-kai Kinyû Bunka-kai daini bukai chûkan hôkoku ni tsuite [The Outline of the Interim Report issued by the 2nd Subcommittee, Sectional Committee on Financial System, Financial System Council]: (2002) 70 Seimei Hoken Keiei [Journal of Life Insurance Management] No. 1, p. 6 at 30.

55 Nihon Keizai Shinbun [Nihon Keizai Newspaper] of 7 September 2001.

VI. Provisional Remarks

As to the financial regulations, the IBL offers plenty of indications to estimate financial soundness, and more detailed disclosure on insurers' calculation bases is to be introduced. Indeed, it is a very difficult time to require full disclosure. Every effort to strengthen the insurers' financial stability that can be done without risk has already been done. Risk-resistible life products have been innovated. It may be the FSA's turn to take the risk in controlling the condition alteration procedure.

Presumably, the FSA's risk-evasive attitude in developing market conduct rules would be better explained if we insist that the supervisory authority shall act only in the interest of public interest. This is the position supported in Germany in justifying Art. 81 para. 1 sentence 3 of the German Insurance Supervision Law 1994 (*Versicherungsaufsichtsgesetz*: VAG). However, we may say that public interest in the context of market conduct rules is equivalent to the total amount of individual policyholders' private interest to be protected in the frame of their own insurance contracts. We should decide if we should follow the same lines as those of the German law.

As described above, the new challenges for the insurance supervisor are mainly in the field of market conduct regulation. Although the FSA often hesitates to play a positive role in creating market conduct rules with private law remedies, not a few market conduct rules directly concern the individual policyholders' contractual right. There is a widely accepted consensus among insurance supervisors at the international level that market conduct rules should be one of the main concerns of the insurance supervisors.[56] I hope the complicated patchwork of regulatory rules and the unclear nature of those market conduct rules will be crystallized in the near future.

---

[56] IAIS, Principles for Conduct of Insurance Business, December 1999, <www.iaisweb.org/content/02pas/02conduct.pdf>.

THE ROLE OF THE IAIS IN INSURANCE REGULATION

by Knut Hohlfeld, Basel

I. Introduction

Professor Kinoshita has described the Japanese insurance supervisory system as an example of a national regulatory system. Professor Roth presented the insurance supervisory system in the European Union (EU) as a model of regional regulation. It covers the fifteen EU member states, but also Iceland, Liechtenstein, and Norway as further contracting parties of the European Economic Area Agreement (EEA). I will set out what I think is possible in global insurance regulation and what has been achieved so far in this respect.

II. The International Association of Insurance Supervisors (IAIS)

I represent the International Association of Insurance Supervisors (IAIS), founded in 1994. Its sister organizations representing the other two financial sectors, the Basel Committee on Banking Supervision (Basel Committee) and the International Organisation of Securities Commissions (IOSCO), were founded twenty years earlier and thus have a much longer history. The IAIS is an association under Swiss private law, with its secretariat in Basel.

J. Basedow, H. Baum, K. Hopt, H. Kanda and T. Kono (eds.), Economic Regulation and Competition, (211-216)

It is hosted by the Bank for International Settlements (BIS) and located in the same building as the Basel Committee. It is financed by its members who represent insurance supervisory authorities from over 100 jurisdictions. As stated in the IAIS by-laws, its goal is to improve supervision in the insurance sector worldwide in order to maintain efficient, fair, safe, and stable insurance markets for the benefit and protection of policyholders.

III. Standard-Setting Activities

Initially, IAIS activities centered on exchanging information and experiences among insurance supervisors. However, in 1997 it began developing international principles and standards on insurance supervision.

So far the IAIS has issued eighteen principles, standards, and guidance papers. These papers consist of three layers: the Insurance Core Principles complemented by several additional principles papers as the first layer; more detailed standards as the second layer; and textbooks and case studies as the third layer.

The Insurance Core Principles comprise seventeen essential principles that need to be in place for an insurance supervisory system to be effective. They set out the basis for insurance supervision, identify subject areas that should be addressed in legislation or regulation in each jurisdiction, and provide a framework on which the IAIS can develop more detailed international standards. In particular, the essential elements for effective insurance supervision are:

- supervision of the insurance industry by an independent insurance supervisory authority with clear and objectively stated powers (Principle 1);
- a system of licensing whereby insurers must be licensed to operate (Principle 2);
- fit and proper requirements for the Board of Directors, senior management, and stakeholders of insurance companies (Principles 2 and 3);
- a framework of corporate governance that sets out responsibilities for the Board of Directors and ensures that internal controls exist and are operating properly (Principle 4);
- capital adequacy/solvency requirements that reflect the size, complexity, and business risks of a company (Principle 8);
- prudential rules that limit or manage the amount of risk that insurance companies retain (Principles 5 and 10);
- monitoring and on-site inspection to enable supervisors to get the information they need (Principle 13);

- principles applicable to the supervision of internationally active insurers and insurance groups and their cross-border business operations (Principles 15 and 16);
- powers to take remedial action where problems involving insurance companies are identified (Principle 14).

This framework is similar to that used in other financial sectors, as are many of the risks that it addresses. Like banks and securities firms, insurance companies face credit, market, liquidity, and operational risks. However, these risks that are significant in the banking and securities sectors are only of secondary importance for the insurance sector, as is the role of capital requirements. The technical provisions cover insurance risk. The investment risk that includes credit, market, and liquidity risks is covered by strict investment rules. Capital adequacy or solvency is only a necessary additional safety cushion to cover non-technical risks and other unexpected losses, e.g., from operational risk. The required solvency margin should therefore be considered as the last resort after all other measures taken by the insurer to secure its financial stability have failed.

The Core Principles are complemented by an Insurance Concordat which contains principles applicable to the supervision of international insurers and insurance groups and their cross-border business; principles on capital adequacy and solvency, particularly important as a first step to harmonization of solvency requirements, which differ considerably worldwide; principles for the conduct of insurance business; principles on the supervision of insurance activities on the Internet; a guidance paper for fit and proper principles and their application; a guidance paper on public disclosure by insurers; and anti-money laundering guidance notes for insurance supervisors and insurance entities.

As a second layer under the Core Principles, the IAIS has developed and adopted several detailed insurance standards with regard to licensing, on-site inspections, derivatives, asset management, indirect supervision of reinsurance, group coordination, and the exchange of information. In case of cross-border business – either by establishment or by providing services – both the Supervisory Standard on the Exchange of Information and the Insurance Concordat request full information exchange between home and host country supervisor.

The third layer under the Core Principles and the standards is textbooks and case studies. These are educational tools that support the implementation of the IAIS principles and standards.

At present, the IAIS is working on a number of additional papers setting out principles and standards for different areas of insurance supervision. First priorities are given to:

- solvency requirements – developing a supervisory standard, or at least more detailed guidance, to complement the principles paper that has just been issued;
- reinsurance supervision – developing a principles paper on direct supervision of reinsurance companies;
- accounting – cooperating with the International Accounting Standards Board (IASB) in the development of harmonized accounting rules for insurance companies; and
- electronic commerce/Internet – finalizing a paper dealing with risks associated with the use of the Internet as a distribution channel for insurance products.

In addition, the Financial Stability Forum (FSF) has asked the IAIS to prepare a study paper on credit risk transfer between banks and insurance companies, particularly by using credit derivatives. Recently the market for these products has grown rapidly.

IV. Cross-Sectoral Cooperation

Globalization and the blurring of the boundaries between the financial sectors have heightened the need for cross-sectoral cooperation. The IAIS works closely with other international organizations, especially the Basel Committee and IOSCO, on a number of cross-sector committees and working groups. The best-known and most important cross-sector groupings are the Joint Forum and the Financial Stability Forum (FSF).

The Joint Forum has just published two papers that compare the Core Principles and risk management practices and regulatory capital across the three financial sectors. The FSF is a high-level discussion forum set up by the G7 finance ministers and central bank governors dealing with financial sector issues affecting financial stability. The IAIS is represented on the FSF by the Chairman of the Executive Committee and the Secretary General. In response to FSF requests, the IAIS prepared a general paper on risks posed in the insurance sector, noting their potential impact on financial stability. In addition, it is working on a paper on credit risk transfer from banks to insurance and the possible risks for financial stability arising from this risk transfer. The IAIS further updates the FSF about the impact of the 11 September terrorist attack on the insurance sector and financial stability.

The IAIS also keeps close contacts and cooperates with many international organizations, such as the OECD, IMF, World Bank, Asian Development Bank, UNCTAD, and WTO.

V. Final Remarks

The IAIS has achieved a lot in a relatively short period of time. However, much remains to be done. Additional principles and standards need to be elaborated and existing principles and standards need to be updated to reflect market developments.

Insurance principles and standards do not have any practical impact if they are not put into practice. In this respect, the IAIS has committed itself to supporting their implementation by encouraging self-assessments, co-sponsoring training seminars, and arranging technical assistance. Thus 'soft standards' can become 'hard rules'.

The IAIS has just carried out a self-assessment exercise on the observance of the Insurance Core Principles by its members. Two-thirds of the members participated. In their self-assessments, the Japanese and, as an example from the EU, the German supervisory authorities both judged their insurance supervisory regime to be nearly fully compliant with the Insurance Core Principles.

The IAIS has no authority to enforce implementation of its principles and standards. It relies on voluntary compliance by its members. This is encouraged by the work of the IMF and World Bank, which regard the implementation of the core principles developed by the IAIS, Basel Committee, and IOSCO as the necessary basis for an effective supervisory system. In their Financial Sector Assessment Programme (FSAP) reviews in developed as well as developing countries, they assess observance with the core principles and thus provide external pressure for compliance.

In conclusion, the IAIS has been quite successful to date in setting and implementing international standards of effective insurance supervision, thus harmonizing insurance supervision and, at the same time, preventing regulatory arbitrage.

In developing its principles and standards, the needs and interests of the insurance industry are taken into account. In 1999 the IAIS introduced a new category of membership called 'observers'. Institutions that are interested in contributing to the work of the IAIS but are not insurance supervisors are invited to join the IAIS as observers. More than sixty institutions, mainly associations of insurers and internationally active insurance companies, have done so thus far. These observers are formally consulted on each paper the IAIS develops on insurance supervision before it is presented to the IAIS membership for approval. This ensures that the IAIS principles and standards are practicable and sensible.

Part 4:

REGULATION OF TELECOMMUNICATIONS SERVICES

EUROPEAN TELECOMMUNICATIONS LAW: UNAFFECTED BY GLOBALIZATION?

by Christoph Engel, Bonn*

I. Introduction

Good politicians are experts in the art of insulting. A decade ago, American politicians demonstrated their expertise by coining the term 'Fortress

* I am grateful to Adrienne Héritier, Dominik Böllhoff and Wolf Osthaus for their comments to an earlier version of this paper, and to Darrell Arnold for the linguistic trimming of the paper.

J. Basedow, H. Baum, K. Hopt, H. Kanda and T. Kono (eds.), Economic Regulation and Competition, (219-252)

Europe'.[1] It took quite some time, and a good many concessions during the Uruguay Round negotiations over the WTO, before the pejorative label fell into oblivion. The bottom line of this paper is: perhaps too early. Communications is a global phenomenon these days, one should think. The conduits of communications, the telecommunications networks, are connected worldwide. Yet the pertinent legal rules of the European Community take surprisingly little notice of globalization. They read as if telecommunications were an exercise in organizing life within the fortress only, with just a few well guarded drawbridges crossing the dangerous moats that surround it.

The paper is organized as follows: It starts by presenting the different meanings of the term globalization (II.). For a theoretical foundation, it relies on work by political scientists on governance across multiple arenas. From this work the paper derives a series of hypotheses of how a European regulative policy might be expected to react to globalization (III.). It contrasts these exiting theoretical hypotheses with the sobering reality of current European telecommunications legislation (IV.). The paper tries to explain this reality (V.). It concludes with a normative outlook (VI.).

A caveat is in place. Although it relies on work of political scientists, this is the paper of a lawyer. This feature plays itself out in two respects. The evidence is strictly limited to the law in force, legislative drafts or policy documents officially introduced into the legislative process. More specifically, the paper exclusively uses the current revision of the telecommunications framework as evidence.[2] Political scientists would certainly double check this material by other empirical methods, and interviews with relevant actors in particular.[3] Since the evidence is restricted, the paper cannot make claims of causality. It is confined to functionality: if A is the goal, then B helps further it; or vice versa: if B is the action, the actual goal cannot be A. At one point of our argument, this limitation will become relevant. Among the legislative practice we will find a good number of actions that are functional for both globalization and Europeanisation. Due to the methodological

---

1 See e.g. *G.C. Hufbauer* and *C. Schmitz*, 'The North American Argument about a 'Fortress Europe' in: T. Oppermann and J. Molsberger (eds), A New GATT for the Nineties and Europe '92 (Nomos, Baden-Baden, 1991), pp. 307–323.

2 All documents are made available at <http://europa.eu.int/information_society/topics/telecoms/index_en.htm> (visited on August 21, 2001). For details see below IV.

3 On their methodology see *G. King, R.O. Keohane*, et al., Designing social inquiry: scientific inference in qualitative research (Princeton University Press, Princeton N.J., 1994).

restriction, we will not be able to actually prove that they are indeed the result of the latter. We will only be able to demonstrate the (high) plausibility of this thesis.

II. Dimensions of Globalization

There is much controversy about globalization. Obviously there are those who think it is a bad,[4] and others who think it is a good thing.[5] But an equally lively controversy concerns the question what globalization actually means. It partially is also a controversy over the appropriate conceptual tools for understanding the phenomenon. A first distinction concerns the object of globalization. In this context, the globalization of markets is not itself of interest.[6] When applied to government, globalization characterizes a – partial or even total – loss of autonomy of the nation state. Those who use the term in this way disagree, however, about the dimension of the loss.

The most basic dividing line is between rational choice and constructivist approaches.[7] The former look at individual actors maximizing some utility, the latter at the social context into which individual action is embedded. Another way of putting the dividing line is: the former look at interests, the latter at ideas.[8]

On the interest side, those are most prominent who equate globalization and regulatory competition.[9] In the terminology of economic competition

---

4 Characteristic *H.-P. Martin* and *H. Schumann*, Die Globalisierungsfalle. Der Angriff auf Demokratie und Wohlstand (Rowohlt, Hamburg, 1996).

5 Characteristic *C.C. von Weizsäcker*, Logik der Globalisierung (Vandenhoeck & Ruprecht, Göttingen, 1999.

6 See below on the possible repercussions of global markets on regulatory autonomy.

7 Comprehensive on this, and stimulating *T.A. Börzel* and *T. Risse*, Die Wirkung internationaler Institutionen. Von der Normanerkennung zur Normeinhaltung, Preprints aus der Max-Planck-Projektgruppe Recht der Gemeinschaftsgüter Bonn 2001/15.

8 On this distinction *V. Vanberg* and *J.M. Buchanan*, 'Interests and Theories in Constitutional Choice' (1989) 1 Journal of Theoretical Politics, 49–62; *A.S. Yee*, 'The Causal Effects of Ideas on Policies' (1996) 50 International Organization 66–108.

9 On regulatory competition see only *L. Gerken* (ed.), Competition Among Institutions (MacMillan, Houndmills, 1995); *Monopolkommission*, Systemwettbewerb (Nomos, Baden-Baden, 1998); *M. Müller*, Systemwettbewerb, Harmonisierung und Wettbewerbsverzerrung (Nomos, Baden-Baden, 2000); and critical *H.I.T. Tjiong*, Breaking the Spell of Regulatory Competition. Reframing the Problem of Regulatory Exit, cont. ...

theory: the nation states no longer have a monopoly of governance. They shift into a situation of monopolistic competition.[10] Other nation states offer different bundles of public goods. Regulatees are able to move to these substitutes.[11] A related concept might be more appropriate to understand the effect. It replaces the metaphor of competition on a market with the metaphor of members controlling the management of an organization. There are two conceivable mechanisms for doing that: voice and exit.[12] Within a traditional nation state, regulatees can only avail themselves of the former mechanism. Globalization adds the second. Exit becomes so easy that it is turned into a practical option, at least for some actors. If an actor can credibly threat government with exit, his voice also becomes much louder. Market entry by outside suppliers can be a functional equivalent to the exit of formerly captive regulatees. This is so, if the new entrants into the national market can at least partly operate under the less stringent rules in force at their place of origin. The importing country may be able to impose their product regulation on them. But it will normally not have an opportunity to control production, organization or funding.

In this perspective, a link to the globalization of markets becomes visible. On a market, globalization affects what antitrust lawyers call the geographically relevant market.[13] Globalization can also change what they call the relevant product market,[14] e.g. if consumers only ask for a telecommunica-

---

Preprints aus der Max-Planck-Projektgruppe Recht der Gemeinschaftsgüter Bonn 2000/13. For the equation see only *F.W. Scharpf*, Globalisierung als Beschränkung der Handlungsmöglichkeiten nationalstaatlicher Politik, Max-Planck-Institut for Gesellschaftsforschung Discussion Paper 1997.

10 Fundamental on this concept *E. Chamberlin*, The theory of monopolistic competition (Harvard University Press, Cambridge Mass., 1933); for modern views see *J. Tirole*, The theory of industrial organization (MIT Press, Cambridge Mass., 1988), chapter 7.

11 Clear on this *W. Schäfer*, 'Globalisierung: Entmonopolisierung des Nationalen' in: H. Berg, Globalisierung der Wirtschaft. Ursachen – Formen – Konsequenzen (Berlin, 1999), pp. 9–21, pp. 10 et seq.

12 Basic *A.O. Hirschman*, Exit, voice, and loyalty; responses to decline in firms, organizations, and states (Harvard University Press, Cambridge Mass., 1970).

13 More in our context from EC Commission Working Document On Proposed New Regulatory Framework for Electronic Communications Networks and Services Draft Guidelines on market analysis and the calculation of significant market power under Article 14 of the proposed Directive on a common regulatory framework for electronic communications networks and services of March 28, 2001, COM (2001) 175, par. 46–52.

14 More ibid. (note 13) par. 56 and 58.

tions service that offers global coverage. To the extent that one of these effects takes place, the physical location of the headquarters of a firm becomes less relevant. If this is the case, exit becomes easier. This is often not a strong effect, however. Usually, the switching cost still is considerable. For doing local business, regularly local premises must remain and are regulatory targets.

More important is another link between the globalization of markets and the autonomy of national governments. It is difficult for a single nation state to regulate a truly global market. The nation state is not entirely devoid of means. It can apply its own rules extraterritorially.[15] It can engage in international cooperation. Or it can go for governed self-governance,[16] to cite only the most important options.[17] But each of these options comes at a cost, or a risk, or both.

Not by coincidence, political scientists interested in European governance have coined a term analogous to globalization, Europeanisation.[18] Their prime interest, however, is not pressure on member states' autonomy originating from fundamental freedoms as guaranteed by the EC-Treaty; that would be the strict parallel to globalization as discussed so far. They look at how national politics change once Europe as an additional arena for policy making is introduced. Obviously there is no strict parallel to this on the world level. There is no sign of supranational governance at the global level. But here we are interested in limitations to national regulatory autonomy. And such limitations do not exclusively stem from exit options of regulatees or from the enlargement of regulatory issues beyond national borders. They also ground in – limited – international regulatory powers that partly or even fully escape national control.

One may discuss whether ordinary international treaties do already fall into this category. For treaties must be ratified by each and every nation state

---

15 Basic *A.K. Schnyder*, Wirtschaftskollisionsrecht. Sonderanknüpfung und extraterritoriale Anwendung wirtschaftsrechtlicher Normen unter besonderer Berücksichtigung von Marktrecht (Schulthess, Zürich, 1990); *W. Meng*, Extraterritoriale Jurisdiktion im öffentlichen Wirtschaftsrecht (Springer, Berlin/New York, 1994).

16 More at *C. Engel*, 'Hybrid Governance Across National Jurisdictions as a Challenge to Constitutional Law', (2001) European Business Organisation Review 569–583.

17 *C. Engel*, 'The Internet and the Nation State', in: C. Engel and K.H. Keller, Understanding the Impact of Global Networks on Local Social, Political and Cultural Values (Nomos, Baden-Baden, 2000) pp. 201–260 (245 et seq).

18 See only *A. Héritier*, in: A. Héritier (ed.), (2001). Differential Europe. The European Union Impact on National Policy Making (Lanham, Rowman & Littlefield, 2001), pp. 1–21.

before it becomes bound by their rules. But globalization clearly happens when a framework treaty endows an international organization with some uncontrolled regulatory powers.[19] In our context, the International Telecommunications Union[20] and the World Trade Organization Agreement on Basic Telecommunications Services are the most prominent instances.[21] One can even close the conceptual circle and couch regulatory competition in these terms. It means that functionally some regulatory power shifts away to foreign nation states. This interpretation allows to properly classify what one might in economic terms dub regulatory yardstick competition. The term yardstick competition has been developed for understanding how managers are controlled by the product markets, even if they earn a fixed salary. If their firm performs significantly worse than its competitors, shareholders receive a relatively reliable signal for poor managerial quality. The manager must justify himself, if he is not simply fired.[22] The intensity of yardstick competition depends on transparency. Not only data on foreign performance must be available; also must the foreign and the domestic case be sufficiently similar. On both grounds, globalization can have a similar effect on national regulation.[23] It makes access to information about foreign regulatory practice much easier than before. If globalization extends product markets across national borders, it also partly standardizes the regulatory issue.[24]

All these have been rational choice arguments. An analogy to research on risk helps understand how the constructivist understanding of globalization differs. In a rational choice perspective, classifying risks seems relatively easy: multiply the conceivable damage by its probability. If you do not know any of these elements precisely, build rational expectations on the basis of what information you have. If you find more information, update your

19 More on this difference from *C. Engel*, Völkerrecht als Tatbestandsmerkmal deutscher Normen (Duncker & Humblot, Berlin 1989), pp. 258–328.

20 Comprehensive, though somewhat dated, *A. Tegge*, Die Internationale Telekommunikations-Union: Organisation und Funktion einer Weltorganisation im Wandel (Nomos, Baden-Baden, 1994).

21 For the moment see only *C. Blouin*, 'The WTO Agreement on Basic Telecommunications. A Reevaluation.' (2000) 24 Telecommunications Policy 135–142.

22 *Tirole*, supra note 10, pp. 41–48.

23 Cf. *S. Weber*, Globalization and the European political economy (Columbia University Press, New York 2001), p. 13: globalization yields information about 'best regulatory practices'.

24 Cf. *R.W. Crandall* and *L. Waverman*, Who pays for universal service?: when telephone subsidies become transparent (Brookings Institution Press, Washington D.C., 2000).

expectations.[25] This leads into a quest for measurable indices, like dollars per lives saved.[26] Many have objected that people perceive risks differently.[27] They consequently call for 'perceived risk' as the appropriate regulatory standard.[28] By the same token, one might distinguish globalization from 'perceived globalization'. The decisive fact is whether policy makers think that the regulatory environment has changed, and that they have lost some of their autonomy.[29] In the extreme, even the regulatory discourse could no longer be national or European, but become global.[30] And in the constructivist perspective too, there is a link between the globalization of markets and of politics. For constructivists, an industry has an identity, created by communication among its members.[31] If this identity is no longer national, but global, the regulatory problem changes. For in the constructivist perspective, successful regulation is tantamount to altering the internal communication of the addressees as a group. If they now think global, they are likely to ignore purely national governance attempts as mere irrelevant

---

25 More from *R. Eichenberger*, 'Wissen und Information in ökonomischer Perspektive' in: C. Engel, J. Halfmann and M. Schulte, Wissen, Nichtwissen, Unsicheres Wissen (Nomos, Baden-Baden, 2001), pp. 75–92.

26 As in the famous *Morrall* table, *J.F. Morrall*, 'A Review of the Record' (1986) Regulation (Nov/Dec) 25; critical *L. Heinzerling*, 'Regulatory Costs of Mythic Proprotions' (1998) 107 Yale Law Journal, 1981–2070.

27 See only *R.H. Pildes* and C.R. Sunstein, 'Reinventing the Regulatory State' (1995) 62 University of Chicago Law Review, 1–129; *T.O. McGarity*, 'A Cost-Benefit State' (1998) 50 Administrative Law Review, 7–79; see also *Symposium*, 'Cost-Benefit Analysis. Legal, Economic, and Philosophical Perspectives' (2000) 29 Journal of Legal Studies, 837–1153.

28 See in greater detail *C.R. Sunstein*, 'Legislative Foreword. Congress, Constitutional Moments, and the Cost-Benefit State' (2000) Stanford Law Review, 247–309; but *W.K. Viscusi*, (2000) 'Risk Equity', Harvard John M. Olin Center for Law, Economics, and Business Discussion Paper, 2000, p. 32.

29 Cf. *Weber*, supra note 23: 'Ultimately, institutional change happens only when political actors understand a challenge in a particular way and fashion a response'.

30 Sceptical on empirical grounds *V.A. Schmidt*, 'Discourse and (Dis)integration in Europe. The Cases of France, Germany, and Great Britain' (1997) 126 Daedalus 167–197.

31 Basic *H.C. White*, Identity and control: a structural theory of social action (Princeton University Press, Princeton N.J., 1992).

noise. Governments will only be successful, if they adapt their interventions to the new internal logic of the industry.[32]

III. Exiting Hypotheses: A System of Multi-Level Governance Facing Globalization

The European Union is a functioning system of multi-level governance. There is Europe, the Member States, in federal States like Germany also the members of this national federation, the municipalities, often also autonomous regional bodies. There are many functional governmental regulatory bodies at all these levels, like the independent *Regulierungsbehörde Telekommunikation und Post*. Finally, there is a multitude of private or hybrid regulatory institutions, like the European Telecommunications Standardization Institute ETSI. Globalization potentially affects their policies (A.), but also the institutional framework for policy making (B.). The individual elements, and the system as a whole, in theory have three options for reacting to the challenge: mitigation (C.), adaptation (D.) and preference change (E.). Here the focus is on the options of European actors, exercising their powers for autonomous reaction.

A. Effects of Globalization on Policies

The effect of globalization on policies is obvious.[33] It directly follows from the definition of globalization. We have defined globalization as a (partial) loss of regulatory autonomy. In a rational choice perspective, European regulators must subdue to competitive pressure from abroad, or to the regulatory activities of foreign regulatory bodies.

---

32 These are insights from systems theory, one strand of constructivist thinking. The details are heavily disputed among systems theorists. The interpretation offered here is close to *G. Teubner*, Recht als autopoietisches System (Suhrkamp Frankfurt, 1989); more discussion in: *C. Engel*, The Constitutional Court – applying the proportionality principle – as a subsidiary authority for the assessment of political outcomes, Preprints aus der Max-Planck Projektgruppe Recht der Gemeinschaftsgüter Bonn 2001/10, pp. 15–19.

33 One might further distinguish the effect on policy patterns from the one on policy outcomes, *Héritier*, supra note 18, p. 3.

In a constructivist perspective, the limitation results from the outside influence on the canvas of ideas. Europe looses some autonomy of choosing political preferences.[34] There are many ways of explaining how this might result from globalization. Discourse theory points to a potential change of prevailing belief systems.[35] Others would investigate whether the dominant problem solving approach[36] or even identity change.[37] Historical institutionalists would look out for new 'rules of appropriateness'.[38] Organization ecologists would investigate how 'coercion, mimetism and normative pressure' play themselves out under the new circumstances.[39]

B. *Effects of Globalization on Political Institutions*

Less obvious, but not less important, are the potential impacts of globalization on formal and informal political institutions.[40] Again, a rational choice and a constructivist perspective can be distinguished.

In a rational choice view, changes in the political opportunity structure are decisive. How are the games changed that political actors play with each other?[41] Already introducing Europe makes the analysis complicated.[42] In

---

34 Cf. for Europeanisation *C.M. Radaelli*, The politics of corporate taxation in the European Union: knowledge and international policy agendas (Routledge, London/ New York 1997; *M.J.A. Green Cowles*, *J.A. Caporaso* et al., Transforming Europe: Europeanization and domestic change (Cornell University Press, Ithaca N.Y., 2001).

35 *Schmidt*, supra note 35.

36 *P.A. Sabatier*, 'Advocacy-Koalitionen, Policy-Wandel und Policy-Lernen. Eine Alternative zur Phasenheuristik' in: A. Héritier, Policy-Analyse. Kritik und Neuorientierung (Westdeutscher Verlag, Opladen, 1993) 116–148.

37 *Green Cowles*, *Carporaso* and *Risse-Kappen*, supra note 34.

38 *J.G. March* and *J.P. Olsen*, Rediscovering institutions: the organizational basis of politics (Free Press, New York 1989); *J.P. Olsen*, 'Europeanization and Nation State Dynamics' in: S. Gustavsson and L. Lewin, The Future of the Nation-State (Routledge, London 1996) 245–285.

39 *P.J. diMaggio and W.W. Powell*, 'The Iron Cage Revisited. Institutionalised Isomorphism and Collective Rationality in Organisational Fields' in: P.J. diMaggio and W.W. Powell, The New Instutionalism in Organizational Research (Chicago University Press, Chicago, 1991), 63–82; *Radaelli*, supra note 34).

40 In the language of *Héritier* in: Héritier, supra note 18, p. 3: Europeanisation, and hence also globalization, can have an impact on administrative structures, but also on patterns of interest intermediation.

41 Basic *F.W. Scharpf*, Games real actors play: actor-centered institutionalism in policy research (Westview Press, Boulder Colo., 1997).

game-theoretic terms, political actors are now playing a two-level game.[43] What they do at the national level has repercussions on their policy options at the European level, and vice versa.[44] Their policy variables explode, once a more realistic picture of governance across multiple arenas is introduced. Globalization is one more element of this picture. Due to the enormous complexity of the ensuing nested game[45] it becomes almost impossible to predict strategic moves. Is Europe an independent, additional driving force for change, along with globalization? Is it, instead, the strategic environment where political actors try to moderate and control how they are affected by globalization? Or is the European Union no more than a pipeline transmitting global causes to Member States and firms?[46]

Only case studies of specific political conflicts might define opportunity structures, and to all likeliness their results would be confined to narrow issues at one point of history. They would often even differ from Member State to Member State.[47] No more than some possibilities can be listed here, as an illustration of the potential impacts of globalization on the European multi-level game. If firms can muster a realistic threat of exit, this gives them a stronger veto point in negotiations over future regulation.[48] If they stand to become superfluous after the globalization of a market, administrative agencies are likely to combat it fiercely.[49] Any new arena for policy making tends to give informal political actors a greater potential, because

---

42 *Héritier* in: Héritier, supra note 18, p. 9: 'the complex dynamics of political processes induced by European policy outcomes' in the Member States.

43 Basic *R.D. Putnam*, 'Diplomacy and Domestic Politics. The Logic of Two-Level Games.' (1988) 42 International Organization, 427–460.

44 *Héritier* in: Héritier, supra note 18, p. 10: 'European and national policy making as two separate, but parallel, policy streams which intermittently interlink'; *Héritier* in: Héritier, supra note 18, p. 2: 'Member state actors exert influence in the shaping of policies at the European level by which they themselves are subsequently transformed'.

45 On this game-theoretic category more from *D.G. Baird, R.H. Gertner* et al., Game theory and the law (Harvard University Press, Cambridge Mass., 1994), pp. 188–218.

46 *Weber*, supra note 23, p. 289 offers all three hypotheses and claims that each has some truth in it.

47 Cf. *Héritier* in: Héritier, supra note 18, pp. 9 et seq.

48 On the concept of veto points basic *E.M. Immergut*, Health politics: interests and institutions in Western Europe (Cambridge University Press, Cambridge/New York, 1992).

49 Cf. *Héritier* in: Héritier, supra note 18, p. 15.

they gain additional 'access points'.[50] The more important it becomes that Europe can externally speak with one voice, the more unitary European organs, and the Commission in particular, are likely to gain.

From a functionalist perspective, one might expect that globalization will increase the urge for a unitary 'European regulatory culture'.[51] Practice seems different, however, not only in the case of telecommunications. The political systems of Members States seem to be much more likely to react to the increased (feeling of) uncertainty by renationalizing political discourse.[52] This is in line with the observation that there is no such thing as a true European *demos* yet. Solidarity as still very much perceived as a national endeavour, as is (political, national) identity.[53]

C. Mitigation

Theoretically, the European political system, or any of its components, can parry the challenge of globalization in three distinct ways: by mitigation, adaptation, or preference change.[54] Mitigation is a defence strategy. Feasible defences mirror the reasons for globalization.

If globalization comes in the form of regulatory competition, the previously autonomous regulatory body must strive for making exit more difficult.[55] There are many ways of doing this. An outright prohibition is only the

---

50 Ibid., p. 11.

51 This is indeed what the Commission calls for in the Explanatory Memorandum, B 2, to the Amended proposal for a Directive on a common regulatory framework for electronic communications networks and services of July 4, 2001, COM (2001) 380 final.

52 *V.A. Schmidt*, 'Discourse and the Legitimation of Economic and Social Policy Change in Europe', in: S. Weber, Globalization and the European Political Economy (Columbia University Press, New York, 2001), pp. 229–272.

53 For a legal voice see *G. Lübbe-Wolff*, 'Europäisches und nationales Verfassungsrecht' (2001) 60 Veröffentlichungen der Vereinigung der Deutschen Staatsrechtslehrer, 246–287; for a voice from political sciences see *F.W. Scharpf*, Governing in Europe: effective and democratic? (Oxford University Press, Oxford/New York, 1999), sec. 1.2.

54 It is no coincidence that these same options do also exist if a constitution considers how best to react to private or hybrid governance, see *Engel*, supra note 16, sec. V.

55 More at *C. Engel*, 'Legal Experiences of Competition Among Institutions' in: L. Gerken, Competition Among Institutions (MacMillan, Houndmills 1995), pp. 89–118.

most obvious form. But throughout history many states have made emigration impossible or at least dependent on an explicit permission.[56] The most popular strategy is making exit more costly. This can be done via asymmetric taxation. This is what the famous conflict over removing headquarters within the EC is about. After *Centros*, going abroad is much more of a practical option than before.[57] We also implicitly used the idea of considerable exit costs when we characterized regulatory competition as an instance of monopolistic competition. Normally, firms do not have the option of customized exit from those provisions of national law that they dislike. They have to swap whole regulatory packages, taking the British instead of the German, for instance. There is a constructivist option, too. Nation states, or the European Union, could try to discourage private actors from exit by shaming them if they go. The famous 'buy British' campaign is an instance. It shamed customers who bought foreign products, and thereby circumvented any national regulation not directly affecting product quality.

In principle, the same options do also exist if a loss of regulatory autonomy originates in the globalization of regulated markets. But they are more difficult to apply. For then it is not sufficient to specifically target those national actors who might be tempted to exit. Instead, the whole market must be (re-)nationalized.

Legally, it is easy to prevent regulatory authority from being siphoned away by international regulators. Their jurisdiction depends on the ratification of a treaty by the national parliament. Yet politically, not conferring, or pulling back, jurisdiction is not always easy to do. Private regulatory bodies do not need an explicit transfer of authority from the national sovereigns at all. In principle, the nations, and Europe, might apply the same techniques of mitigation as in the case of regulatory competition. They might, by autonomous rules, prohibit their subjects to apply these foreign rules; they might make this prohibitively costly; or they might shame those who rely on these foreign rules. But these individuals are themselves the addressees of these foreign rules. They will therefore object that, unlike in the case of regulatory competition, the loss of national regulatory autonomy is not their fault. Maybe the foreign and the competing national rules are even contradictory. In that case, addressees would rightly ask to be protected against tragic choices. For all these reasons, the practical options will therefore usually

[56] For the evidence see *S.E. Finer*, 'State-Building, State Boundaries and Border Control' (1974) 13 Social Science Information, 79–126.

[57] ECJ 9.3.1999, C-212/97, Reports 1999 I 1459.

boil down to an open political fight between the national regulator and its foreign adversary. If the foreign rules must be implemented by the nation state, non-implementation is another option.

Remains perceived globalization. If the national, or European, regulator itself perceives the issue such that autonomous action no longer makes sense, enlightenment by outside observers might help. If this regulator is itself the observer of prevailing social construction, strategic action is conceivable, but difficult to perform. The regulator would have to mould public perception differently. Or maybe it is enough to offer the public other salient issues. It then might be content with the maintenance of previous national regulation, once the globalization issue is no longer centre stage.

D. *Adaptation*

The terms mitigation and adaptation are culled from the discussion of climate change.[58] Introducing adaptation into this discussion was a strategic move of countries that did not want to take on rigorous mitigation obligations. They objected that adapting to a different climate would be much cheaper for many regions of the world. Likewise, regulators exposed to globalization are not faced with a choice between mitigation or withdrawal. Not so rarely, they can adapt to the changed environment. This can be (politically) cheaper, or even more effective.

If the effect of globalization is on a policy, adaptation means altering this policy so that globalization no longer affects, or damages, it. For this to be an instance of adaptation, the underlying policy preferences should not change. But regulators might find less vulnerable ways of reaching their constant goals. A very popular reaction is a shift from pure public to hybrid regulation. This is characteristic for many Internet related issues, like data protection, consumer protection or speech control.[59]

Likewise, if globalization affects political institutions, the underlying constitutional goals should not change via adaptation. But a polity might find ways to reach these same goals by different, less vulnerable means. Another way of putting the task is: make the institutional framework more robust against outside influences. In the parallel context of Europeanisation, it has

---

58 See only *S.M. Kane* and *G.W. Yohe*, Societal adaptation to climate variability and change (Kluwer Academic Publishers, Dordrecht/Boston, 2000).

59 For details see *C. Engel* and *K.H. Keller* (eds), Global Networks and Local Values (National Research Council, Washington, 2002), chap. 8.

been observed that nations possessing a greater 'reform capacity' do adapt much better.[60] Europeanisation, or globalization for that matter, can therefore become a stimulus for constitutional reform. A most likely target of such reform are historically grown, but no longer functional veto positions.[61]

There is a less benevolent perspective on adaptation, however. It inevitably opens up internal political debate anew. Previous compromises can crack. Interested actors can seize the opportunity for gaining on other grounds. The general insight into regulative policy holds: there is almost ever more than one option for addressing a true social problem. And these solutions almost ever differ on distributional grounds. Effectively imposing one solution, and not any other, is therefore the safest way for securing distributional gains. For after the fact, all actors would lose by abolishing it, even those who lose on the distribution side. In game-theoretic terms: the distributional gain is a Nash equilibrium.[62] One application of this general idea is particularly likely: the Commission of the EU could use adaptation to globalization as a reason for extending its powers to the detriment of Member States or other European political organs.[63]

E. Preference Change

If you can't beat them, join them. If globalization affects specific policies, regulators have the same option.[64] They can make their cause what originally was the political will of a foreign or superior regulator only. They also can interpret regulatory competition as a healthy stimulus to internal betterment. For individuals, the parallel process is well studied by psychologists. A change of attitude is a mechanism to preserve self-esteem. Psychologists call

---

60 *Héritier* in: Héritier, supra note 18, p. 9 et seq. and 19 comparing the Member States of the European Union in this respect.

61 This is the central claim of *F.W. Scharpf*, Politikverflechtung: Theorie u. Empririe d. kooperativen Föderalismus in d. Bundesrepublik (Scriptor-Verlag, Kronberg/Ts., 1976).

62 This is the central idea of *J. Knight*, Institutions and social conflict (Cambridge University Press, Cambridge England/New York N.Y., 1992).

63 Cf. *Héritier* in: Héritier, supra note 18, p. 7 on a similar strategy of the Commission in other areas. It repeatedly has promoted the representation of associations at the national or local level, in the interest of weakening Member States, and of using the associations as their watchdogs.

64 Cf. ibid., p. 1: Europeanisation can add new policy goals to the political agenda.

it a reduction of cognitive dissonance.[65] But there is the opposite reaction too. Psychologists call it reactance.[66] A loss of utility seems still better than subduing to unjust pressure. Which reaction is more likely depends on the character and representation of the outside pressure.[67] None of these mechanisms does directly carry over to group behaviour.[68] Even less can they mechanically be applied to the institutionally embedded political process. But we need not understand the mechanism here. It suffices to point to a change of political preferences as a third option for a previously autonomous regulatory body.

IV. Sobering Reality: European Telecommunications Law Hardly Affected by Globalization

Against this rich theoretical backdrop, the reality of European Telecommunications Law in the making is quite sobering. European Telecommunications Law is in the process of a major overhaul, called the new telecommunications framework.[69] There are, it is true, a number of explicit references to international issues to be found in these documents (1). But most of them read as if globalization just did not take place. The small exceptions concern rather marginal issues. There is hardly a sign of mitigation (2). Adaptation is the only debatable issue (3). But it at least is highly plausible that the apparent signs of adaptation are mere instances of Europeanisation. Are we thus faced with a neglect of globalization by the European Community, and by the Commission in particular (4)?

---

65 Comprehensive *D. Frey* and *A. Gaska*, 'Die Theorie der kognitiven Dissonanz', in: D. Frey and M. Irle, Theorien der Sozialpsychologie I, Kognitive Theorien (Hans Huber, Bern, 1993), pp. 275–326.

66 Comprehensive *D. Dickenberger, G. Gniech*, et al., 'Die Theorie der psychologischen Reaktanz', in: D. Frey and M. Irle, Theorien der Sozialpsychologie I Kognitive Theorien (Hans Huber, Bern, 1993), pp. 243–274.

67 A graphic example of both options is to be found in *B. Frey*, and *F. Oberholzer-Gee*, 'Natural Environment. Fair Siting Procedures', in: B. Frey, Economics as a Science of Human Behaviour (Boston, 1999), pp. 23–48.

68 For an overview see *C. Sedikides*, J. Schopler, et al., Intergroup cognition and intergroup behavior (Lawrence Erlbaum Associates, Mahwah N.J., 1998).

69 All documents can be accessed at <http://europa.eu.int/information_society/topics/telecoms/index_en.htm> (visited on August 21, 2001).

A. Explicit References to International Issues

In all the many documents on the new regulatory framework for telecommunications, the term 'globalization' is merely mentioned once, and at a totally marginal place:

> 'Numbering requirements in Europe, the need for the provision of pan-European and new services and the *globalization* and synergy of the electronic communications market require the Community to harmonize national positions in accordance with the Treaty in international organizations and fora where numbering decisions are taken.'[70]

Apart from that, there is a good number of references to the international dimension of telecommunications. But most of them concern issues that were no different ten years ago, when nobody spoke about globalization.[71] There is, of course, respect to the international legal obligations of the Community and its Member States (1.). The Community organs and the Member States must specify who speaks for them externally (2). In antitrust law, markets sometimes must be defined in a way that transgresses Community borders (3.). Finally, there is the Internet, by definition a global enterprise (4.).

1. Respect for International Legal Obligations

At several instances, the new telecommunications framework points to the commitments of the Community and the Member States under the WTO

---

70 Draft Framework Directive (supra note 51) preamble (17), emphasis added. See also Regulation of the European Parliament and of the Council on unbundled access to the local loop of Dec. 5, 2000, 2000/0185 (COD): 'In accordance with the principle of subsidiarity as set out in Article 5 of the Treaty, the objective of achieving a harmonised framework for unbundled access to the local loop in order to enable the competitive provision of an inexpensive, *world-class communications infrastructure* and a wide range of services for all businesses and citizens in the Community cannot be achieved by the Member States in a secure, harmonised and timely manner and can therefore be better achieved by the Community'. – emphasis added.

71 For the elder law, see in detail *C. Engel*, 'Trade in Services Between the European Communities and Third Countries – Its Regulation by Community Law', in: D. Friedmann and E.J. Mestmäcker, Rules for Free International Trade in Services (Nomos, Baden-Baden, 1990), pp. 107–176, 130-134 in particular.

Agreement on Basic Telecommunications Services.[72] There are also references to the international obligations relating to the use of radio frequencies and of orbital positions, as enshrined in the law of the International Telecommunications Union (ITU), and in the rules of the Conference Européenne des Administration des postes et des télécommunications (CEPT) at the European level.[73] Further references are to international technical standards that are part of ITU law or of the secondary legislation of other international standardization bodies;[74] but the Community stresses that it prefers its independent European standards.[75] The new rules also make occasional caveats for international commitments in the case of conditional access systems for digital television services;[76] reporting obligations under international treaties;[77] and ex ante regulatory obligations in general.[78]

2. External Relations

The many references to international issues in the Draft Radio Spectrum Directive boil down to a conflict between the EU and its Member States over external powers. Until now, the Community has not much of a say on radio spectrum management.[79] The Community pushes Member States on two

---

72 Draft Framework Directive (supra note 51) preamble (22); Amended proposal for a Directive on access to, and interconnection of, electronic communications networks and associated facilities of July 4, 2001, COM (2001) 369 final, preamble (8); Proposal for a Directive on universal service and users' rights relating to electronic communications networks and services of July 12, 2000, COM (2000) 392, preamble (3); par. 102 Draft Market Analysis Guidelines (supra note 13); see also Sixth Report on the Implementation of the Telecommunications Regulatory Package of Dec. 7, 2000, COM (2000) 814, at 5.

73 Amended proposal for a Directive on the authorisation of electronic communications networks and services of July 4, 2001, COM (2001) 372 final, Art. 7 IV (2); Proposal for a Decision on a regulatory framework for radio spectrum policy in the European Community of July 21, 2000, COM (2000) 407, Explanatory Memorandum, at 1.

74 Draft Framework Directive (supra note 51) Art. 15 II (3)-(4); Draft Access Directive (supra note 72) preamble (3).

75 Draft Framework Directive (supra note 51) Art. 15 II (1)-(2).

76 Draft Access Directive (supra note 72) preamble (9).

77 Draft Authorisation Directive (supra note 73) preamble (14).

78 Draft Framework Directive (supra note 51) preamble (20).

79 Explicitly Draft Decision Radio Spectrum (supra note 73) Explanatory Memorandum at 3; see also Green Paper on radio spectrum policy in the context of European cont. ...

grounds. It wants management issues to be decided within the Community framework, rather than by international organizations like the ITU or CEPT.[80] At least the Community should speak with one voice in these bodies.[81] To this effect, joint negotiation position should be agreed upon beforehand,[82] and the Community should get involved in the implementation of international agreements vis-à-vis Community actors.[83] The Commission does even ask for the power to give standardization mandates to CEPT in the area of radio spectrum.[84]

3. Market Definition in Antitrust Affairs

The Draft Guidelines on Market Analysis explicitly envisage the possibility of geographically relevant markets that transgress Community borders,[85] including potential competitive pressure from abroad.[86] But the Guidelines point to the impact of network coverage and regulatory instruments on market definition.[87] A legal definition contained in the Draft Framework Directive also highlights that global markets is not what the Commission is interested in. 'Trans-national markets' are defined such that their 'geographical dimension comprises the whole of the Community or a substantial part thereof',[88] not any area beyond that.

The Guidelines occasionally also use an international element for the definition of the relevant product market. They point to 'international voice and data communications services',[89] to the 'resale of international transmission capacity'[90] and to 'enhanced global telecommunications services'.[91]

Community policies such as telecommunications, broadcasting, transport, and R&D, COM (98) 596 final.

80 Ibid, at 3; preamble (2).
81 Ibid, preamble (8); preamble (14); Art. 1 (4); Explanatory Memorandum at 3.
82 Ibid, Art. 10 III 2.
83 Ibid, Art. 6 III, see also Explanatory Memorandum at 3.
84 Ibid, Art. 6 II.
85 Draft Guidelines on Market Analysis (supra note 13) par. 51.
86 Ibid, par. 49.
87 Ibid, par 50.
88 Draft Framework Directive (supra note 51) Art. 2 (m).
89 Draft Guidelines on Market Analysis (supra note 13) par. 56, see also par. 58 and note 38.
90 Ibid, par. 58.
91 Ibid.

Further market definitions are also inherently international, like the ones for 'satellite services' or 'seamless pan-European mobile telecommunications services to internationally mobile consumers'.[92]

4. Internet

The most outspoken acknowledgement of the global character of telecommunications is to be found in the Draft Data Protection Directive for Telecommunications Services. It reads:

> 'The Internet is overturning traditional market structures by providing a common, global infrastructure for the delivery of a wide range of electronic communications services. Publicly available electronic communications services over the Internet open new possibilities for users but also new risks for their personal data and privacy'.[93]

But compared to political reality, even this almost sounds like camouflage. For data protection is the one success story of EU Internet policy. The US would have preferred a pure self-regulatory regime. EU pressure has forced a compromise upon the US. They have accepted an oversight role of the Federal Trade Commission, thus transforming the regime into one of international hybrid regulation.[94]

The idea of the Internet becoming an infrastructure is also behind the only act of the regulatory package already in force. For the regulation on unbundled access to the local loop, the Community gives the following reason:

> 'The conclusions of the European Council of Lisbon of 23 and 24 March 2000 note that, for Europe to fully seize the growth and job potential of the digital, knowledge-based economy, businesses and citizens must have access to an inexpensive, world-class communications infrastructure and a wide range of services. The Member States, together with the Commission, are called upon to work towards introducing greater competition in local access networks before the end of 2000 and unbundling the local loop, in order to

---

92 Ibid.

93 Proposal for a Directive concerning the processing of personal data and the protection of privacy in the electronic communications sector of July 12, 2000, COM (2000) 385, preamble (5).

94 *H. Farrell*, 'Negotiating Privacy across Arenas. The EU-US "Safe Harbour" Discussions', in: A. Héritier, Common Goods. Reinventing European and International Governance (Rowman & Littlechild, London, 2002) pp. 105–126.

> help bring about a substantial reduction in the costs of using the Internet. The Feira European Council of 20 June 2000 endorsed the proposed Europe Action Plan which identifies unbundled access to the local loop as a short-term priority'.[95]

But apart from that, the EU is still hesitant to develop its own Internet policy.[96]

B. Mitigation

If one looks at telecommunications legislation, European actors do not seem to be concerned by globalization. There is hardly a trace of attempts to mitigate its impact. The only explicit reference to market access by foreign firms is to be found in the Draft Decision on the Radio Spectrum. The Commission considers the conclusion of international treaties on access with third countries on a reciprocal basis.[97]

There are considerable efforts to draw a strict line between telecommunications regulation and the regulation of communication contents.[98] Theoretically, one might interpret this as an attempt to fence a protected core off from a set of rules that otherwise has to respect the global character of telecommunications.[99] But this is not a plausible interpretation. There is, as we have seen, hardly a sign of awareness of globalization in these texts at all. It seems much more likely that the mentioned rules respond to Member States', and in particular French, concerns with a loss of cultural autonomy.

---

95 Local Loop Regulation (supra note 70) preamble (1).

96 Characteristic The results of the public consultation on the 1999 Communications Review and Orientations for the new Regulatory Framework of April 26, 2000, COM (2000) 239 final, at 6: 'This Communication does not set out a specific regulatory framework for the Internet. But it does aim to facilitate vigorous competition and innovation in the networks and services which make up the Internet, and over which the new knowledge economy is going to be delivered.'; more from *R. Werle*, 'Internet@Europe. Overcoming Institutional Fragmentation and Policy Failure.' (2001) 5(7) European Integration online Papers, 1–14.

97 Draft Radio Spectrum Decision (supra note 73) preamble (13).

98 Draft Framework Directive (supra note 51) preamble (7), see also Explanatory Memorandum, at 2; Draft Authorisation Directive (supra note 73) Explanatory Memorandum, at 2.

99 For the idea of areas of the economy protected against globalization see *Scharpf* (supra note 53) sec. 4.1.2.

C. Adaptation

In the same vein, it is quite dubitable whether any legislative measures can be interpreted as signs of adaptation to a globalized regulatory environment. There are two sets of rules that do indeed have an adaptation effect. But the regulatory context makes it not plausible that they are meant for that.

The first set of rules makes Europe stronger vis-à-vis the Member States. This could in principle be interpreted as an exercise in making Europe as a whole more robust towards global challenges. These changes increase the reform capacity of Europe, to use the language of political scientists.[100] But again, there is hardly a sign of legislative awareness for globalization. It seems much more likely that these measures are just attempts of the Commission to push Europeanisation forward.[101]

Let us have a look at the details. According to the will of the Commission, Member States' regulatory authorities shall in the future no longer be allowed to define relevant telecommunications services markets. Instead, they must rely on authoritative definitions by the Commission,[102] as laid down in its (draft) Guidelines.[103] If they think a case is exceptional, they are obliged to reach prior agreement with the Commission before defining a market differently.[104] Under normal circumstances, Member States are only allowed to define the geographically relevant market.[105]

A host of other substantive issues is also to be harmonized under the new regulatory package: authorization, i.e. legal impediments to market access;[106] access to, and interconnection with, the networks of other operators,[107] in particular to the local loop;[108] the management of the radio spectrum;[109]

---

[100] *Héritier* in: Héritier, supra note 18, p. 9 et seq.

[101] For an overview of the rich literature on Europeanisation see ibid., pp. 3-9. A further hint is Draft Framework Directive (supra note 51) Explanatory Memorandum, at 2, where the Commission rejects all amendments suggested by the European Parliament 'which jeopardise harmonisation'.

[102] Draft Framework Definition (supra note 51) Art. 14 I; see also The results of the public consultation on the 1999 Communications Review and Orientations for the new Regulatory Framework of April 26, 2000, COM (2000) 239 final, at 18.

[103] Supra note 13.

[104] Draft Framework Directive (supra note 51) Art. 14 I (3).

[105] Draft Guidelines on Market Analysis (supra note 13) par. 27.

[106] Draft Authorisation Directive (supra note 73), in particular preamble (1).

[107] Draft Access Directive (supra note 72).

[108] Local Loop Regulation (supra note 70).

technical standardization;[110] numbering, naming and addressing;[111] rights of way;[112] co-location and facility sharing;[113] accounting separation and financial reporting for undertakings possessing significant market power;[114] universal service;[115] data protection.[116] The Commission does even want to avail itself of the following general clause:

> '1. The Commission may, where appropriate, [...] issue Recommendations to Member States. Member States shall ensure that national regulatory authorities take the utmost account of those Recommendations in carrying out their tasks. Where a national regulatory authority chooses not to follow a Recommendation, it shall publish its reasoning.
>
> 2. Where the Commission finds, inter alia, that divergence in regulation at national level creates a barrier to the single market, or where the High-Level Communications Group advises that a binding harmonization measure is necessary, the Commission may, [...] take the appropriate technical implementing adopt binding harmonization measures. The Commission may consult the Advisory Communications Group about its views in this matter'.[117]

The Commission also defines regulatory goals strategically so that the need for harmonization increases. It for that purpose tries to establish the principle of 'technologically neutral regulation'. Due to pervasive convergence between communications technologies,[118] this principle almost gives the Commission *carte blanche* for regulatory intervention.[119]

---

109 Draft Framework Directive (supra note 51) Art. 8; Draft Radio Spectrum Decision (supra 73).

110 Draft Framework Directive (supra note 51) Art. 15.

111 Draft Framework Directive (supra note 51) Art. 9.

112 Ibid. Art. 10.

113 Ibid. Art. 11.

114 Ibid. Art. 12.

115 Draft Universal Service Directive (supra note 72).

116 Proposal for a Directive concerning the processing of personal data and the protection of privacy in the electronic communications sector of July 12, 2000, COM (2000) 385.

117 Draft Framework Directive (supra note 51) Art. 16.

118 See only Green Paper on the Convergence of the Telecommunications, Media and Information Technology Sectors, and the Implications for Regulation. Towards an Information Society Approach of December 1997, COM (97) 623; *B. Clements*, 'The impact of convergence on regulatory policy in Europe' (1998) 22 Telecommunications Policy, 197–205.

119 Cf. the criticism reported in 1999 Communications Review, supra note 102, at 7.

A second line of Community action targets regulatory institutions. The Draft Framework Directive obliges Member States to set up independent regulatory authorities[120] and to make them strong actors.[121] These authorities shall have the right to exchange information without informing their governments.[122] Their representatives shall form an independent European Communications Group, to become the Commission's watchdog at the national level.[123] The activities of the National Regulatory Authorities will themselves be under strict Commission supervision. In many instances, they have to notify draft decisions to the Commission; their measures do only take effect if the Commission does not declare otherwise within a month.[124] Under the Draft Access Directive, National Regulatory Authorities must also notify the names of operators deemed to have significant market power, and the obligations imposed on them.[125]

Finally, private actors is given the opportunity to by-pass national governments. They can bring claims to the Group of National Regulatory Authorities.[126] If National Regulatory Authorities fail to resolve a cross-border dispute between private actors, they can submit it to the Commission. 'In so doing, the parties renounce any further action under national law'.[127]

Similar observations can be made with respect to a second set of rules that has an adaptation effect. At several instances, the new regulatory

---

120 Draft Framework Directive (supra note 51) Art 3, see also preamble (11).

121 See in particular ibid. Art. 3 II: 'Member States shall guarantee the independence of national regulatory authorities by ensuring that they are legally distinct from and functionally independent of all organizations providing electronic communications networks, equipment or services. Member States that retain ownership or control of undertakings providing electronic communications networks and/or services shall ensure full and effective structural separation of the regulatory function from activities associated with ownership or control. Member States shall ensure that national regulatory authorities are able to act freely, without further authorisation or control from any other agency or body, subject only to the provisions of Articles 4 and 6 of this directive.'; see also ibid. Explanatory Memorandum, at B 4: The success of the new framework will depend on the provisions being implemented in a consistent manner by strong and independent NRAs'.

122 Ibid. Art. 3 II, see also preamble (27).

123 Ibid. Art. 21; the original plans of the Commission went even further, see 1999 Review, supra note 102, at 19.

124 Draft Framework Directive (supra note 51) Art. 6 II 1 and 6 IV, see also preamble (14).

125 Draft Access Directive (supra note 72) Art. 16 II, see also preamble (16).

126 Draft Framework Directive (supra note 51) Art. 21 VII.

127 Ibid., Art. 18 III.

framework calls for hybrid forms of governance, combining public and private inputs:[128] for technical standardization,[129] for spectrum management[130] and for data protection.[131] This could be a means for getting hold on governance activities that would otherwise, due to their global character, escape Community influence. In a 'better less than nothing' attitude, Europe changes its own, internal governance structure. But the pertinent provisions speak the language of Europeanisation, not of globalization. The Community can oust national standardization activities by transferring the issue to a hybrid European body.[132] The Commission grudgingly accepts CEPT activities in the domain of spectrum management, although they escape its control. But if the Commission is not pleased with the outcomes, it can step in with autonomous regulatory activities.[133] This gives the Commission considerable threat power for informal negotiations with CEPT.

D. Neglect

In the theoretical part of this paper, we have presented a third option. Regulators can react to globalization by a change of their own preferences. Since we find neither mitigation nor adaptation, this would thus be the theoretical prediction. But there is not the remotest sign for preference change in the documents of the new regulatory package. What one finds, however, is pervasive Euro-centricity. The new rules aim at the creation of a true *internal* market for telecommunications services.[134] 'Trans-national' markets are defined as markets transgressing Member States, not Community borders.[135]

---

[128] For the general attitude of the Commission see 1999 Review, supra note 102, at 7; more on hybrid governance in: *C. Engel*, 'Institutionen zwischen Staat und Markt' (2001) 34 Die Verwaltung, 1–24; *Engel*, supra note 16.

[129] Draft Framework Directive (supra note 51) Art. 15, see also Explanatory Memorandum, at B 5.

[130] Draft Radio Spectrum Decision (supra note 73) Art. 6 II-IV.

[131] Draft Data Protection Directive (supra note 116) preamble (8), see also Explanatory Memorandum, at 4.

[132] Draft Framework Directive (supra note 51) Art. 15 I 2.

[133] Draft Radio Spectrum Decision (supra note 73) Art. 6 IV.

[134] Draft Framework Directive (supra note 51) Art. 7 III; Draft Guidelines on Market Analysis (supra note 13), par.10; Draft Authorisation Directive (supra note 73) preamble (3).

[135] Draft Framework Directive (supra note 51) Art. 2 (m) and Art. 14 I (2).

Internet policy is discussed as if the Community had autonomy to decide.[136] The evidence thus points to a simple neglect of globalization by the new regulatory package.

V. Explanations

How come? There are two possible lines of explanation. Thus far, we have only presupposed, not actually shown, that telecommunications are affected by globalization. Maybe regulatory practice knows better. Maybe at closer sight telecommunications turn out to be one of the happy protected sectors of the economy[137] (A.). If not, we are faced with an interpretative choice between involuntarily 'unperceived globalization' and strategic neglect (B.). Given the limited evidence on which this paper is based, we cannot fully decide. But it at least seems much more plausible that strategic neglect is the correct interpretation.

A. Telecommunications as a Protected Sector of the Economy?

We have offered four complementary definitions of globalization. The first definition points to regulatory competition. Competitive pressure rests on credible threats of exit. At first sight, telecommunications operators do not seem to possess threat power. For telecommunications in essence is the transportation of signals. This makes it inexorably a local business. The local character is obvious for the physical grid dug into national territory, or hanging on poles erected along national streets. It also holds for cellular communications. They presuppose a dense network of senders and receivers within the territory.

Moreover,[138] national telecommunications companies are relatively well protected against market entry by foreign competitors. Consequently, they normally cannot credibly argue that they have to compete with suppliers working under less stringent rules. There are, in other words, important barriers to entry[139] in this industry. The sunk costs for rolling out a new tele-

[136] 1999 Review, supra note 102, at 9.

[137] On the general idea of protected sectors see again *Scharpf*, supra note 53, sec. 4.1.2.

[138] International rules notwithstanding, see below V.B.

[139] Basic von *C.C. Weizsäcker*, Barriers to entry: a theoretical treatment (Springer-Verlag, Berlin/New York, 1980).

communications network are substantial.[140] Network externalities make a piecemeal approach to market entry difficult.[141] Newcomers must make a substantial investment upfront. The market position of incumbents is strong, due to their previous monopoly. End-users have no interest in single components of communications services. Guaranteeing compatibility of components is therefore paramount. Newcomers do accordingly depend on existing compatibility standards.[142] These standards tend to be tuned to the network of the incumbents.

Newcomers will hardly ever be able to offer all these complementary components on their own. If not, market access depends on contracting with the incumbent, or on a regulatory authority forcing a contract upon him. In the former case, the incumbent can protect himself easily.[143] In the latter case, the regulatory authority can see at making conditions for market entry unattractive for foreign suppliers. If they want to build independent networks, newcomers must get rights of way. This also normally means that they need help from a regulatory authority.[144] They also must dispose of numbering resources, provided by a regulated numbering plan.[145] They are in other words operating on a market organized by way of regulation.[146] Government can use its power of organization to make market access for foreign providers cumbersome. Finally, as long as taking up business in the telecommunications industry presupposes a public authorization, government

---

140 This is the basic concern of the Local Loop Regulation (supra note 70) and of the Draft Access Directive (supra note 72).

141 See on network externalities only the classical texts of *M.L. Katz* and *C. Shapiro*, 'Network Externalities, Competition, and Compatibility' (1985) 75 American Economic Review, 424–440; *J. Farrell* and *C. Shapiro*, 'Dynamic Economics with Switching Costs' (1988) 19 Rand Journal of Economics, 123–137.

142 Cf. Draft Framework Directive (supra note 51) preamble (23).

143 Cf. Draft Guidelines Market Analysis (supra note 13) par. 51 note 26: 'Physical interconnection agreements may also be taken into consideration for defining the geographical scope of the market, Case No IV/M.570 – TBT/BT/TeleDanmark/Telenor, par. 35'; see also ibid. par. 58 note 38: 'Case No IV/M.856 – BT/MCI (II), OJ L 8.12.1997. These services are provided on the basis of existing international transmission facilities existing between the countries concerned or through the use of international private leased circuits hired from facilities based operators'.

144 Cf. ibid. preamble (18).

145 Cf. Draft Framework Directive (supra note 51) preamble (17).

146 On organised markets see *C. Engel* and *U.E. Schweizer*, 'Organising and Designing Markets' (2002) 158 Journal of Institutional and Theoretical Economics, 1–4.

can use the authorization procedure, and its terms and conditions, for making market access difficult.[147]

At closer sight, however, national telecommunications operators are much less dependent on their government. Technically, there is satellite communications as a way out. If an economically important nation state were to exercise pressure on national telecommunications companies, the general high speed of innovation in this field[148] is likely to generate further loopholes quickly. The pervasive convergence[149] would make it easy to shift traffic away to less controllable substitutes. The nation states, and Europe for that matter, can at most credibly threat the local loop. All other telecommunications services can fairly easily be substituted by less vulnerable alternatives. The practically most important way of doing this is packet switching, as used by the Internet. Communication is portioned into small data packages, each finding its way through the world communications networks separately. Packet switching originally has precisely been invented to secure communication even in the event of nuclear war.[150] The Commission itself demonstrates by the Regulation on unbundled access to the local loop[151] that this monopolistic bottleneck can to a large extent be separated from the remaining telecommunications services. Finally, and most importantly, for economic reasons nation states, and Europe, are not likely to take the owners of the local loop as hostages for their regulatory autonomy. The opportunity cost would be prohibitive. For state of the art, internationally connected communications networks are an infrastructure for almost any other business.[152] No industrially developed country would conceive of cutting itself off from these networks, or making them considerably less effective.

---

147 Cf. Draft Guidelines Market Analysis (supra note 13) par. 50 note 24: 'In practice, this area will correspond to the limits of the area in which an operator is authorised to operate. In Case No COMP/M.1650 – ACEA/Telefonica, the Commission pointed out that since the notified joint venture would have a licence limited to the area of Rome, the geographical market could be defined as local; at par.16'.

148 This is acknowledged by the Commission itself: Draft Framework Directive (supra note 51) preamble (21); Draft Guidelines Market Analysis (supra note 13) par. 24.

149 It also is acknowledged by the Commission, Draft Framework Directive (supra note 51) preamble (7); Draft Guidelines Market Analysis (supra note 13) par. 38; Green Paper on Convergence (supra note 118).

150 More on the history of the Internet by *Engel* and *Keller*, supra note 59, chap. 2.

151 Regulation Local Loop (supra note 70).

152 The Commission acknowledges this fact in Framework Directive (supra note 51) preamble (6).

Our second dimension of globalization relies on market definition. In this perspective, globalization is characterized by a definition of the geographically relevant market that transcends territorial boundaries. In the alternative, the relevant product market can have an international element in its definition. Obviously, not all telecommunications markets are global in one of these senses. But if one takes complementarity into account, the picture changes. Most telephony customers will rarely make transatlantic calls. But they are not likely to contract with a telephone company if international calls are technically impossible, even if their services are cheaper. They accordingly attribute option value to the possibility of making or receiving international calls. While these considerations may seem a little speculative for ordinary telephony, they are obvious for customers buying Internet access. They want worldwide access. Their Internet Service Provider can only guarantee this, if he has concluded transmission contracts with backbone providers. Otherwise, the routers will not let this traffic pass.[153] If nation states do not want to put this complementarity at risk, they lose at least some of their regulatory authority over telecommunications.

Our third dimension of globalization originates in independent, superior regulatory authority. This time, the relationship between appearances and underlying forces is the other way round. Appearances clearly point into the direction of globalization. All Members States of the Community, and the Community itself, have made commitments under the WTO Agreement on Basic Telecommunications Services. These commitments cover all segments of the telecommunications services sector.[154] The following quote from a report of the United States International Trade Commission highlights why this is an important factor of globalization:

> 'EU members were under no obligation to extend market access privileges to non-EU members, nor were they subject to any penalty should they treat non-EU carriers in a discriminatory manner. Through the 1997 WTO commitments, the EU made a binding commitment to extend its current internal level of market access to non-EU service providers'.[155]

There is controversy, however, how far the liberalizing effect of these commitments actually reaches. For lifting legal barriers to entry is not enough in

[153] For the details see EU Commission: Internet Network Issues, CEPT, ETNO & EICTA WTSA-2k doc. (00)122 Rev. 002 of September 11, 2000.

[154] *Blouin*, supra note 21, at 137.

[155] United States International Trade Commission (USITC): Recent Trends in US Services Trade: 1998 Annual Report, Investigation No. 332-345, pp. 4-42, cited after ibid., 139.

telecommunications markets. All the other barriers to entry listed above may still prevent foreign suppliers from entering European markets. The WTO has not been blind to this challenge. It has supplemented the Agreement with a 'Reference paper', addressing anticompetitive behaviour of incumbents, interconnection, rules on universal service, licensing procedure and the obligation to set up an independent and impartial regulatory authority.[156] All EC Member States have signed the Reference Paper.[157] Observers are divided, however, over the efficacy of these rules.[158]

B. Unperceived Globalization, or Strategic Neglect?

Remains our last dimension of globalization, the constructivist. If there is such a thing as perceived globalization, the opposite must also exist. The indicators of globalization analysed with tools from rational choice theory could be masked in collective perception. Globalization could go 'unperceived'. Is this what explains the conspicuous lack of concern for globalization in the documents of the new regulatory package?

There is one element in this package that might support the hypothesis. The Commission is strongly preoccupied with the transitional dimension of telecommunications policy. The Commission stresses the difficulties inherent in getting from national monopolies to true competition.[159] For the time being, it opts for asymmetric regulation. Incumbents are forced to grant newcomers access to the local loop[160] and to other elements of their networks, if appropriate.[161] Accounting separation and reporting obligations

---

156 Ibid., 137 s.

157 Ibid.

158 Among the sceptics are *M. Bronkers* and *P. Larouche*, 'Telecommunications Services and the World Trade Organisation' (1997) 31 Journal of World Trade, 5–48; *M. Fredebeul-Krein* and *A. Freytag*, 'Telecommunications and WTO Discipline. An Assessment of the WTO Agreement on Telecommunication Services' (1997) 21 Telecommunications Policy, 477–491; see also *E. Noam*, 'Assessing the WTO Agreement on Basic Telecommunications', in: G.C. Hubauer and E. Wada, Unfinished Business. Telecommunications After the Uruguay Round (Institute for International Economics, Washington DC 1997) pp. 27–61; *Blouin*, supra note 21, is considerably more optimistic.

159 Draft Framework Directive (supra note 51) preamble (1).

160 Regulation Local Loop (supra note 70), and preamble (3) in particular.

161 Draft Access Directive (supra note 72).

shall make it easier to supervise them.[162] Administrative charges may not be flat, in order not to implicitly discriminate against smaller newcomers.[163] But asymmetric regulation is to be phased out, once the newcomers are strong enough. Should new bottlenecks become visible, however, ex ante rules must step in early enough.[164]

Has this concern with transition been so dominant that the Commission, and the other actors involved in the political process preceding the adoption of the regulatory package, just have overlooked the challenge of globalization? Possible, but not likely. In other, related areas the Commission has been quite concerned with globalization: electronic commerce,[165] youth protection,[166] data protection[167] and the discussions of the White paper on governance stand out.[168]

We do already possess the key to an alternative, more plausible interpretation. We have demonstrated how much ground the Commission stands to gain by this new regulatory package, to the detriment of Member States.[169] It has not won the battle yet. But chances are it will. Introducing globalization into this discourse would open up an entirely new political flank. Had this been the battleground right from the beginning, the Commission might have argued that making Europe stronger helps parry the global challenge. But for the Commission, introducing this line of argument now is dangerous. Adversaries in the Member States' governments might argue that Europe is not the right arena for solving global problems, and try to bring the issue into the arenas of the WTO, the OECD, or other international bodies. Since none of these organizations can muster the political power of the EU, they might hope to preserve their autonomy this way. They might already have won, once they succeed in seriously protracting negotiations over the regulatory package. The 'window of opportunity' for the Commission might be lost.

---

162 Draft Framework Directive (supra note 51) Art. 12.
163 Draft Authorisation Directive (supra note 73) Explanatory Memorandum, at 2.
164 Draft Access Directive (supra note 72) preamble (8).
165 Directive on certain legal aspects of information society services, in particular electronic commerce, in the Internal Market (Directive on electronic commerce) of June 8, 2000, OJ 2000 L 178/1, preamble (58-62).
166 Illegal and Harmful Content on the Internet, COM (1996) 487.
167 See again *Farrell*, supra note 94.
168 Characteristic: White Paper on Governance Working Group No. 5: An EU Contribution to Better Governance beyond Our Borders, Report: Strengthening Europe's Contribution to World Governance, of May 2001, <http://europa.eu.int/comm/governance/areas/group11/report_en.pdf> (visited on August 24, 2001).
169 See above IV.C.

Our evidence is, as repeatedly stressed, insufficient for actually proving this explanation. But considered all we have, strategic neglect seems by far the most likely interpretation.

VI. Normative Outlook

These are interesting findings for a social scientist. But what is in it for a lawyer? Not much, to be honest. Had our theoretical hypotheses turned out true, a host of normative questions would have ensued: is globalization a justification for interferences with fundamental freedoms, or human rights? Does the European legislator, under fundamental freedoms or human rights, possess a larger margin of appreciation when he reacts to globalization?[170] Do the three options of mitigation, adaptation and preference change rank differently under these constitutional rules? How is the principle of subsidiarity affected by globalization? Does the European Community gain a larger space of action vis-à-vis the Member States when it acts in a globalized environment?

But we have not found a proactive Community policy addressing globalization. The Community organs might just have overlooked the globalization of telecommunications. More likely is, however, that they are aware of, but deliberately ignore globalization. One might think that the just mentioned normative questions would just be mirrored. Member States might blame the European Community for unduly interfering with their legislative autonomy. Some individuals and firms surely stand to loose if the Community strategically neglects the global character of telecommunications. But it is difficult to transpose this normative issue into legal dogmatics. The logical tool would be a duty to protect. Constitutionalists have indeed ere long discussed whether government is constitutionally obliged to grant its nationals diplomatic protection. By this term, public international law characterizes an intervention by one against another sovereign state on behalf of the nationals of the former state. But constitutionalists agree that there cannot be a strict obligation to grant diplomatic protection, given the imponderables of foreign policy. Government is only obliged to exercise its discretion properly.[171]

---

[170] More from *Engel*, supra note 16, pp. 8–11.

[171] Under German law, the leading case is BVerfGE 55, 349 – Hess; comprehensive *E. Klein*, 'Anspruch auf diplomatischen Schutz', in: G. Ress and T. Stein, Der diplomatische Schutz im Völker- und Europarecht (Nomos, Baden-Baden, 1996) pp. 125–136.

More importantly, our question is not identical to the one constitutionalists were concerned with. If our interpretation of the findings is correct, the Commission does not shy away from international conflict; it does not want to treat telecommunications in its internal policy-making as a globalizes issue. The normative question is thus one political scientists would address in terms of policy cycle analysis. Roughly speaking, the policy cycle consists of the following elements: agenda setting, problem definition, policy formulation, implementation, assessing outcomes. Our question is one of problem definition. Given the strong indications of globalization, the Commission defines the problem of telecommunications policy inappropriately.

Proper problem definition is certainly a normative issue. But courts seem rightly reluctant to impose a more appropriate problem definition on political organs. The danger of a *gouvernement des juges* looms large.[172] This is so for two combined reasons. The first is conceptual, the second factual. Problem definition is a normative endeavour. To criticize one problem definition, one thus needs a normative starting point. Unfortunately, there is not just one such starting point, but a good number of competing ones, like efficiency, liberty, fairness, or equality. These starting points cannot be translated one into the other. There is no single normative currency, so to speak. Decisions must be taken that cannot fully be justified. In a democracy, this is what Parliaments exist for.[173] The factual reason is uncertainty. The legislator hardly ever has all the facts one might theoretically wish to know before deciding. Again, decision is the only way out.[174]

The most one can envisage are thus procedural rules. But European Community law anyhow is advanced in this respect. Art 253 ECT obliges the Community to give reasons for its legislative acts. In practice, a long preamble precedes the operative part of regulations, directives and decisions. Actually, it is mostly due to these preambles that we have been able to trace the neglect of globalization in the new regulatory package on telecommuni-

[172] More from *C. Engel*, 'Delineating the Proper Scope of Government: A Proper Task for a Constitutional Court?' (2001) 157 Journal of Institutional and Theoretical Economics, 187–219; *Engel*, supra note 32.

[173] More from *C. Engel*, Offene Gemeinwohldefinitionen, Gemeinschaftsgüter: Recht, Politik und Ökonomie. Preprints aus der Max-Planck-Projektgruppe Recht der Gemeinschaftsgüter Bonn 2000/16.

[174] More from *I. Spiecker gen. Döhmann*, 'Staatliche Entscheidungen unter Unsicherheit: Juristische und ökonomische Vorgaben', in: J. Lege, Gentechnik im nichtmenschlichen Bereich – was kann und was sollte das Recht regeln? (Arno Spitz, Berlin 2001) pp. 51–88.

cations. This is what the law can do. It is up to the political actors involved in European legislation to prevent the Commission from strategically defining the policy problem inappropriately. Occasionally, science can help by pointing policy makers to such a neglect. This is what this article has intended to do.

REGULATING TELECOMMUNICATIONS SERVICES: GLOBALIZATION IN VIEW OF JAPAN

by Yasuo Hasebe, Tokyo

I. Introduction

When the organizers of this conference invited me to give a paper on the impact of globalization on telecommunications regulation, it occurred to me that the term 'globalization' often has different meanings in different contexts. These meanings bear only a family resemblance to each other, so it is important to clarify how we are employing the term. In this paper, I will consider three particular senses in which globalization is discussed, each revealing a different context in which globalization and the regulation of telecommunications intersect.

J. Basedow, H. Baum, K. Hopt, H. Kanda and T. Kono (eds.), Economic Regulation and Competition, (253-264)

First, as discussed in Section II, globalization sometimes refers to the movement toward defining standards or, indeed, the contents of regulation through international organizations or intergovernmental negotiations, as well as the legal and/or practical obligation of national governments to conform to such 'global standards'.

Second, as considered in Section III, globalization sometimes focuses upon the opening of the domestic market of a given nation more widely to international competition. When foreign corporations either enter a new market or plan to do so, foreign governments take an interest in whether the regulatory regime of that nation is sufficiently fair, transparent, and stable for their corporations to compete.

Third, as addressed in Section IV, the term globalization also applies, conversely, to the entry or planned entry of the corporations of a given nation into foreign markets, as well as to the requirements of foreign governments that these corporations not only comply with their regulatory regimes, but also do business transparently enough for domestic players to compete fairly.

Understandably, the conference organizers who invited me here today might expect me to present the Japanese perspective on globalization and telecommunications regulation. However, I question whether or not a distinctively Japanese perspective on these issues exists. When one confronts a given problem, the solutions that occur to one are more or less reasonable regardless of nationality. The case of Japan is illustrative, but the ideas presented in this paper are strictly my own, and do not necessarily represent the views of my fellow citizens.

II. International Coordination

A. Globalization and Ethical Challenges

In the sense that globalization entails the increased setting of regulatory agendas and standards by international organizations, globalization can be problematic with regard to serious moral issues in a wide range of areas. From bioethics to whale hunting, international organizations have been producing agenda- and standard-setting documents that reach general conclusions on controversial questions, but often these conclusions are not well supported by well-thought-through arguments.

For example, Unesco declares the following in Article 11 of the Universal Declaration on the Human Genome and Human Rights: 'practices which are contrary to human dignity, such as reproductive cloning of human beings, shall not be permitted'.[1] Despite the sweeping breadth of this conclusion, the declaration provides neither scientific nor moral arguments in support of it.

Such documents are generally the result of international meetings at which high-level representatives achieve some face-saving consensus on a particular issue despite holding mutually incompatible and conflicting viewpoints. Conclusions thus reached are usually framed in terms of highly abstract principles; in order to avoid controversy, supporting arguments are not presented. As such, international protocols are increasingly cited in ethical justifications, and moral arguments in areas of global concern have become increasingly poor.[2]

B. The International Telecommunication Union

Fortunately, moral issues rarely present problems in the area of telecommunications regulation, at least as far as the International Telecommunication Union (ITU) is concerned. Meetings of the ITU are usually limited to dealing with technical matters such as allocating radio frequencies or setting standards for new technologies.[3]

The purpose of ITU decisions is, essentially, to solve coordination problems, which Joseph Raz describes as 'situations where the vast majority have sufficient reason to prefer to take that action which is taken by the vast majority'.[4] In such situations, people are willing to conform to a standard set by any sufficiently authoritative body because they expect that the 'vast majority' is also likely to conform to it. Substantive argument to support such a standard is not necessary, because having some standard is more important than having the right standard in a coordination problem situa-

1 See <www.unesco.org/ibc/en/genome/projet/index.htm>.

2 See *John Harris*, Introduction: The importance of bioethics, in: John Harris (ed.), Bioethics (Oxford, Oxford University Press, 2001), pp. 5-7. The Universal Declaration on the Human Genome and Human Rights of Unesco is an example Harris discusses.

3 In addition to standard-setting and radio frequency allocation, a new basic purpose was added to the ITU mission in 1982: 'to promote and to offer technical assistance to developing countries in the field of telecommunications, and also to promote the mobilization of the material and financial resources needed for implementation'. Constitution of the ITU, Cm 3145 (HMSO, 1996), article 1(1)(b).

4 *Joseph Raz*, The Morality of Freedom (Oxford, Clarendon Press, 1986), p. 49.

tion.[5] Once the ITU sets technical standards for third-generation mobile phone service, for example, every player will be able to create business plans with legal certainty; without standards, players cannot conduct the planning needed to create a market. In the event that players do not perceive the necessity of coordination, they remain free to opt-out of the standards. Coordination can then proceed without them.[6] In this respect, the globalization of telecommunications regulation does not present serious problems for telecommunications players.

III. 'Capturing' Regulators?

A. The WTO and the Convergence of Regulatory Regimes

International negotiations and the accords that they produce can significantly affect domestic policy decisions that should be informed by more substantial considerations, as the Japanese case demonstrates regarding telecommunications regulation.

Demands by foreign governments for Japan to liberalize its telecommunications market have had a strong influence on domestic policy; for example, interconnection fees for Japan's dominant fixed-line carriers, NTT East and NTT West (which are controlled by the NTT holding company), are to be reduced by 22.5% over the course of three years as a result of an agreement negotiated between Japan and the U.S. in 2000.[7] The negotiations leading to this agreement were undertaken because the U.S. (and the EC) had threatened to take action against Japan over its purported 'failure' to introduce the long-run incremental cost methodology for setting interconnection rates. The U.S. government maintained that the fully allocated cost methodology

---

[5] For more on the concept of the coordination problem, see, for example, *David Lewis*, Convention (Cambridge/Mass., Harvard University Press, 1969); and *Edna Ullmann-Margalit*, The Emergence of Norms (Oxford, Clarendon Press, 1977), chapter III. As *Christoph Engel* points out, possible solutions might differ as to their distributional aspect. See his contribution, III.D.

[6] See *Christoph Engel*, contribution, IV.A.1. Engel provides illustrative examples in the context of telecommunications regulation.

[7] See *Ministry of Posts and Telecommunications*, Jôhô Tsûshin Hakusho 2001 [The Annual Report on Information and Communications of 2001] (Gyôsei, 2001), p. 250.

employed by Japanese regulators did not conform to the 'cost-oriented' principle required under the WTO agreement on basic telecommunications.[8]

As this example demonstrates, initiatives by foreign governments and international organizations have contributed much to bring the Japanese regulatory approach into alignment with the approaches of Western countries, making it more acceptable to Western operators. Nonetheless, distinctively Japanese characteristics remain, and these have been viewed with suspicion by foreign observers. One difference that has raised particular concern is that rather than being independent of the central government, the regulator of telecommunications in Japan is one of its ministries, namely, the Ministry of Posts and Telecommunications.[9]

By way of background, in January 2001 the Ministry of Posts and Telecommunications was integrated along with several other ministries into a gigantic, newly created department called the *Sômushô*, which might roughly be translated as the 'Ministry of General Affairs'. However, the official English name of this new department is the 'Ministry of Public Management, Home Affairs, Posts, and Telecommunications', and this long English name reveals its true nature: the old ministries have not been integrated at all, but rather continue to behave autonomously. I therefore use the term 'Ministry of Posts and Telecommunications' in this paper to refer to the governmental regulatory authority.

---

8 See Reference Paper included in the Fourth Protocol to the General Agreement on Trade in Services, which came into force in February 1998. The Fourth Protocol is also known as the Basic Telecommunications Agreement. It is generally assumed that the incremental cost methodology is superior to the fully allocated cost methodology, because the latter is less likely to reflect the true replacement cost of assets, and therefore sends the wrong signal to market players. However, as incremental costs are notoriously difficult to calculate, it is not clear whether or not this theoretical superiority translates into practical benefits. See *Lisa Correa*, The economics of telecommunications regulation, in: Ian Walden/John Angel (eds), Telecommunications Law (London, Blackstone, 2001), pp. 42-46.

9 The Reference Paper in the Fourth Protocol requires that the 'regulatory body is separate from, and not accountable to, any supplier of basic telecommunications services' (section 5). Notably, the Reference Paper does not require that the regulator be independent of the government.

B. *The Government: Owner of the Incumbent*

Those who are suspicious of direct regulation by the government are usually most concerned with the potential for collusion between the regulator and the regulated – in this case, between the Ministry of Posts and Telecommunications and the incumbent, dominant operator, NTT. Although I question whether a government ministry is necessarily more prone to 'capture' than an independent regulator, the Japanese case bears closer consideration.

First, when NTT DoCoMo and the NTT holding company recently faced proposals to regulate 'dominant carriers' in the mobile phone market, they lobbied politicians of the governing parties to pressure the Ministry of Posts and Telecommunications to enlarge the concept of 'dominant carriers', thereby extending the new regulation to other significant operators as well.[10] To resist these political pressures, the ministry sought to strengthen its argument for narrowly targeting NTT DoCoMo by sending delegations to Western countries to study their regulatory experiences.[11] Such studies of foreign experiences have a strong influence on Japanese policy formulation, though in this case the effect was limited and NTT succeeded in weakening the regulation.[12]

Similar interactions between the same players arose during the attempted break-up of NTT in 1997. To maintain its unified structure as far as possible,

---

10 This measure corresponds to the Reference Paper's requirement that 'major suppliers' be regulated. A similar regulation had been introduced into the fixed-line market. According to the Reference Paper, major suppliers are obligated to provide for interconnection on non-discriminatory terms, at cost-oriented rates, and on an unbundled basis.

11 Masayuki Funada, a member of the Council on Telecommunications Regulation, argues that Japan's mobile phone market has already become sufficiently competitive so that there is no need to introduce European-type, broad-range regulation such as that advocated by NTT. His conclusion is that only NTT DoCoMo, which both maintains a market share in excess of 50% and remains under the control of NTT, should be the target of the newly introduced regulations. See *Masayuki Funada*, On the interim report on the competition policy by the Council on Telecommunications Regulation: (2001) 1199 Jurist 54-57. The Interim Report on the Competition Policy of Telecommunications, made public by the Council on Telecommunications Regulation in December 2000, shared Funada's view.

12 Under the Telecommunications Act as amended in 2001, concrete conditions to trigger 'dominant carriers' regulation, including the market share of the carriers, are to be specified by a ministerial order. The order was publicized in September 2001. According to the order, the trigger of the regulation is set at 25% of the market share, not at 50% as the Ministry of Posts and Telecommunications advocated.

NTT lobbied politicians and government officials extensively, and as a result, NTT has survived as the holding company of the NTT group, to which NTT East, NTT West, and NTT DoCoMo belong.

Admittedly, some of the arguments that NTT presented during these efforts might be defensible on their merits. If telecommunications networks fell into the hands of not one but several operators, none of whom were dominant, it might indeed be necessary for all operators with 'significant market power' to be required not to abuse them.[13] Furthermore, the structural separation of existing, dominant operators might not alleviate problems resulting from their dominance, and worse still, might instead institutionalize a structure that technological advances or regulatory change could render obsolete. Finally, the accounting separation for which NTT lobbied as an alternative to a break-up might prove both more flexible and easier to implement than a complete separation.[14]

However, NTT often successfully employs a more problematic argument to dissuade politicians and governmental departments (other than the Ministry of Posts and Telecommunications) from supporting regulatory measures to liberalize the market: namely, that jeopardizing NTT's dominance entails risking a reduction in prospective governmental revenues. The real problem that can lead to collusion between NTT and the government is not that the regulatory authority for the telecommunications industry is part of the government, but rather that the government still owns a large percentage of NTT shares.[15] As long as the government has an interest in maintaining the equity value of the dominant operator, it cannot be expected to promote robust competition in the telecommunications market.

In light of this problem, it is by no means certain that an independent regulator with no voice in the Cabinet will be more successful than a government ministry in resisting the direct and indirect pressures exerted by the incumbent operator. Indeed, a large ministry with a wide range of responsibilities might be less prone to 'capture' by the regulated, not least because it could rotate personnel every two or three years between various offices, as is common in the Japanese ministries. A smaller, more narrowly focused independent authority, on the other hand, would run a greater risk of undue influ-

---

13 *Edward Pitt*, Competition Law in Telecommunications, in: Ian Walden/John Angel (eds), supra note 8, at p. 264.

14 See *Correa*, supra note 8., at pp. 22-23.

15 According to the NTT Financial Report issued in May 2001, the Ministry of Finance retains 45.96% of NTT's total shares. Article 4(1) of the NTT Act requires the government to retain not less than one third of NTT's total shares.

ence, because its officials would become intimately acquainted with people in the regulated industry.[16]

C. Dispute Resolution

Through an amendment to Japan's Telecommunications Act,[17] the Telecommunications Dispute Resolution Commission[18] was created within the Ministry of Posts and Telecommunications in June 2001, with the mission of facilitating the resolution of disputes over interconnection issues by means of conciliation and arbitration. Apparently, the creation of this commission was motivated by the WTO's requirement that 'a service supplier requesting interconnection with a major supplier will have recourse [...] to an independent domestic body [...] to resolve disputes' promptly.[19] The term 'independent' here specifically refers to independence from 'any supplier of basic telecommunications services', rather than from the government.

The long-term merit of spending taxpayers' money on such an alternative dispute resolution (ADR) mechanism seems dubious. With or without an ADR, operators can always bring their disputes to the judicial courts, which are ideally independent and impartial. Furthermore, parties who are dissatisfied with the outcomes of the ADR process can also turn to the judicial system, where they can seek more favorable outcomes. Yet government ministries always welcome the birth of new fiefdoms under their control.

D. Other Ostensible Advantages of Independence

It can be argued that an independent regulatory authority (that is, independent of the government) provides at least a greater appearance of impartiality than a government ministry. However, pursuing the appearance of impartiality rather than the substance is nonsensical.

It might also be argued that by hiving off the task of implementing regulatory policy to an independent body, the ministry could better concentrate

---

16 For similar reasons, I doubt the wisdom of conferring the authority for economic regulation in general, including telecommunications regulation, on independent commissions.

17 Denki tsûshin jigyô-hô, Law No. 86/1984, last amended by Law No. 62/2001.

18 Denki Tsûshin Jigyô Funsô Shori Iinkai.

19 The Reference Paper in the Fourth Protocol, section 2.5.

on policy formulation. However, in light of the British experiences with executive agencies, the wisdom of such a division of labor appears questionable.[20] As the British discovered, it is not easy to draw a line between policy formulation and its implementation. A ministry and its ministers can in effect interfere with the day-to-day business of an ostensibly independent regulatory body, but disclaim responsibility for the results of their interference on the pretext of that body's independence. On the other hand, a Japanese-style integrated regulatory approach might make policy formulation more responsive to the day-to-day effects of regulation, and might also make ministers more accountable.

E. *Remaining Hope*

It follows from these arguments that the only way to fundamentally improve the telecommunications environment in Japan is for the government to dispose of its NTT shares. However, with the Japanese economy in a deep recession and the government in serious financial difficulty, this is not likely to occur in the foreseeable future. Thus, with progress toward a domestic solution to the current problems in Japan's telecommunications market stymied, we can only hope that foreign governments and international bodies will continue to pressure the Japanese government toward further liberalization.

IV. Semi-Official Self-Regulation: The Mobile Internet Business

A. *Business Models*

The Annual Report on Information and Communications of 2001, issued by the Ministry of Posts and Telecommunications,[21] refers to the proposals of a study group that I chaired on regularizing the business framework for mobile phone content providers. The group included representatives of mobile phone operators, including NTT DoCoMo, J-Phone, and KDDI, mobile

---

20 *Vernon Bogdanor*, Politics and the Constitution (Aldershot, Dartmouth, 1996), pp. 32-33; *Gavin Drewry*, The New Public Management, in: Jeffrey Jowell/ Dawn Oliver (eds), The Changing Constitution, (4th edn, Oxford, Oxford University Press, 2000), pp. 179-83.

21 The Annual Report, supra note 7, at p. 268.

Internet content providers, and legal experts. The study group published its proposals in July 2001.[22]

The task of the study group was to conceptualize a new, self-regulated framework for Japan's burgeoning wireless Internet services, that is, NTT DoCoMo's iMode, J-Phone's J-Sky, and KDDI's EzWeb. In general, the business models of mobile Internet operators in Japan work as follows: the operator provides both a handset and mobile Internet service that allow the user access to e-mail and to an installed browser in the mobile phone. The browser offers a menu of 'official' mini-Web sites, and users can navigate to other 'unofficial' Web sites as well, though no direct links are provided. The operator generates revenue both from charges for time spent on-line, and from fees paid by the 'official' Web site content providers.

At the same time, 'official' site providers are able to charge for their services through the operators' billing systems; however, 'unofficial' sites that are not indexed on the handset menus are not allowed access. Instead, these sites must rely on credit cards as their only effective means of accepting payments, a cumbersome method for the petty transactions typical of their business models.[23] Thus, designated 'official' site providers enjoy major competitive advantages over 'unofficial' sites that have not partnered with operators.

The mobile Internet business faces other problems as well. The process by which service operators have chosen their designated 'official' sites has not been transparent. Furthermore, since the Telecommunications Act prohibits operators from controlling the content that they distribute, they cannot be held accountable when even 'official' sites provide socially harmful information or handle the personal information of users improperly.

Nonetheless, with the advent of third-generation mobile telephone, Japan's wireless Internet services are expected to expand worldwide. NTT DoCoMo intends to launch similar businesses in the U.S. and Europe. It is widely believed that J-Phone's parent company Vodaphone plans to utilize the expertise that J-Phone has accumulated in this business.

---

22 Môbairu kontentsu bijinesu no kankyô seibi ni mukete [Toward a More Transparent Regulatory Framework for Mobile Contents Business], 26 June 2001.

23 For further discussion on the wireless Internet business model, see *Charles Bickers*'s exposition in his 'The Way of the Mobile Warrior': (21 June 2001) Far Eastern Economic Review 46-50. According to the Ministry of Posts and Telecommunications, the number of wireless Internet users in Japan rose to 46,180,000 in October 2001.

Japan thus faces the somewhat embarrassing prospect of exporting a business model that is not supported by any regulatory framework able to assure both fair access and accountability for contents. Complicating this situation, the Japanese government is prohibited under both the Telecommunications Act and the Constitution[24] from controlling or interfering with the contents of telecommunications. The only feasible solution would appear to be a system of self-regulation on which both common carriers and content providers could agree.

B. Proposal

Under the system proposed by the study group that I chaired, an independent body would create a code of standards for content-providers. On the basis of this code, a separate body will evaluate the applications of content providers and either grant or deny accreditation. Accredited providers will have the right to use operators' billing systems, but operators will not be obligated to list them on handset menus, which will continue to be edited at the operators' sole discretion. These proposals are intended to clarify the distribution of responsibilities in the mobile Internet business, and to create opportunity by making the business more transparent.[25]

The Ministry of Posts and Telecommunications set up the study group that produced this plan, and played the role both of preparing draft proposals and brokering an agreement between group members. The proposed system will neither be enacted as law, nor enforced by the government. Rather, it will be run on a self-regulating, voluntary basis.[26]

V. Conclusion

As mentioned at the outset of this paper, I suspect that there might not be any distinctively Japanese viewpoint on telecommunications regulation. As

---

24 Kempô, 3 November 1946.

25 In developing this proposal, the study group considered several self-regulated e-commerce systems in the United States, including BBBOnLine and TRUSTe.

26 This method of regulatory system-building is similar to the one A. Michael Froomkin calls 'semi-private rulemaking'. See *A. Michael Froomkin*, Semi-private international rulemaking, in: Christopher T. Marsden (ed.), Regulating the Global Information Society (London, Routledge, 2000), chapter 11.

argued in Section III, the discretion of national policymakers is, to a large extent, limited by both international standards and economic and financial conditions. Furthermore, there is often more than one way to solve a given problem, particularly if it is a coordination problem – that is, the sort of problem that many regulatory issues touch upon. Even when Japan takes a different course from other countries, the Japanese approach may be no more idiosyncratic or less reasonable than others; however, it may appear out of context.

STATEMENT ON THE REGULATION OF TELECOMMUNCATIONS SERVICES

by Klaus-Dieter Scheurle, Frankfurt/Main

Today, there is no doubt that telecommunications is the key to the development of an information society and to the international competitiveness of each region of the world. It has also become clear that the enormous potential for innovations and economy can only be exploited in a liberalized and open framework.

This was seen differently when telecommunications first started in Germany in the 19th century. It was a German named Philipp Reis (1834–1874) who developed the world's first telephone. But when he presented his invention to the public on 26 October 1861, in Frankfurt, there was no major interest and he could not convince anyone to invest money in its further development to start a commercial business. The American Alexander Graham Bell (1848–1922) was more successful in this respect, and he very quickly succeeded in deploying telecommunications services on a commercial basis in the major and mid-sized towns of North America. In Germany the Postmaster General Heinrich von Stephan began his country's first experiments with Bell's telephones in Berlin on 26 October 1877. This was the beginning of a state-owned monopoly, as in the other states of Europe; in the United States, Mr. Bell founded a private monopoly that he successfully defended for more than a century.

During the 1970s, however, opinions began to change as it became more and more obvious that large amounts of money needed to be invested in order to exploit the great potential of the new high-tech capabilities in the telecommunications industry. The liberalization in the United States and Great Britain began in 1984 and showed that a competitive framework is a more appropriate instrument than a monopoly for creating incentives for new

J. Basedow, H. Baum, K. Hopt, H. Kanda and T. Kono (eds.), Economic Regulation and Competition, (265-268)

investments, providing more efficiency in the sector, and delivering lower prices and better products to end users.

But it is not easy to open an infrastructure-based market such as telecommunications, and the question was how it should be done. The German fixed-line infrastructure has a value of far more than 50 billion Euro. It makes no sense to force competitors to invest such a huge amount of money in a comparable second or third infrastructure. But even if entrepreneurs had to do so, it would not be a guarantee for their success. Therefore, any new legal framework for creating workable competition must tackle the situation that the incumbent actually possesses all the citizens of a country as its customers, and competition would mean that a significant number of them must be convinced to move from the incumbent to one of the new entrants. And, of course, it is not of interest to the incumbent to let them go. Keeping them would be a very easy task for the incumbent if it would not be forced to interconnect its network with the networks of its competitors. Nonetheless, such rules compelling incumbents into open network provision are not enough. Additionally, there must be clear rules about the tariffs an incumbent can demand from the entrepreneurs and its customers on a fair cost-oriented basis. Such rules are not provided by the existing general competition legislation. That means there must be a clear legal, sector-specific framework for regulation to liberalize the telecommunications market. A large amount of literature and experiences confirms this.

In Germany, the German Telecommunications Act entered into force on 1 August 1996. Besides rules about open network provision (i.e., interconnection and unbundled access in the local loop) and rate regulation, the act also governs numbering, licensing, frequency management, and universal service. Through this Telecommunications Act, Germany has implemented the European legal framework set by roughly two dozen EU directives. According to the international rules of the GATS, the EU directives, and the German legal framework, an independent regulatory agency was established on 1 January 1998, when the liberalization finally became effective.

We have had very good experiences with this regulatory framework, which is reported to be one of the most effective worldwide. The German market rose from 43 billion Euro in 1998 to 55 billion Euro in 2000, and more than 250 players are now offering telecommunications services in Germany. The entrepreneurs won 40 percent of the German market in total, i.e., 18 percent of the fixed-line business, 70 percent in the mobile telecommunications sector, 42 percent of the lease-line markets, and 46 percent of the cable business. At the same time the tariffs, especially for long-distance and international calls, dropped significantly by over 90 percent. At present, for a call to the U.S., German customers have to pay only 7 percent of the tariff they had to pay before liberalization started in 1998.

In light of these speedy developments, the incumbent – the Deutsche Telekom AG – started a discussion as to whether the tough regulation requiring approval for all tariff changes could not be softened. Additionally, the incumbent applied to define some parts of the German telecommunications market as single independent markets, a step that would remove them from the jurisdiction of the regulation. Deutsche Telekom argued that it had lost market dominance in this regard, thereby negating the necessity of sector-specific regulation and making general competition law the appropriate legal yardstick. In this context, Deutsche Telekom regarded calls to Turkey, the United States, Denmark, Japan, Australia, Russia, Ukraine, and other countries as independent markets. Additionally, it applied to define business calls in the local market of Berlin as an independent market. Deutsche Telekom's applications met with partial success, in particular concerning international sales to specific countries; however, its other applications were rejected by the regulator.

Although some academics are currently supporting Deutsche Telekom in its efforts to soften the regulation in Germany, others have a different opinion. The so-called monopoly commission, which is composed of academics and businesspeople who advise the German government on economic policy issues, published a special report at the end of 2001. This report stated that because of the strong position of the incumbent regarding infrastructure, and according to the situation in the local loop in Germany where Deutsche Telekom still holds a market share of 97.9 percent, regulation has to be continued at the existing level.

The experiences made in Germany are clear, and they are in line with other international experiences:

1. A competitive framework rather than a monopoly pushes the sector and the whole economy forward dramatically.
2. To move a monopoly toward a workable competitive framework, sector-specific regulation is needed. The general competitive legislation is not sufficient to achieve competition. The regulatory framework will come to its end when workable competition exists.
3. The incumbent also benefits from a competitive framework because only under such conditions will it achieve efficiency and more productivity.
4. Liberalization provides many benefits for the customers.

References

J. Große, Deregulierungsbedarf bei Ferngesprächen: (2000) 80 Wirtschaftsdienst 409.

G. Knieps, Rückführung der sektorspezifischen Regulierung auf dem deutschen TK-Markt. Die verpaßte Chance des Sondergutachtens der Monopolkommission: (2000) 3 Multi-Media und Recht 266 et seq.

P. Bolton/J. F. Brodley/M. Riordan, Predatory Pricing: Strategic Theory and Legal Policy: (2000) 88 Georgetown Law Journal 2304 et seq.

Sondergutachten der Monopolkommission: Wettbewerbsentwicklung bei Telekommunikation und Post 2001: Unsicherheit und Stillstand.

A. Picot/W. Burr, Regulierung der Deregulierung des Telekommunikationssektor: (1996) 48 Schmalenbachs Zeitschrift für betriebswirtschaftliche Forschung 173-200.

E. Witte, Die Entwicklung zur Reformreife, in: L.M. Büchner (ed.), Post und Telekommunikation: Eine Bilanz nach zehn Jahren Reform (Heidelberg, 1999), pp. 59-85.

E. Witte, Die Liberalisierung des deutschen Telekommunikationsmarktes: (1999) 48 Zeitschrift für Wirtschaftspolitik 315 et seq.

Part 5:

ASPECTS OF PRIVATE INTERNATIONAL LAW

CONFLICTS OF LAW IN THE FINANCIAL SERVICES MARKETS

Anton K. Schnyder, Basel*

I. Globalization and Co-ordination

Banks, insurers, and other enterprises offering financial services are the target of a special supervision exercised by the State. They are subject to the control exercised by specialized supervisory bodies that are themselves subject to constant structural adjustment on account of interdependence of financial services and the resulting need for so-called consolidated or conglomerate supervision. It remains to be seen whether such structural adjustment will ultimately improve the effectiveness of the supervision of money market transactions.

Increasing globalization of the markets would actually imply regulating standards and mechanisms to apply worldwide: the more comprehensive and

* I wish to express my thankfulness to my assistant, Mr. Lukas Bopp, attorney-at-law, whose contribution to the present treatise has proved most valuable.

J. Basedow, H. Baum, K. Hopt, H. Kanda and T. Kono (eds.), Economic Regulation and Competition, (271-286)

global the events on the market and their relating effects upon the markets become, the more limited and dysfunctional the national supervising mechanisms appear that are meant to control them. It follows that legal provisions destined to assume a regulatory function with the financial markets must, as it were, be symmetrically matched to the markets they intend to regulate. Domestic provisions lose their effectiveness with regard to market control to the extent that international inter-linking of economic systems and cross-border transactions are gaining in importance.

However, a coherent symmetry between market conditions and regulatory law has not yet become manifest.

As an example, we might refer to the wide field of application of e-commerce. Electronic business transactions are almost invariably concluded by means of communication that are not impeded in any way by national borders. Its international and transnational character is the very essence of modern behaviour with regard to offer and demand. Such 'denationalization' of economic events is somehow in contrast with private international law (PIL), which still stipulates that each of the acting parties have a domicile or seat, respectively, to be located in any given State; or, in the least, it provides for such a domicile or seat to be determinable under regulatory provisions. It is the helplessness shown in the realm of criminal liability and the execution of sentences that can hardly be overlooked where computer-assisted crime is concerned, which again is to be traced back to the dilemma existing between globalization and internationalization with regard to factual conditions and, on the other hand, domestic and regional legislation. This helplessness where e-commerce is concerned actually accounts for the existence of a regulatory no-man's land. These phenomena may be observed mutatis mutandis also in the realm of private law.

Regulation principles such as unilateral application of the law (unilateral conflict of laws provisions) or the effects principle, may, as we know, give rise to serious jurisdictional conflicts.

The ultimate goal to be achieved in the domain of international market control must therefore be the *co-ordination* of competencies and the supervising instruments. In order to get closer to this aim, an analysis of prevailing mechanisms and an appreciation of international commercial law (as conflicts of law) are indispensable.

II. Conflicts of Law in the Area of Market Regulations

For many years – decades even – a controversy has surrounded the question of whether and to what extent *regulatory provisions*, in particular those relating to commercial law, are to be dealt with independently of 'classical' private international law (PIL). Some of the topics under discussion have been the dependency of provisions applicable to the facts, the special connection of qualified mandatory law, and the determination of the proper law designated by the conflict of laws rules. Meanwhile, related literature dealing – approvingly or disapprovingly – with independent methods of international commercial law as a body of conflict of laws rules has become immeasurable.[1] The controversy reached its peak in the 1990s when *Stefan Habermeier's*[2] monograph in the form of a pamphlet was published, a desperate and inappropriate attempt at denying – in the (alleged) light of critical rationalism – all independent effects of supervisory provisions as conflict of laws rules, insinuating that the authors advocating such effects have fallen victim to an untenable positivistic minimization of the controlling function of commercial law.

However, it has become quite obvious that supervisory provisions or commercial law of any kind whatsoever must, as conflict of laws rules, be given special treatment, especially since the present development of European private international law, in particular within the EU, inevitably calls for a qualified discussion on the statement of problems and related methods to be implemented. What (still) remains to be settled are the system and particulars of the road network yet to be built, both European and worldwide.

The independent nature of problems to be dealt with within the realm of commercial conflict of laws rules and the necessary search for special rules of application becomes ever more manifest in the area of transnational *takeovers,*[3] for instance.

Just as in the event of a domestic takeover of a company various legal domains are involved, a transnational takeover involves a great number of

---

1 For the conceptual classification, see, among others, *A. K. Schnyder*, 'Internationales Wirtschaftsrecht – zu Begriff und Phänomenologie', in: Th. Baums/K.J. Hopt/ N. Horn (eds), Liber Amicorum Richard M. Buxbaum, 2000, pages 515 et seq.

2 'Neue Wege zum Wirtschaftskollisionsrecht', habilitation thesis, Saarbrücken, Baden-Baden 1997.

3 *A.K. Schnyder*, Takeovers and the Conflict of Law, in: G. Ferrarini (ed.), Capital Markets in the Age of the Euro, 2002, 427 et seq.

sources of law that have to be taken into account simultaneously. Public law rules and criminal law provisions may have to be applied in addition to rules of private international law and international procedural law, eventually leading to the application of substantive civil law. Legal provisions applicable in any particular case are, as a rule, assigned to domestic law. A cross-border, truly international substantive law or conflict of laws rules and/or procedural rules that would settle transnational takeovers, either do not exist at all or – within the territory of the European Union – exist only in a rudimentary form.

Whoever means to take over a non-domestic company must allow for subsequent difficulties arising when considering related legal aspects of the transaction. An answer must be found to the question of which State might assert its competence to deal with one or more aspects of the case and which substantive law provisions would consequently become applicable. If the company operating a takeover fails to do so, it is in danger of being sanctioned in one way or another by any of the legal orders involved. A highly complex conglomerate of provisions must therefore be penetrated, a task that is rendered even more difficult by an interpretation of rules of law that in many cases leaves some doubts. This legal situation is far from being satisfactory, in particular if one bears in mind the need for certainty from the law.

The legislators and authorities called upon to apply the law should be aware of these difficulties: the former when they are about to put the tenor of domestic law into words and upon entering into negotiations aiming at the conclusion of bilateral agreements with other States, and the latter when they are actually concerned with an international takeover. In these cases, to avoid making decisions that cannot (in the end) be enforced, or ordering measures to be taken that prove impracticable for the persons concerned, it is indispensable that national authorities always be aware that foreign laws may also become involved.

As will be shown below, questions arising from conflict of laws provisions in the matter of regulation may be dealt with in the light of the following supranational or national competencies:

- jurisdiction to adjudicate
- jurisdiction to prescribe
- jurisdiction to co-operate (to enforce).

III. Jurisdiction to Adjudicate

International jurisdiction to adjudicate is concerned with the designation of authorities – such as law courts, administrative bodies, and others – that have competence to carry through (supervisory) commercial law proceedings and to order acts of enforcement if this should prove necessary.

Swissair, an example drawn from recent events, may serve to illustrate: Which aeronautical authority shall have jurisdiction to order supervisory acts and determine the nature of such acts? What are the competencies to be exercised by the States as supervisory bodies and what competencies are to be exercised by the company's organs? Where are the dividing lines and what conflicts may arise with regard to jurisdiction where the need for regulation and 'private' commercial law rules clash?

From doctrine on jurisdiction under public international law there is not very much to be derived in the way of bearings to be taken and restrictions to be imposed on the *extraterritorial enforcement* of commercial (supervisory) law of any State. Furthermore, the classical connecting elements (territorial or personal) appear more and more accidental on account of the interdependence of national economies and the increasing mobility of the respective actors. Homogenous factual situations are often linked with several countries and can no longer be grasped exclusively by means of the classical connecting factors provided for by private international law.

The basis of jurisdiction enabling authorities to act is the *market connection*, which must be defined more precisely for each domain of regulation. Such definition is provided (increasingly) by explicit ordinances dealing with the matter.[4] It should not, however, be overlooked that the competen-

4 Regarding financial market supervision, reference is made to Art. 49 et seq. of Council Directive 85/611 EEC of 20 December 1985 on the co-ordination of laws, regulations, and administrative provisions relating to undertakings for collective investment in transferable securities (UCITS). It is incumbent on the supervisory authorities of the seat State to exercise control of the business activities of the UCITS in the whole of the EU territory. There is but one exception to this rule, i.e., the territory of distribution, where the principle of control being exercised by the seat State does not apply, so that the supervision of distribution activities is incumbent on the supervising authorities of the State where the UCITS distributes its shares. Type and extent of measures to be taken by the competent supervising authority are determined by domestic law. See also Art. 26 of the Directive 2000/12/EC of the European Parliament and the Council of 20 March 2000, relating to the taking up and pursuit of the business of credit institutions: 'The prudential supervision of a credit institution (...) shall be the responsibility of the competent authorities of the home Member State

cont. ...

cies to decide (on which we shall expand later) are still dependent to a large extent on the applicability and admissibility of application or provided for by the *lex fori*, i.e., by substantive law.

Connecting factors include the following: seat of a company; establishment/branch establishment; any other form of 'doing business' (including solicitation across national borders); place of the stock exchange; place of business; place of dispatch; place of processing; or, for example, the mobility of possible connecting factors – such as the transfer of a company's domicile or a supplier's change of location (such as the provider of services) – constituting an increasing challenge to their determination.

Markets are supranational/global and sometimes overlapping, thus giving rise, among other things, to the phenomenon of *competing jurisdiction*. The resulting conflicts of jurisdiction can be either positive or negative. Commercial enterprises find themselves confronted with a variety of competencies exercised by several authorities cumulatively.

The (increasing) probability of multiple jurisdiction calls for a more thorough co-ordination of competencies. Such *co-ordination* has to be implemented in the first place meta-legally, for instance, (as within the EC) by way of an allocation of competencies based on the distinction between the supervisory authority of the country of domicile on the one hand and that of the country where the business activity is performed on the other.[5] To

(...).' 'Host Member States shall retain responsibility in cooperation with the competent authorities of the home Member State for the supervision of the liquidity of the branches of credit institutions pending further coordination'; (Art. 27 Directive 2000/12/EC).

5 See, for instance, Art. 9 of Council Directive 92/49/EEC of 18 June 1992 on the coordination of laws, regulations, and administrative provisions relating to direct insurance other than life assurance and amending Directives 73/239/EEC and 88/357/EEC (third non-life insurance Directive): The financial supervision of an insurance undertaking, including that of the business it carries on either through branches or under the freedom to provide services, shall be the sole responsibility of the home Member State (See also Art. 15 Second Council Directive 89/646/EEC of 15 December 1989 on the coordination of laws, regulations and administrative provisions relating to the taking up and pursuit of the business of credit institutions and amending Directive 77/780/EEC and Art. 24 Council Directive 93/22/EEC of 10 May 1993 on investment services in the securities field). By the introduction of the principle of supervision exercised by the country of origin, a uniform competence regulation applying to all EU Member States has been created. This principle ensures that every enterprise acting within the EU internal market is subject to the control of its country of origin. By a control exercised by the country of origin, gaps or overlapping in the

cont. ...

renounce jurisdiction altogether cannot (in any event, not as a general principle) be accepted as a goal. The aim should be the co-ordination of the various claims to regulation, which, viewed from the perspective of market law, are necessarily extra-territorial in their orientation.

Cumulative jurisdiction (without any actual co-ordination) entails serious consequences for the parties called upon to act. They are bound to measure the whole of their activities against the rules imposed by the most stringent supervisory regime.[6] This may lead to further consequences as 'competition of legal systems' encourages a (general) decrease of the density of regulation.

IV. Jurisdiction to Prescribe

A. In General

Under regulation conditions, the conflict of laws regime often follows the jurisdiction of the authority concerned: concurrence of *forum* and *ius*. In many cases, authorities have jurisdiction only (but at least) where the *lex fori* supervisory rules are meant to apply. Here again prevailing connecting factors are those derived from the market.

As a more recent example, we cite the order made by the Takeover Division of the Federal Banking Commission (EBK) of 30 September 1999, in the matter LVMH Moët Hennessy Louis Vuitton/TAG Heuer International SA:[7]

TAG Heuer International SA is a company incorporated under the law of Luxembourg with a registered office in Luxembourg. TAG Heuer International SA is quoted at the Swiss Stock Exchange through its 100% daugh-

---

exercise of supervision may be avoided altogether as there can be no doubt as to the competence of the authority called upon to exercise control.

6 This constellation makes itself felt most clearly in cases of *cross-border mergers*. Due to sales achieved and shares held both at home and abroad, mergers become increasingly liable to control under the jurisdiction of several countries. This will, as may be gathered from the cases Honeywell/General Electric and Boeing/McDonnell Douglas, result in internationally diverging decisions or obligations producing duplicate effects. In the first case, the EU Commission prohibited the merger altogether, whereas the U.S. Federal Trade Commission approved of it without more ado. In the second case, where the U.S. authority did not put forth any objection either, the EU Commission made its approval dependent on stringent conditions.

7 See CFB-EBK-BULL (Bulletin of the Federal Banking Commission) 39, 27 et seq.

ter TAG/Heuer SA with a seat in Marin. It ranks among the leading designers, producers, and distributors of top-of-the-line Swiss sports watches and chronographs marketed under the trade name of 'Tag Heuer'.

On 21 September 1999, the Federal Takeover Board issued a recommendation within the scope of the takeover bid made by LVMH Moët Hennessy Louis Vuitton, stating that due to the foreign registered office, TAG Heuer International SA was not subject to Swiss takeover rules. Furthermore, the offering party had renounced the opportunity of filing an application for voluntary submission.

The Federal Banking Commission was informed of the tenor of the recommendation made by the Takeover Board pursuant to pertinent rules of procedure on 23 September 1999. On 30 September 1999, the Takeover Division of the Federal Banking Commission made an order stating that it would decide the issue itself and that the recommendation by the Board of 21 September 1999, was to be replaced by the following regulation: the takeover bid made by LVMH Moët Hennessy Louis Vuitton is subject to the Stock Exchange Act so that publication and handling of the offer shall be subject to such stock exchange rules as govern public purchasing offers.

The central statements of this decision are:

1. A company whose shares are quoted in Switzerland and which has its registered office abroad but whose factual administration is located exclusively in Switzerland with resident staff, and whose operative activities are likewise directed predominantly in and from Switzerland with the decisive decisions being taken in Switzerland, is subject to the Swiss Stock Exchange Act.
2. The decisive element is not the legal construction (incorporation) but rather the place where business activities are actually undertaken. In the realm of the law governing the supervision of financial services markets, the local connection, that is the place where the registered office is actually located, constitutes the decisive criterion.
3. In the event of a takeover bid being submitted, the rules governing takeovers of the Stock Exchange Act shall apply. Thus, the publication and handling of the offer shall be done in accordance with the rules governing public offers provided for by the Stock Exchange Act.

A comprehensive application of *foreign* supervisory law by domestic authorities – after the manner of the universal rules of private international law – will hardly ever occur. However, there is a marked tendency to also 'take into account' foreign rules in the event of

– co-ordinated supervision

– 'renunciation' of supervision, provided foreign authorities ensure equivalent control (either autonomous or prescribed by a higher organ).

As an example, see the recommendation given by the Swiss Takeover Board of 20 March 2001, in the matter of *De Beers Centenary Linked Units*. We cite from the factual statements:[8]

The De Beers Centenary AG (DBC-AG) is a stock corporation with seat in Lucerne. Its share capital amounts to Sfrs 901,495,200.--, divided in 4,507,476 registered shares with a par value of Sfrs 200.--.

The De Beers Consolidated Mines Ltd. (DBCM) with registered office in South Africa was founded in 1888. It is concerned mostly with the extraction of raw diamonds, their processing and marketing, as well as the production and distribution of synthetic diamonds. In the year 1990 the De Beers group changed its structure. Shares held in other companies abroad and spheres of business located outside South Africa were brought into the newly founded DBC-AG. Centenary Holdings, the company with registered office in Luxembourg, which at that time already managed shares held by the De Beers group outside the Republic of South Africa, became in the following a 100% daughter of DBC-AG, whereas all shares held and activities undertaken within South Africa remained with DBCM as before.

In the course of the restructuring, the De Beers group decided to create a new type of negotiable instruments. Thus, all the shares of DBC-AG and all the profit-sharing certificates of Centenary Holdings were taken over by Century Depository AG (CD-AG), another 100% daughter of DBC-AG. One share each of DBC-AG and one profit-sharing certificate of Centenary Holding were merged into a 'Centenary Unit'. CD-AG on its part issued 'Centenary Depository Receipts' (CDR), each one of them representing the hundredth part of the rights arising from a Centenary Unit. These CDR were then combined with the ordinary shares of DBCM so as to form the 'De Beers Centenary Linked Units' (Linked Units) and can henceforth be assigned to a third party only together with the latter. These Linked Units were quoted in the Stock Exchange of Johannesburg, London, Frankfurt, Paris, and Brussels, as well as at the then existing Stock Exchange in Switzerland, i.e., Zurich, Basel, Geneva, and Lausanne. Registered shares that had been negotiated before the restructuring of the Swiss Stock Exchange as so-called Swiss Certificates and the DBCM bearers shares were exchanged, at the rate of one to one, for Linked Units.

---

8 see <www.takeover.ch/transactions/mo_offers/mo_debeers/mo_debeers.html>.

DBC-AG and DBCM requested by letter dated 9 February 2001, that the Takeover Board make it clear, in view of the forthcoming takeover of De Beers by a South African syndicate of companies, that De Beers Centenary Linked Units negotiated in Switzerland be not subject to the provisions governing public purchasing offers pursuant to section 5 of the Stock Exchange Act.

Quotations from the decision rendered by the Takeover Board.

De Beers Centenary Linked Units shall be exempt from the application of the provisions on public purchasing offers of the Swiss Stock Exchange Act *under the following conditions:*

a) A confirmation is handed over to the Takeover Board at the beginning of the tender offer, wherein the South African supervisory authorities declare that they will use their competence to handle takeover proceedings.
b) The South African takeover bid must apply to the whole of Switzerland. To this end, related information shall be published both in German and in French in two or more daily papers and shall also be made available to one of the electronic media undertakings of primary importance concerned with the circulation of stock exchange information.
c) The result of the takeover bid shall be published in those media where the tender offer had previously been made.

Foreign and domestic *rules determining the governing law* may be described as commercial law/commercial conflict of laws rules in the narrow sense of the term, or within the meaning of private international law. In a case with international connections, such rules determine the applicable law destined to govern claims under private (commercial) law arising from economic transactions. Although said conflict of laws rules reveal their likeness to the classical private international law, they still remain very often – bearing in mind a country's domestic interests – 'unilateral' in their tenor. However, as may be gathered – for instance, from Art. 156 of the Swiss Private International Law Statute (conflict of laws rule dealing with claims arising from prospectus liability) – an extension of connections in every possible direction appears to be feasible.

B. Special Connection of Mandatory Market Supervision Law

The *more open* connecting systems become regarding rules determining the governing law in the matter of regulation, the more topical becomes the complex problem of *special connections*, which, by departing from the regular connections, reserve the application of (qualified) 'mandatory', particularly domestic, law. In this respect, the discussion on conflict of laws rules determining the governing law has become quite explicit with regard to consumer law, employment protection law, insurance law, and in other 'sensitive' domains.

1. Object of the Special Connection

Special connection means 'separate' application of *supervision law,* undertaken in accordance with special regulation principles, to cross-border facts. The resulting methodical independence makes itself felt particularly when measured against traditional private international law and in the application of private law.

The special connection does not, however, presuppose that the question of the applicability of such substantive law provisions be dealt with – as a *partial question* – at the moment of the enforcement of penal or private law. Rather, the special connection may also arise as the so-called *principal question* where jurisdiction regarding supervisory law provisions in commercial matters is solely concerned. This is the case, for instance, when authorities supervising competition are called upon to decide on the admissibility of a merger or distribution system. Civil courts – either in ordinary proceedings or by way of an interlocutory order – may also be concerned with a principal question arising from commercial conflict of laws rules. What must invariably be determined are cross-border implications and the application of domestic and foreign supervisory provisions in the event of factual circumstances that – looked at from the perspective of the application of the law – do not relate to one legal system only.

Therefore, this is the question to be answered: What provisions shall apply in the event of a multiple connection? There can be no abstract or general answer to this question. Bearing in mind related rulings of the European Court of Justice, the relevant provisions are those meant to control the behaviour of actors engaged in economic activities and to exercise some influence upon any other commercial transactions. After all, it appears to be of merely secondary importance whether related regulations are described as 'interference provisions', 'qualified imperative law', or in any other way. Even the specific orientation of such provisions deemed suitable for connection may vary just like the kind of interests they are intended to serve. It may therefore be said that regulations that are intended to serve above all (or even exclusively?) the purpose of balancing private interests may also become suited for special connection. In any given particular case, it is decisive to know whether, and to what extent, a provision shall be taken into account, independently of any other *lex causae*. The answer to this must be derived from any explicit or 'hidden' connection reference that is at the root of the substantive law provision concerned.

The recent ruling of the European Court of Justice of 9 November 2000, in the matter of Ingmar/Eaton Leonard Technologies constitutes a vivid example of the problems that are dealt with here.[9] According to this decision, protective Community law provisions granting the commercial agent certain claims on the termination of his contract, shall apply even if the commercial agent has exercised his activities in a Member State, whereas the employer has his registered office in a third country and the parties have made a choice of law whereby the contract is governed by the law of that third country. The imperative protective law therefore must, *if need be*, be taken account of independently of the proper law of the contract. According to the European Court of Justice, these provisions must prevail, in particular with a view to ensuring protection of both freedom of establishment and undistorted competition within the internal market by way of the group of commercial agents (consideration 24). In its consideration 25, the Court states literally: 'It therefore is of fundamental importance for Community law that an employer whose registered office is in a third country, but whose commercial agent is active within the Community, should not be in a position to evade such provisions simply by resorting to a choice of law, as the purpose aimed at by said provisions is their application irrespective of the law the parties intended to govern the contract, provided the facts of the case reveal a close Community connection, such as the commercial agent's activity within the territory of a Member State.'

2. Connection Standards

a) *Lex Fori* Determined by Supervisory Law

With respect to 'qualified' mandatory provisions of domestic law, it is to be determined both under the aspect of the principal and the partial question (particularly within the scope of the application of private law) whether the provision concerned shall be enforced across borders. The answer to this

---

9 Rs. C-381/98, see. IPRax 2001, 225.

question is dependent in particular on the nature of domestic and foreign connections of the case, and to what extent protection purpose and the interest in the application of a domestic substantive law provision calls for the provision concerned to be enforced abroad in any particular case. Such legally uncontested examination of the special connection shall be undertaken in particular where the domestic regulation clashes with foreign provisions, and where the *lex causae* determined by private international law is not to be applied according to the domestic legal system as well. The procedure to be followed in a case like this has been enlarged upon by the European Court of Justice in its *Ingmar* decision mentioned above. From this case, however, there is nothing really new to be gathered and proclaimed as a dogma relating to special connection, although the aspect of the legally relevant connection, i.e., the determination of a domestic interest in the enforcement of a provision and the application order arising therefrom, has clearly been established and designated as European supervisory law ranking as an autonomous reservation clause when the special connection is established. However, this emanation is not new either. Domestic supervisory law of any EU member state is enlarged in such a way as to encompass the provisions of Community law.

b) Foreign Supervisory Law

Taking account of foreign mandatory law within the meaning of a *primary connection* when establishing a special connection, mirrors, as it were, the problems outlined above. In the light of the rulings given by the European Court of Justice we have referred to, it is of no consequence for the subject under discussion whether it is a domestic or a foreign supervisory provision that gives rise to considerations as to the establishment of a special connection. A foreign provision (of a Member State) that demands to be observed is suited for application if its intended purpose is identical to that aimed at by domestic law. These principles apply – *mutatis mutandis* – also to the observance of supervisory provisions of *third countries*.

A closer look into the more recent rulings given by the European Court of Justice on the application of mandatory law reveals, on the whole, that they may be inserted without any difficulty, or emphatically, in previous endeavours to devise independent special connections in the realm of economic conflict of laws provisions. A closer look into the matter even makes it clear that more detail work is quite unavoidable with a view to finding a *rule of reason* to be applied to *economic conflict of laws provisions*, taking account in particular its impact on European Community Law.

V. Jurisdiction to Co-operate

Territorial economic supervision leads to a regulatory deficiency where factual circumstances show international implications. Increased economic globalization translates into a growing dysfunction of supervision exercised by individual States. Therefore, international supervision imposes itself as a matter of paramount importance in international co-operation through international supervisory bodies, whose recommendations and guidelines relating to global supervision are capable of exercising considerable influence upon national legislators.[10]

Co-operation of supervisory authorities toward achieving a concerted jurisdiction to enforce results in a *conflict* between the need to observe constitutional protective principles and the demand for effectiveness, a conflict that is most conspicuous in the domain of data protection, money laundering, or internal transactions and combinations operated by commercial enterprises, to name but a few.

Thus, the question invariably arises, with regard to the *principle of legality*, if, to what extent, and to what purpose an authority is entitled to pass on to a foreign authority any knowledge it has gained in an official capacity. As an example, reference is made to Art. 38 par.2 of the Federal Stock Exchange Act providing for the Federal Banking Commission to make available, under certain circumstances, information and pertinent documents that are not accessible to the public. The authorities supplied with such information and documents must be 'supervising authorities controlling stock exchange traders and dealers in securities' who are bound to use the information exclusively for the direct control of the Stock Exchange and securities trading (Art. 38 par. 2, lit. a; 'speciality principle' and are also bound to official and professional secrecy (Art. 38 par.2 lit. b of the Stock Exchange Act). Information may be made available only after the prior consent given by the Federal Supervising Authority or within the scope of a general authorization based on a State Treaty to competent authorities and organs entrusted with supervising activities in the public interest ('Long-Hand Principle'). Information must not be made available to criminal prosecution authorities where judicial assistance in criminal matters would not be granted. The matter is decided on by the supervisory authority in mutual agreement with the Federal Office for Justice. Insofar as the information to

---

[10] Examples: Basler Ausschuss für Bankenaufsicht; International Organization of Securities Commissions; Joint Forum on Financial Conglomerates.

be made available concerns individual clients of securities dealers ('client-related information') the Federal Law on Administrative Procedure shall apply. No information on persons that are obviously not involved in the matter under investigation shall be made available (Art. 38, par. 3 of the Act: 'not involved third parties').

Legal instruments relating to co-operation, as well as jurisdiction and endowment of supervisory authorities, must be improved with a lasting effect. Measures to be taken to this end comprise the development and implementation of early warning systems, a code for the behaviour of authorities, and the creation of competencies in the domain of rehabilitation. What is to be avoided, however, are inefficient bureaucracies.

DEREGULATION IN THE FIELD OF SECURITIES LAW AND PRIVATE INTERNATIONAL LAW FROM A JAPANESE PERSPECTIVE

– The Extraterritorial Applicability of the Japanese Securities and Exchange Law and its Restriction –

by Toshiyuki Kono, Fukuoka

I. Deregulation and its Effect: Competition among Markets

After the bursting of the stock market and real estate bubbles in Japan in the early 1990s, it was discovered that many legal and regulatory systems for the

J. Basedow, H. Baum, K. Hopt, H. Kanda and T. Kono (eds.), Economic Regulation and Competition, (287-302)

financial industry were not adequate.[1] Therefore, in 1996 the so-called 'Big Bang' project to reform the financial system with drastic deregulation and regulatory restructuring was commenced. According to the original schedule, the year 2001 was to be the last year of the Big Bang project. In this context, the Securities and Exchange Law (SEL)[2] was vastly amended.[3] Several important measures taken in this framework are as follows: The firewall between the banking sector and the securities sector was removed, so that banks can now do securities-related business through establishing subsidiaries.[4] Permission of the authority is no longer required to commence securities transaction business. Only registration suffices.[5] The requirements for foreign institutions to start business were also relaxed.[6]

The 'playing field' was also enlarged. Securities companies can offer more services than before, such as investment consultation, or futures, commodities, or derivatives trading.[7] The statute of the Tokyo Stock Exchange (TSE) was amended, so that now transactions of the listed stocks can be made outside of the stock exchange, although customers must clearly state that they want this particular type of trade.[8]

---

1 For example, there was no proper legal instrument for insolvent banks or insurance, while creating a pure holding company was prohibited.

2 Shôken torihiki-hô, Law No. 25/1948, last amended by Law No. 134/2001.

3 See *Hideki Kanda*, Globalization of Financial Markets: Law and Regulation from a Japanese Perspective, in: Kitagawa et al. (eds), Das Recht vor der Herausforderung eines neuen Jahrhunderts (1996); *Harald Baum*, Struktureller Wandel der Finanzmärkte und regulatorische Herausforderungen – Deutschland und Japan: (1997) 4 Zeitschrift für Japanisches Recht 3-8; *Hideki Kanda*, Globalization of Financial Markets and Financial Regulation in Japan: (1997) 4 Zeitschrift für Japanisches Recht 9-17; *Harald Baum*, Modernisierung des japanischen Kapitalmarktrechts: (1998) 5 Zeitschrift für Japanisches Recht 19-30.

4 However, it should be pointed out that banks and other financial institutions are not yet allowed to operate securities-related businesses by themselves (Artt. 65, 65-3 SEL).

5 Art. 28 SEL.

6 Before the reform, foreign securities companies had to obtain permission for each branch. Under the new Art. 3 of the Law on Foreign Securities Companies (Gaikoku shôken gyôsha ni kansuru hôritsu, Law no. 5/1971, last amended by Law no. 129/2001), when the business is registered at the main branch in Japan, nothing is required for doing business at the other branches in Japan.

7 Art. 34 SEL.

8 Art. 37 SEL. About the practice of this type of transactions, see *Satoshi Takahashi*, Torihiki shôgai torihiki wo meguru saikin no ugoki ni tsuite [Recent Trend of Securities Transactions Outside the Exchanges]: (2001) 6 Shôken [Securities] 7-23.

While exchanges in different regions can merge,[9] several exchanges can be established in one region.[10] Foreign securities companies can also establish exchanges.[11] An exchange can open several markets.[12] Before the year 2000, only the markets established by the exchanges were considered as the 'securities market' under the SEL. Therefore, the over-the-counter market operated by the Japanese Association of Securities Companies was not an 'exchange' under the SEL. But now this is also classified as a competing 'securities market' under the SEL.[13] Even the demutualization of exchanges is allowed,[14] which would strengthen the competition among the exchanges. The operation of a PTS (proprietary trading system) is now possible as a type of securities-related business[15] that has very similar functions to those of stock exchanges.

As a whole, we now have different types of exchanges and securities markets competing with each other[16] and involving more brokers and investors.

Just as the 'market fragmentation' caused by inter-market competitions has been a big concern shared by market participants in the United States,[17]

---

9 Art. 136 SEL. The Hiroshima Stock Exchange and the Niigata Stock Exchange were merged with the Tokyo Stock Exchange.

10 The reformed Art. 82 SEL no longer mentions the number of exchanges in one region. This means that establishing several exchanges has become possible.

11 Art. 80 SEL.

12 Art. 81 SEL, which allowed an exchange to open only one market, was deleted.

13 Art. 67 SEL. The types of traded stocks in the over-the-counter market are still different from those in exchanges.

14 The Tokyo Stock exchange was demutualized and transformed into a public corporation as of 1 November 2001. For a critical comment on this demutualization, see *Sadakazu Osaki*, Shijô-kan kyôsô to shôken torihikisho no arikata [Competitions among Capital Markets and Security Exchanges]: (2000) Shihon Shijô Quarterly [Capital Market Quarterly], autumn issue, 2-11. Also see *Johannes Köndgen*, Ownership and Corporate Governance of Stock Exchanges: (1998) 154 Journal of Institutional Theoretical Economics 224-249. Cf. *Horst Hermann*, Börsenorganisationsrecht im Wandel: (2001) AG 549-567.

15 Art. 2, no. 7. See *Sadakazu Osaki*, Wagakuni no atarashii PTS Kisei [The New PTS Regulation in Japan]: (2001) Shihon Shijô Quarterly [Capital Market Quarterly], winter issue, 66-75.

16 On the competition among the securities markets on an international scale and in Japan, see *Sadakazu Osaki*, Kabushiki shijô-kan sensô [Wars among the Securities Markets] (2000); *Sadakazu Osaki*, Honkaku-ka suru wagakuni no kabushiki shijô kyôsô [Severe Competition among Capital Markets in Japan]: (2000) Shihon Shijô Quarterly [Capital Market Quarterly], winter issue, 10-22.

it may also occur in Japan through this competition among the securities markets. However, it is clear that the competition will bring many advantages to investors: brokers will offer more reasonable conditions for securities transactions, and investors can choose a market that is more suitable to their investment purposes. The deregulation and the resulting competition definitely make the securities markets attractive.

II. The Effect of Globalization for Investors

If a deregulated market is not attractive enough, some investors will seek other markets to invest in. Until we can establish a global exchange,[18] the most effective forum for this purpose would be the 24-hour trading system.

The 24-hour trading system is feasible in the following cases:

- a broker has establishments worldwide and deals with 24-hour trading, or
- by transactions at exchanges,
  (1) when the same stocks are listed in several exchanges in different continents and these exchanges have common members, or
  (2) when an exchange is open 24 hours, all major stocks are listed in this exchange, and many foreign securities companies are members of this exchange.

Twenty-four-hour trading through exchanges will become easier. Because of the demutualization of the major exchanges in the world, the exchange is losing its character as a closed-member society; as a result, it will be less difficult for securities companies to obtain trading licenses in different countries. This is a typical phenomenon of globalization. Investors can

---

17 Market fragmentation has been defined as the inability of an order in one market to interact with an order in a competing market. An example is the phenomenon that, through the diversification of securities transactions to many markets, even important information for pricing is not shared by all market participants. Investors then could not know which market would be the most advantageous for their transactions. On the situation in the U.S., see *Sadakazu Osaki*, Shin-kyokumen wo mukaeru beikoku no kabushiki shijô-kan kyôsô [New Aspects of the Competition among Securities Markets in the U.S.]: (2000) Shihon Shijô Quarterly, spring issue, 24-42. Cf. *Yakov Amihud/Haim Mendelson*, A New Approach to the Regulation of Trading Across Securities Markets: (1996) 71 N.Y.U. L. Rev. 1411, at 1434-1435.

18 *John Moon*, The Dangerous Territoriality of American Securities Law: A Proposal for an Integrated Global Market: (2000) 21 J.Intl.L.Bus. 131, at 182-187.

pursue the most effective methods of investment. Those who benefit most from such a globalized capital market are the institutional investors, since they have enough human and financial resources for this purpose. They are like top tennis players who travel worldwide, at the French Open this month and at Wimbledon next month. For such investors, strong regulation for securities transactions is unnecessary. They can choose effective ways to invest and protect themselves. The issuer can also count the investors as 'top players'; therefore, for example, the issuer would not need to care if the disclosure were sufficient or not. If the institutional investors think that the disclosure is sufficient, they will invest. If not, nothing from this issuer will be purchased. In this context, the SEL, which aims at the protection of investors (Art. 1), could be less useful for the institutional investors concerned.[19] An ambitious proposal, the portable reciprocity approach,[20] seems more suitable to the institutional investors. According to this theory, the market participants are allowed to choose the most appropriate regulatory regime for themselves. Any combination of issuer nationality, investor nationality, regime choice, and transaction location is deemed permissible under that concept. Under this scheme, for example, a Japanese company may issue its shares at the New York Stock Exchange following the German disclosure rule. As a consequence, the regulatory regime 'travels' with the securities it issues.[21] Since the players here are well informed and equipped, they can make this choice at their own risk. This theory seems to me a variation of the party autonomy rule in the private international law.

However, we should not forget that we also have individual investors, without whose participation the securities market could not exist.[22] The securities business has benefited the most from the development of the Internet.[23,24] It opened possibilities to individual investors to access information that was not available before, and to trade with new brokers/dealers in their own country or another part of the world around the clock, an activity that

19 See *Hideki Kanda*, in Kitagawa et al (eds), supra note 3 at 259.

20 *Stephan Choi/Andrew Gutzman*, Portable Reciprocity: Rethinking the International Reach of Securities Regulation: (1998) 71 S. Cal. L. Rev. 903, at 942-951.

21 Id. at 922.

22 The absence of individual investors is one of the important reasons for the current situation at the Tokyo Stock Exchange.

23 See IOSCO Report on Securities Activity on Internet II in 2001, pp. 8-15. This report is available at <www.iosco.org/>.

24 *Sadakazu Osaki*, Internet Finance (in Japanese)(1997); cf., Internet Securities Transactions (in Japanese)(2000).

was previously only feasible for institutional investors. As individual investors expand their investment activities, what should be the role of regulation?

III. The SEL: Its Enforcement, Applicability, and Territoriality

A. The Enforcement of the SEL

The aims of the SEL, as mentioned above, are the protection of investors and also, as its means, maintaining the appropriate function of the market through various regulations.

To enforce the regulations, there are three instruments available: (1) criminal punishment, (2) administrative measures, and (3) recovery of damage. They are designed to be effective mainly in purely domestic cases: the criminal punishment and administrative measures have effect only within the scope of the sovereign power of Japan. Recovery of damages could be ordered in Japan if its jurisdiction could be confirmed, but this judgment would have effect only when it could be recognized and enforced in a country where the defendant has assets. In other words, these measures to implement the regulations by the SEL, if applicable to foreign issuers or securities companies, function effectively only in cases where they hold some enforceable assets in Japan and will continue to carry on business in Japan.

B. The Applicability of the SEL: The Territoriality and the Extraterritoriality

The applicability of the SEL must be examined separately from its enforceability, since it may have a de facto effect on foreign transactions regardless of its enforceability.

The prevailing opinion was that the SEL was not internationally applicable.[25] However, the Japanese Financial Services Agency (JFSA) took the so-called target approach to cross-border securities transactions through the

[25] See *Misao Tatsuta*, Shoken torihiki-hô no ikigai tekiyô [Extraterritorial Applicability of the SEL]: (1993) 2 International Economic Law (Yearbook of the Japanese Association of International Economic Law) 23-39, at 24. Tatsuta himself takes a different approach: he examines individual types of regulations in the SEL and interprets some regulations as exterritorially applicable, such as Art. 159 SEL.

Internet.[26] In December 2000, the Japanese Financial Services Agency (cited below as 'the Agency') issued a guideline concerning the Law on Foreign Securities Companies.[27] According to Art. 3 of this law, a foreign securities company that was incorporated in a foreign country and does securities-related business in a foreign country is not allowed to do securities transactions with parties residing in Japan, unless the company registers and establishes its Japanese branch as the base of its business in Japan. On the other hand, a company without a registered base in Japan is allowed to do securities transactions with parties residing in Japan when the company receives orders from the parties, as long as the company did not solicit the transactions.[28] The Agency considers uploading advertisements or information on securities transactions as 'solicitation'. However, the Agency makes an exception 1) if a disclaimer is made that investors in Japan are not targeted for their services,[29] and 2) if measures to prevent transactions with investors in Japan are taken.[30] If no reasonable measure is taken, the foreign securities company must prove that no transaction with an invitation has taken place. Thus the Agency has taken the target approach supported by IOSCO in its 1998 Report on Securities Activity on the Internet.[31] This Anglo-American approach[32] premises the territoriality of the law and its

---

26 Great Britain, Canada, Germany, and Australia take the same approach. *John Moon*, supra note 18 at 175.

27 <www.fsa.go.jp/news/newse.html>, December 2000.

28 Art. 2 of the Ordinance to Implement the Law on Foreign Securities Companies (Gaikoku shôken gyôsha ni kansuru hôritsu shikô-rei, ordinance no. 267/1971, last amended by ordinance no. 4/2001).

29 This is understood to be so when no extra operation is necessary to read the disclaimer and the disclaimer is written in a language which investors in Japan could reasonable understand.

30 This is considered to be so when an investor supplies the place of residence by producing postal address, e-mail address, method of payment, etc., and the company pays attention to not accepting those orders from investors who apparently reside in Japan and not inviting investors in Japan to securities transactions. If the company were to open a call-center in Japan or hypertext linked to the portal sites targeted at Japanese residents, appropriate attention would not be being paid.

31 <www.iosco.org/iosco.html>, public documents, 83.

32 Use of Internet Websites to Offer Securities, Solicit Securities Transactions, or Adverse Investment Services Offshore, *SEC*, Release No. 33-7516, 34-39779, IA-1710, IC-23071, International Series Release No. 1125 (23 March 1998); Treatment of material on overseas internet world wide websites accessible in the UK but not intended for investors in the UK, *FSA*, Guidance Release 2/98 (28 May 1998); Art. 21 of the Financial Services and Markets Act 2000.

extraterritorial applicability. The latter was not the prevailing one among Japanese scholarly opinions. In other words, with this guideline, Japan made clear its intention to apply the SEL to activities carried out in other jurisdictions.

C. *How should Territoriality and Extraterritoriality be Evaluated?*

Here we have to evaluate the territoriality of the regulation by the SEL and its extraterritorial applicability. If we stick to strict territoriality, no conflict with other regulation would occur, but it may create a legal lacuna. It should be avoided.[33]

On the other hand, the extraterritorial application has been criticized.[34] Probably the most popular criticism is that extraterritoriality would cause conflicts of regulations and may close the market off to regulatory competition.[35] As a counterargument, the author who supports extraterritorial application claims that conflict of regulations is more acceptable than the race-to-the-bottom, which could be caused by the coordination of regulations in different jurisdictions.[36] The race-to-the-bottom may also be created by regulatory competition.[37]

The decisive points here are (1) whether or not the race-to-the-bottom would occur, and (2) if it occurs, what is the problem? For the first question, the authors say that only 'in a world in which all issuers and all investors are the same (meaning that all issuers present the same risk to investors and all investors have the same attitude toward risk), there can exist either a race-to-the-top or a race-to-the-bottom. Issuers and investors, however, are not all the same'.[38] But, as the same authors say, 'countries will find themselves unable to attract all types of issuers and investors.... In response, countries

33 *Misao Tatsuta*, supra note 25, at 35.

34 For example, *Harald Baum*, Globalizing Capital Markets and Possible Regulatory Responses, in: Jürgen Basedow/Toshikyuki Kono (eds), Legal Aspects of Globalization (2000), 79-132, especially at 90-93; *Stephan Choi/Andrew Gutzman*, The Dangerous Extraterritoriality of American Securities Law, (cited below as 'Dangerous'): (1996) 17 J.Int.L.Bus 207, at 220-229.

35 *Stephan Choi/Andrew Gutzman*, supra note 34, at 227.

36 *Misao Tatsuta*, supra note 25, at 35. Baum also says, 'Harmonization may only be possible on some kind of shared minimum standard', supra note 34, at 106.

37 See *Lucian Arye Bebchuk*, Federalism and the Corporation: The Desirable Limits on State Competition in Corporate Law: (1992) 105 Harv. L. Rev. 1435.

38 *Stephan Choi/Andrew Gutzman*, supra note 20 ('Portable'), at 917.

will target only a part of the overall market'.[39] Therefore, unless we abandon the entire regulatory system, and as long as more or less regulation should exist, we have to focus on a prototype of investors, and therefore the race-to-the-bottom may occur.

The race-to-the-bottom would be problematic because 'investors' could not be 'protected' enough through lowering the hurdle. Here we have to examine two things: the first is what the prototype of the investors is, and the other is what is meant by 'protection'. If the prototype of the investors here were the institutional investors, the race-to-the-bottom might be desirable, since the race would lower the hurdle of regulation and would create more freedom for them. Therefore, for the race-to-the-bottom to be considered problematic, the prototype here should be individual investors.

What then should be the 'protection' of the investors? According to Choi/Gutzman, who allow the market participants to choose their favorite regulatory regime, the protection of investors aims at ensuring that investors are able to understand and anticipate the legal regime that will apply to them when they invest.[40] Even if the investor suffers a loss, in their view, it is the nature of securities to be risky, and it is up to the investor to assess the risk prior to investing.[41] However, is this enough protection? This understanding of protection seems to be far from the usual concept of investor protection. Except for institutional investors who can understand the details of the regulation system of foreign countries, many individual investors engage in securities transactions without even knowing their own law.[42] In addition, not all countries have an abundant supply of specialized lawyers like the United States. We have to remember that the party autonomy rule in private international law, to which the portable reciprocity theory seems equivalent, premises the same type of person who can understand foreign legal systems. Therefore, the choice of law is allowed. However, since the applicable law chosen for some particular types of contract may harm the weaker party, we need to find a special applicable law, such as that for consumer protection or labor contract. If we have individual investors as the prototype of the inves-

39 *Stephan Choi/Andrew Gutman*, ibd.
40 *Stephan Choi/Andrew Gutzman*, supra note 34 ('Dangerous'), at 227.
41 *Stephan Choi/Andrew Gutzman*, ibd.
42 This can be the case not only on the investor side, but also on the trader side. According to the Agency, the people in charge at one of the penalized banks for the violating of short-selling rules did not know the basic rules. There was one person who had never read the SEL. Financial Times, 6 March 2002, at 19.

tors, we could not reply on such an understanding of protection.[43] An understanding of the foreign regulatory regime by the individual investors would never be achieved or remain as an assumption. Ensuring an understanding of the regulatory regime to which a transaction is subject is not enough protection.

In short, the prototype of the investors that the regulation should focus on is the individual investors. Therefore, to the extent that it is necessary for the protection of individual investors, the extraterritorial applicability of the regulation could be justified.[44]

D. *How can the SEL be Applied Extraterritorially?*

If this is so, when should the SEL be internationally applicable? The most famous test is the conduct test and the effect test in United States case law.[45] In Germany there are also a few opinions on the connecting point: the place of market[46] or the place of effect.[47,48]

The conduct test may easily lead to an exorbitant jurisdiction of the regulatory regime. We should therefore search for another way. In my view, the effect test (or the place of effect occurrence) and the place of market would often lead to the same result: the effect of actions made in a foreign country becomes influential in Japan, since Japan is the place in which the interests of all related parties are concentrated and weighed in the best form.[49] However, since we now have various 'markets', as we saw above, we

---

43 The risk the authors mention is not the same type of risk as the risk in the market caused by price ups and downs.

44 More than 250,000 individuals do securities transactions as so-called 'day-traders'. How to regulate the day-trader is a big issue in the United States. It seems to suggest that individual investors should be carefully and separately treated. See *Sadakazu Osaki*, Beikoku ni okeru day-trader kisei wo meguru ugoki [Trend on the Regulation of Day-Traders in the U.S.]: (1999) Shihon Shijô Quarterly, autumn issue, 30-41; also *Sadakazu Osaki*, Beikoku ni okeru kabushiki no kojin tôshika jikan-gai torihiki [After-Business-Hour-Trading for Individual Investors in the U.S.], ibd., at 42-48.

45 *Stephan Choi/Andrew Gutzman*, supra note 20 ('Portbale'), at 912.

46 For example, *Peter Kiel*, Internationales Kapitalanlegerschutzrecht (1994), 302-318.

47 *Uwe H. Schneider*, Internationales Kapitalmarktrecht: (2001) 6 AG 269-278, at 276.

48 Cf. *Daniel Zimmer*, Internationales Gesellschaftsrecht (1996), at 57, distinguishes according to the nature of regulation.

49 Therefore, the market should be protected first for the purpose of investor protection. *Misao Tatsuta*, supra note 25, takes the same opinion at 34.

cannot simply use the term 'market'. Probably we should focus on 'activities'.[50] In fact, it is not impossible to accept the activity-based connecting point in Japanese law: Japanese case law in the field of international jurisdiction employs the so-called 'special circumstances' test.[51] Although this test was originally introduced to make exceptions, it practically turns out to be the general rule on international jurisdiction. This test, therefore, has similar (or even greater[52]) flexibility to a 'doing business' test in United States case law. As a result, the important thing is how close the relationship between the case and Japan is. We may use it also in the case of the extraterritorial application of the SEL.

The target approach should also be evaluated from this point of view. The fact that simply setting up a Web page for solicitation to Japanese investors suffices to apply the SEL seems exorbitant. However, since the transaction in this case will be completed exclusively in cyberspace, the relationship between the action and Japan, which would justify the extension of the applicability of the SEL, could be less close than the relationship in the real world. From this point of view, setting up such a Web page is acceptable as the 'activity' that could justify the extraterritorial application. However, could the extraterritorial application be effective if the company has no substantive business in Japan? Due to the lack of an effective enforcement measure, the only measure to be taken could be to publicize the names of the companies that did not fulfill the requirement of registration on the homepage of the Agency. This seems to have been effective so far.[53]

If the SEL applies extraterritorially, it may cause conflicts of jurisdiction. In the framework of the above-mentioned 'special circumstances' test, some judgments refrained from exercising jurisdiction.[54] If several authorities will simultaneously exercise jurisdiction over the same actions, depending upon the influences on Japanese investors, Japanese authority can react in flexible manner using this test. Maybe we could describe it as a 'cooperative approach in connecting point'.

---

50 See *Peter Kiel*, supra note 46, 297-311, especially at 306.

51 See *Toshiyuki Kono*, International Civil Procedure in Japan: (1996) 6 Asian Yearbook of International Law 105-134, at 111-112.

52 This is not required by the Japanese Constitution. Some judgments do not mention this test at all, while some judgments refer only to this test without mentioning any provision of the Japanese Code of Civil Procedure.

53 The names were removed, since these companies must have stopped their 'business activities' on the Web. See <www.fsa.go.jp/topics/densie/dee_003.html>.

54 *Toshiyuki Kono*, supra note 51, at 116.

E. The Applicability of the Law on Sales of Financial Products[55]

This new law requests the seller of financial products to explain the risks that the products may cause. If the seller fails to do so, regardless of his negligence, he is obliged to recover damages. The seller has to make principles in advance to keep his solicitations appropriate. If he fails to make the principles, he should be fined. This law is considered as a special law of the tort law in the Japanese civil code.[56] If this were to be applicable to international cases, it should be to cases in which a foreign company sold some financial product to investors in Japan without appropriate explanation on possible risks of the product, and the investors suffered loss. Such cases could be classified as follows:

- The foreign company has an establishment in Japan and this establishment sold the product to investors in Japan.
- The company has an establishment in Japan, but all sales activities were from outside of Japan.
- The company has no establishment in Japan. All sales activities were made from outside of Japan.
- The company has no establishment in Japan, but all activities were made in Japan.

In all these cases – although the last case seems unrealistic – the jurisdiction of the Japanese court could be affirmed either as the place of establishment or as the place of damage occurrence.

The applicable law should then be Japanese law as the law of the place of damage occurrence.[57] Also, the new law could be applied as a part of the applicable law to the tort. We would not have to discuss the extraterritorial applicability.

Only if the applicable law is a foreign law is there room to discuss it. It could be such a case: A Japanese investor residing in Japan purchased some financial product from a foreign company in the country X, in which the Japanese investor has an account and makes investments separately from his account in Japan. The payment to the company was made using this account

---

[55] <www.fsa.go.jp/topics/law_e/law_002.pdf>.

[56] *Keiichiro Omae*, Kinyû shôhin no hanbai-tô ni kansuru hôritsu no gaiyô ni tsuite [On the Outline of the Law on Sales of Financial Products]: (2000) 1185 Jûrisuto 61-66, at 62.

[57] Art. 11 Hôrei [Japanese Private International Law], law no. 10/1898, last amended by law no. 151/1999.

in the country X. The reason he purchased this product was because he received some letters or e-mails in Japan as invitations to the investment. Financial loss occurred at his account in the country X. If this financial 'minus' could be interpreted as his 'damage' in the sense of Japanese private international law, the Japanese law, including the new law, should be applicable. However, if the notion of 'damage' should be interpreted more narrowly, focusing on each jurisdiction, the applicable law should be different from Japanese law. Then the new law would not be automatically applicable and there is room to discuss its extraterritorial applicability.

Through deregulation in the era of globalization, it is becoming popular for individual investors to hold several accounts in different countries. If a loss that occurred in a jurisdiction should be considered the 'damage' of the investor residing in another jurisdiction, 'occurrence of damage' as a connecting point for tort cases would be practically replaced by 'domicile' or 'habitual residence' of the investor. It would then destroy the structure of the international tort law. Therefore 'damage' should be determined in each jurisdiction. Then should the new law be applied extraterritorially? If this should be the case – although from the viewpoint of enforcement the extraterritorial application would not bring much in this case[58] – it may practically urge foreign companies to explain the possible risks of their products. In my view, however, just for this de facto effect the law should not be applied beyond its original border. In short, the Law on Sales of Financial Products should not be applicable extraterritorially.

F. How should the Extraterritorial Application of the SEL be Restricted?

As was suggested at the end of the last section, we have to limit the scope of the extraterritoriality. If its effect is merely a de facto one, we should refrain from using it. Also, since it is just a tool for the protection of the individual investors, if the actions taken in foreign countries clearly focus on the institutional investors only, the SEL should not be applied to them.

Second, although the actions in foreign countries also target the individual investors in Japan, the SEL should be restrictedly applied, i.e., the SEL not as a whole, but the applicability of each regulation should be

---

58 Even if a lawsuit for damage compensation is filed in Japan by the investor, it will be dismissed in most cases due to the lack of jurisdiction.

examined from this point of view. In this article, only some basic regulations are mentioned below:

(1) The regulation for disclosure (Art. 3 et al. and Art. 24) is the most basic regulation for investor protection. It should apply extraterritorially.
(2) Artt. 27-23 require shareholders who own more than five percent of issued shares to make reports. This should apply also to shareholders residing abroad, since this information is important for the market and therefore for individual investors.
(3) TOB (Artt. 27-2 et al.) has many legal aspects. While it affects the interest of individual investors, it is closely related to the organizational structure of the targeted company. Also, fairness between domestic shareholders and foreign investors is another important consideration. Therefore, it cannot be simply said that the regulation on TOB should be extraterritorially applied. One needs comprehensive consideration on the applicable laws to TOB. Could perhaps the alternative application, either the law of the targeted company or the law of the place of shareholders' location, be a feasible idea?
(4) When manipulation of the market is made outside of Japan, regardless of whether it was in the form of securities transactions or not (cf. Art. 159 SEL), it would seriously affect the interests of individual investors. The SEL should be applied extraterritorially.[59]
(5) Insider trading is related to the maintenance of the fair and reliable market. It is the premise of the entire system of securities transactions. The SEL (Art. 167 et al.) should be extraterritorially applied. However, it may cause a conflict of regulations, for example, on the definition of 'insider information' or 'insider'. Therefore, only in those cases in which important parts of the securities transactions (such as order) were made in Japan should the SEL be applicable.

G. *How should the Applicability of the SEL be Restricted? – Creation of a New Market as a Venue of the Portable Reciprocity*

We should limit not only the extraterritorial applicability, but also the applicability of the SEL itself, if the regulation seems excessive or unnecessary. The portable reciprocity theory seems to be unrealistic,[60] but the core con-

59 *Misao Tatsuta*, supra note 25, at. 31.
60 Also *John Moon*, supra note 18, at 192.

cept is adequate to the institutional investors. If the scope of this theory is restricted to the institutional investors only, it is sustainable. One possible restriction of the applicability of the SEL is to establish markets where the hurdles to enter, such as a minimum unit of transactions (for example, a minimum of one million U.S. dollars), are very high, but the freedom is broad. Since, as mentioned above, even foreign companies can establish an exchange in Japan, one further step toward deregulation should be made, i.e., to restrict the applicability of the SEL within Japan through establishing such a market. There the issuers are no longer bound by the SEL. The investors can choose the most attractive offer at their own risk. If some individual investors can afford the requirement for entry, they should not be excluded. If small individual investors are interested in the new investment possibility, they could set up an investment fund that would meet the entry requirements. If this market is established as a Web-based market, it could develop further as a global market. It is like establishing a new Grand Slam tennis competition. In principle, only the top professional players can participate. The risk of losing is high, but the reward can be big. If amateur players wish, they can take part in it at their own cost and effort, as far as they can fulfill the entry requirement.

IV. Summary

With the progress of deregulation, more 'players' take part in the securities market. Japan has made its position clear that it will accept the territoriality of the regulation. As its consequence, Japan decided to take the 'target approach' – i.e., extraterritorial application – when offers are made on the Web that target Japanese investors. Although extraterritorial application has been criticized, this method can be justified when it helps to protect individual investors. In other words, if sales activities made outside of Japan are clearly targeting only the institutional investors, the SEL is not applicable. Even if the SEL should be extraterritorially applicable, its appropriateness should be examined according to the purpose of each regulation. Besides the restricted extraterritorial application, we should perhaps pursue the establishment of a new market as a further step of deregulation, in which not only the SEL but also other laws could be applicable. In other words, a market solely for institutional investors should be developed.

CONCLUDING REMARKS

AND SUMMARY OF DISCUSSIONS

TRANSSECTORAL ISSUES OF REGULATION

– Concluding Remarks on Banking, Capital Market, Insurance, and Telecommunications Regulation –

by Klaus J. Hopt, Hamburg*

At the conclusion of this Max Planck conference at Ringberg Castle, Tegernsee, from 24 to 27 October 2001, the task of closing is mine. Ideally such a conclusion would consist of summing up the insights we gained and the results we reached in the last three days. Yet in the field of theory and practice of regulation, the hope for commonly agreed-upon theories and readily

* Concluding remarks at the European-Japanese Symposion „Comparative Economic Regulation – A Symposium on Regulation of Services in Germany, the EU, and Japan', Ringberg Castle, Tegernsee, 14–17 October 2001. The oral version is more or less retained. A few footnotes have been added in order to give readers who are not familiar with the topic some introductory help. The literature on regulation in general and on regulation in the four specific fields is legion.

J. Basedow, H. Baum, K. Hopt, H. Kanda and T. Kono (eds.), Economic Regulation and Competition, (305-320)

applicable regulatory recipes is futile.[1] All of us – the more theoretically interested academics as well as the practitioners who might focus more an application – seem to agree on this. In itself, this result should not be evaluated as a shortcoming or even a failure, but rather as a valuable insight that creates a challenge: for the academics to shape theories that are more in line with reality, and for the practitioners to be more conscious of the need for underlying principles of regulation that may help not only to make ad hoc decisions from day to day but also in a more consistent and predictable way.

The unsatisfactory state of the art and practice of regulation is partly due to the fact that both are still overwhelmingly discussed and practiced separately in the various regulatory sectors. The practice of regulation in the different fields covered here – bank regulation,[2] securities regulation,[3] regulation of the insurance business and of telecommunications – poses many similar questions, but is still very much sector-specific. Regulation in the four sectors not only has different legal bases, but it also differs considerably as to its aims. In most countries, though not all, this is reflected in the fact that the regulators are separate administrative or self-regulatory agencies without institutional links and more or less routine contacts and cooperation. In addition to this, there are country-specific particularities of regulation in all four sectors. This status is parallel as to the theory of regulation. A generally agreed-upon theory of legal regulation does not seem in sight. This is not just because of the usual academic controversies, but because at least the

---

1 Cf. *Ogus*, Regulation, Legal Form and Economic Theory (Oxford, 1994); *Ogus* (ed.), Regulation, Economics and the Law (Cheltenham, 2001); *Galli/Pelkmans* (eds), Regulatory Reform and Competitiveness in Europe (Cheltenham, 2000); *Hay/Shleifer/Vishny*, Toward a Theory of Legal Reform: (1996) 40 European Economic Review 559. As to the state of the art see *Uche*, The theory of regulation: A review article: (2001) 9 Journal of Financial Regulation and Compliance 67.

2 *Houthakker/Williamson*, The Economics of Financial Markets (Oxford, 1996); *Goodhart et al.*, Financial Regulation, Why, how and where now? (London/New York, 1998); *Jackson/Symons Jr.* (eds), Regulation of Financial Institutions (London, 1999); *Hellmann/Murdoch/Stiglitz*, Liberalization, Moral Hazard in Banking, and Prudential Regulation: Are Capital Requirements Enough?: (2000) 90 No. 1 American Economic Review 147; *Dale*, The Structure of Financial Regulation: (1998) 6 Journal of Financial Regulation and Compliance 326. See also the review article by *Santos*, Bank Capital Regulation in Contemporary Banking Theory: A Review of the Literature: (2001) 10 Financial Markets, Institutions & Instruments 41.

3 *Lo* (ed.), The Industrial Organization and Regulation of the Securities Industry (Chicago/London, 1996); *Steil* (ed.), International Financial Market Regulation (Chichester, 1994).

legal theory of regulation in these fields (as far as it has been developed) is still based on the sector-specific needs, problems, and applications in the various fields; approaches to the general theory of regulation differ widely according to whether they are developed by lawyers, economists, or other social scientists, in particular political scientists and sociologists.

Given this fact, I could confine myself to saying a word on the idea of this conference. It was principally to bring experts together from different regulatory sectors – an event which, surprisingly enough, is far from being a common practice and is still rather exceptional – and to have them exchange their views on why their sector is regulated, what could or should be deregulated, and whether they face common problems in the age of globalization. Of course, this task needed the impact of the practice, i.e., of those who deal with these questions and problems every day. Theory without practice is bound to remain non-committal; equally, practice without theory cannot help but be a more or less short-sighted – if not self-deceiving – muddling-through. On the other hand, the reality of regulation today is no longer purely national, but more and more cross-border and multinational. This has long been true for bank regulation, but in the meantime it is also common ground in securities regulation and insurance regulation. In telecommunications, the very technology, economy, and sheer size of the market participants – many of whom are present or former nationwide monopolists or oligopoists – lead to transnational market and merger activities. With this in mind, we have gathered participants from four countries: Germany, Switzerland, and Austria from the European side, and Japan from the other. The liveliness of the presentations and discussions proved that the old kitchen recipe was right: Just take the right ingredients and boil them together for a good while – preferably isolating them well from outside influences, as we did here ideally at Ringberg Castle, far away from the enticing allures of Munich – and you will get new, possibly excellent outcomes.

Since this was indeed the case, I shall attempt to be a bit more ambitious and sum up some commonly posed issues, to present some questions of my own, and to encourage you to take them home with you for further reflection in the various regulatory sectors and countries you come from.

I. Regulation in Market Economies

Every theory is based on certain premises and – even more – on preconceptions that are usually not even articulated; however, they should be articulated, or at least kept in mind. The basic value judgment shared by all of us who are lawyers is individual freedom as the basic rule of the economic order and competition as the form of its organization.[4] This was rightly mentioned by Jürgen Basedow in his introductory statement. I am not quite sure if such a fundamental consensus would be reached as easily – or at all – with representatives from other disciplines and other systems, such as Professor Scharpf or Professor Streek from the Cologne Max Planck Institute for Social Sciences,[5] for example. Christoph Engel could tell us whether these colleagues would rather look at ideas than interests, what role according to them the political process plays in regulation, and how the corporatist approach differs from the market approach commonly chosen by economic lawyers and economists. Certainly colleagues from other political and economic systems – such as China, for example – would have different ideas on regulation given the fact that they have a system which incorporates bits and pieces of a market economy, though it cannot yet be regarded as a market economy itself, unless in a very early stage of development.

At one point in the discussion, there seemed to be a difference of opinion as to the concept of regulation, whether it should be wider or narrower and whether common private law norms should also be included in the concept. Probably, though, there was no real dissent. If both individual freedom and competition are the basis, and if every regulatory restriction to any of them needs to be justified – and I agree on this – it cannot matter whether this restriction is embedded in a public or a private law norm, whether it stems from the legislators or the regulators or possibly even from a self-regulatory body that looks more after the interests of its members involved in the self-regulatory process than at the costs for third parties and outsiders. In this sense, labor markets, though covered mostly by (mandatory) private law norms, are indeed regulated markets.

On the other hand, it was no coincidence that we chose banking, capital markets, insurance, and telecommunications as the sectors to be covered. They all are fields with intensive state intervention, both by substantive law as well as by supervisory agencies that control access to the market and the continuing market conduct of those admitted to it. It seems that in these and similar sectors of the economy, a number of problems arise that are unique in comparison to the labor markets, be it only because there is active,

---

4 Cf. the contributions to the 18th International Seminar on the New Institutional Economics – The Proper Scope of Government: (2001) 157 JITE 1-230, Editorial Preface by *Engel/Schweizer*, p. 1.

5 Cf. *Mayntz/Scharpf* (eds), Gesellschaftliche Selbstregelung und politische Steuerung (Frankfurt, 1996).

continuous regulatory intervention by state authorities. To put it in other words, or rather in a question: A theory of regulatory intervention would have to explain why, for example, labor markets are basically regulated in market economies by mandatory private law and by self-regulation like works councils, trade unions, and collective bargaining, while in the four sectors mentioned there seems to be need of regulation of access to and conduct at the markets by permanent intervention and supervision through a supervisory body of the state itself or authorized and controlled by the state.

Given the fact that in all of the countries represented here, and indeed nearly all over Europe, regulation in these four sectors is primarily state regulation under particular supervisory acts and legal provisions, it must be remembered that self-regulation is part of regulation. This is cogent if, as Johannes Köndgen put it, individual freedom is the basic yardstick under which to measure regulation and if, for the purpose of justifying regulatory intervention, a presumption for individual freedom and against regulation is maintained.

II. Common Problems and Questions on Regulation across the Four Sectors of Banking, Capital Markets, Insurance, and Telecommunications

Looking at the four sectors dealt with in this conference, it seems that a set of at least six common problems and questions arise across all of them: A. goals of the regulation; B. competition; C. type of risk and regulatory instruments to deal with it; D. type of market participants and need and kind of protection; E. type and jurisdiction of regulators; and F. enforcement.

A. Goals of the Regulation

In a discussion of regulation, the first question must be the purpose of regulation, and if we compare regulation in the different sectors, we must first identify the goals of each form of regulation. There is almost always more than one goal, though one may be primary while the others are secondary. In banking, the primary goal is securing financial system stability. Secondary goals are, among others, monetary policy and protection of depositors as a special form of consumer protection.

In securities regulation, investor protection is the short formula for functioning capital markets as well as for protection of the investing public and thereby individual investors.[6] Sometimes a conflict between market protection and investor protection is postulated. But in most cases, this conflict remains theoretical because functioning capital markets are indispensable for the investors, while investor protection is a precondition for the functioning of the markets. In this sense, so-called protection of functions or markets and protection of individuals has been described as being just two sides of the same coin. The link between both is investor confidence,[7] a fact that is already right at the heart of the U.S. American securities acts of 1933 and 1934, which have set standards for all later securities regulation worldwide.

In insurance, the goal is commonly said to be policyholder protection. But what about insurance markets? While the typical run situations as a consequence of loss of depositor or investor confidence is a phenomenon of banking and of capital markets, it seems that loss of confidence in the insurance markets might also have far-reaching consequences for the insurance policyholders as a group. It would be interesting to know why market protection has been less emphasized in insurance supervisory law and insurance regulation. It might be speculated that this has to do with the degree of intervention in the market process in the insurance field, which is higher than in banking and in capital markets (for example, by prescribing to a considerable degree the actual contract terms in life insurance). If one takes this strong intervention as granted, the focus shifts easily from market protection to policyholder protection.

On the other hand, in the telecommunications field the focus seems to be on opening up a monopolistic market, as Klaus-Dieter Scheurle has showed us. However, this is but another way of saying that there must be more competition and individual freedom, though not to a point that consumer protection is in danger. That means that again both protection of market and protection of individuals goes together.

It is interesting to speculate why the protection of workers seems to be the only goal in legislation and practice of labor market regulation, while legislators and self-regulators – at least the trade unions and in collective bargaining to a certain degree also employers in Germany – hardly care at all about the functioning of labor markets.[8] The result is overregulation and

---

6 *Hopt*, Der Kapitalanlegerschutz im Recht der Banken (München, 1975), p. 51 et seq.

7 Cf. *Rippberger*, Ökonomik des Vertrauens (Tübingen, 1998).

8 Cf. *Engel*, Arbeitsmarkt und staatliche Lenkung: (2000) 59 Veröffentlichungen des Vereins der Deutschen Staatsrechtslehrer 56; *Siebert*, Geht den Deutschen die Arbeit cont. ...

dysfunctional development with dire consequences for the labor markets and the economy as a whole. It might be that this can be explained only be vested interests, both for the legislators as the public choice theory has taught us, and for trade unions and employers who both act as cartels with little concern for the needs of outsiders, such as the unemployed and the consumer.

B. Competition

It was commonly agreed among the participants, though it is still not common in our countries, that competition is of primary importance in all four of these sectors. The old concept of having natural monopolies or specificities in these sectors that bring them out of the scope of antitrust law, or at least considerably restrict its applicability, does not hold any longer. This is certainly true for banking, while for securities regulation it has never played an important role, apart from the stock exchanges perhaps. In the meantime, though somewhat later, it has also become true for insurance. Wulf-Henning Roth has mentioned that European antitrust law is applicable without exception to the insurance industry. Telecommunications is in the process of going in the same direction, though more slowly and with continuing major conflicts and controversies as we constantly witness.

It follows that before and as a condition of each and every regulatory state intervention in these sectors, it must first be asked: Is not competition the better regulator? The force of competition as compared to state regulation can be seen in banking – where state regulation of the interest to be charged for credit has been done away with – or in the field of securities, where the international and even global competition for capital has forced legislators to liberalize their securities markets in a kind of regulatory competition in order to make their national markets more competitive. Lately the stock exchanges have come under intense competitive pressure, both by foreign and even international stock exchanges as well as by alternative or proprietary trading systems (ATS, PTS, also called electronic communication networks, ECN).[9]

---

aus? Wege zu mehr Beschäftigung (München, 1994); *Rieble*, Die Betriebsverfassungsgesetz-Novelle 2001 in ordnungspolitischer Sicht: (2001) ZIP 133.

9 Cf. *Lee*, What is an Exchange? The Automation, Management, and Regulation of Financial Markets (Oxford, 1998).

Competition functions only if there are free markets and – in particular – free access to them. It is the task of antitrust law and of the respective antitrust authorities to look out for this. From a regulatory point of view, it follows that the interaction between the antitrust authorities and the sector-specific regulators is important. In some of our countries, it can be observed that there is not much cooperation between them. Sometimes there seems even to be a tension between them, as possibly in telecommunications. The mistaken belief that antitrust authorities and sectoral supervisors have a task fully separate from each other has led legislators not to prescribe cooperation between them in the sector-specific laws. This is also true for European sector-specific regulation, such as in the banking and securities regulation directives, where cooperation between national regulators is mandated. For stock exchange regulation, the draft Fourth Financial Markets Promotion Act[10] has followed the suggestions of the Max Planck Study on Stock Exchange Law Reform[11] in having a separate provision charging the stock exchange supervisory authority with looking after the observation of antitrust law in the field and helping the antitrust authorities in enforcing antitrust law, also as to the stock exchanges by way of a duty of information. This is a very modern provision that could be a model for other regulatory acts on the national as well as on the EU level.

One might even go one step further: in addition to having a provision making clear that antitrust law is applicable in the specific sector and that the sectoral supervision must look after this and help the antitrust authorities, the goal of having competitive markets could be included under the goals of the sectoral regulation and supervision.[12] Johannes Köndgen seems to agree on this for banking regulation, and Klaus-Dieter Scheurle and – if I am not mistaken – Yasuo Hasebe agree for telecommunications. For stock exchange regulation, section 6 of the above-mentioned draft act points in this direction but does not go quite so far, while in insurance regulation there does not yet seem to be a similar development.

Finally, for all four sectors there is an uneasy relationship between competition on the one side and failures, rescue systems, and state aid on the other. The old view that bank regulation should prevent bank failure has given way to the modern view that in functioning, competitive markets, bank

---

10 As of 3 September 2001, section 6.

11 *Hopt/Rudolph/Baum* (eds), Börsenreform. Eine ökonomische, rechtsvergleichende und rechtspolitische Untersuchung (Stuttgart, 1997).

12 *Hopt/Baum*, Börsenrechtsreform, in: Hopt/Rudolph/Baum, supra note 11, p. 287 at 375 et seq.

failures are a part of the game or even necessary as a consequence of competition that eliminates low performers. This insight leads to the consequence that it is not for regulation to try to uphold failing banks by interfering with the selection process at the market, but rather to accept its outcomes while helping to protect the ordinary depositors from losing their savings in the process. This is even more true for the government bailing out a bank in trouble, as Johannes Köndgen rightly stated. Of course, the practice both in Europe – as evidenced by the Credit Lyonnais case of the European Commission of 1996 – and in Japan is far from being in line with this truth.

C. Types of Risk and Regulatory Response

When we compare regulation in the different sectors, it is of prime importance to see what risks are at stake in the different sectors. Regulatory instruments and response are geared toward these sector-specific risks. Risks in the banking business, to take one example, are different for the most part from risks in the insurance business. As it is sometimes said, most of these risks concern different sides of the balance sheet. Hideki Kanda has made a similar point for derivatives. The first important task, therefore, is a correct functional comparison of what kind of risks are at stake in each specific sector. The difficulty of this is shown, for example, by the European draft directive on supervision of financial conglomerates of 24 April 2001.[13] The proposal addresses the supervisory concerns about intra-group transactions and risk exposures in a financial conglomerate, but concedes readily that it is not yet feasible to introduce quantitative limits in this area. It seeks rather to aim at internal management policy and organizational measures, reporting requirements to supervisors and effective supervisory enforcement powers.

Correspondingly, regulatory reaction to a materialized risk as well as risk-prevention systems must be looked at and evaluated in a functional and comparative way. Capital adequacy and technical provisions for banking – such as the 8 percent rule mentioned by Klaus-Dieter Scheurle – cannot just be compared numerically with the risks, needs, and regulation in insurance, though, as Knut Hohlfeld has stated, the question is posed as to whether capital adequacy may serve as an additional safety cushion in insurance regulation also.

---

[13] (2001) COM 213 fin.

Other questions cannot but be mentioned, such as style of regulation, i.e., more rule-centered versus principle-centered regulation and ex ante versus ex post regulation, as Takashi Kubota has distinguished; and state regulation versus self-regulation as previously mentioned. Another intriguing example is the question of regulation by reserving certain functions and businesses to the state, state enterprises, or at least public bodies under public law, regulation, and supervision, such as German stock exchanges that are still considered by the majority of courts and legal writers as public law bodies. This, of course, has far-reaching consequences for their relationship to customers, for regulation, and for administrative court jurisdiction. Much of all this cannot be explained rationally, but is a consequence of path-dependent and historical developments in the various sectors and countries.[14] The stiff resistance in Germany, for example, against merely opening up the legal possibility for founding and operating stock exchanges fully under private law instead of sticking fully to public law stock exchanges is part of this. Abroad, where the practice of fully private exchanges has long been proven to be not only viable but also beneficial, this is difficult to explain and even more difficult to understand. Modern economic and regulatory theory agrees that stock exchanges should not just be understood as particular markets, but as normal entrepreneurs who act and compete in the markets as other enterprises do.[15]

D. Types of Market Participants and Regulatory Protection

A first comparative issue of regulation in the four fields is whether we can subsume all of them – depositors, private investors, normal policyholders, and consumers in telecommunications – under the general notion of consumer. This is not just a conceptual question of theoretical and dogmatic interest, but has eminently practical consequences. For consumer protection under European law, there are specific bases in the Treaty, specific principles, and specific regulatory jurisdictions. Treating private investors as financial consumers would shift the center of gravity from self-determination to much more legally mandatory protection. This is why in Germany, shareholders are certainly not considered as consumers.

---

[14] Cf. *Ackermann*, Pfadabhängigkeit, Institutionen und Regelform (Tübingen, 2001); more specifically for corporate governance *Hopt*, Gemeinsame Grundsätze der Corporate Governance in Europa?: (2000) ZGR 779 at 798 et seq.

[15] *Ferrarini*, The European Regulation of Stock Exchanges: New Perspectives: (1999) 36 Common Market Law Review 569.

But even if one recognizes certain similarities in the needs for protection of consumers and investors, it is important to differentiate between different types of market participants as Toshiyuki Kono has pointed out. In securities regulation this is done by distinguishing between wholesale and retail markets and between professional, institutional, and possibly also well-informed investors on the one side and normal private investors on the other side. Only the latter need extended protection; the former certainly do not, otherwise competition and the functioning of the market would be impaired.

Which persons are on the other side and need to be regulated? Susanne Kalss has distinguished between issuers, firms offering financial services and related services, and investors. Koji Kinoshita mentioned the rating organizations. Where do the stock exchanges stand, and what about public law institutions providing particular financial services? A proposal has been made to broaden the scope of the Investment Services Directive and to include, among others, the stock exchanges as 'market organizers', as well as PTS/ECNs. The former would form the upper end of the regulatory scale, the latter the downside end. Regulation and supervision would adapt to the different layers, functions, and needs of protection.

Further questions are what to regulate (products, prudential regulation of players, conduct of business – in particular, conduct of financial intermediaries[16] – in the different sectors?) and how to regulate. As to the latter question, there seems to be a trend away from substantive regulation to procedural regulation. Information regulation becomes more important as the role of transparency increases in a more competitive environment.

E. Types and Jurisdiction of Regulators

Regulation is only as good as the regulators. But what types of regulators are needed and what should be their jurisdiction? Politically and institutionally, the most controversial discussion in Europe right now is whether the system of sector-specific regulators as in traditional state regulation should be kept or rather changed by establishing a more or less far-reaching cross-sectoral supervisory and regulatory body. In many countries, such as Belgium and Switzerland, bank regulation and securities regulation are in the hands of the same regulatory body, such as the Commission bancaire et financière in

16 *Pacces*, Financial intermediation in the securities markets law and economics of conduct of business regulation: (2000) 20 International Review of Law and Economics 479.

Belgium or the Swiss Banking Commission. In the UK, the Financial Services Act 2000 goes hand-in-hand with the establishment of a fully cross-sectoral Financial Services Authority that regulates capital markets, banking (instead of, as formerly, the Bank of England), and insurance. In Germany, a draft act is underway which would lead to a combination of capital markets, banking, and insurance regulators, though this innovation has led to stiff resistance from the *Länder,* which might lose jurisdiction and influence, and by the German Bundesbank, which has lost important functions to the European Central Bank and would like to move increasingly into bank supervision. Of course, in the United States there is still full dispersion of regulators, not only between securities regulators, bank supervisors, and insurance supervisors, but even within specific sectors themselves, such as the complicated system of various authorities involved in bank supervision.

The European Union sees the merits and even necessity of supervision for financial conglomerates, as the above-mentioned draft directive shows. After all, the phenomenon of all finance, or – as the French say – 'bancassurfinance',[17] has become a reality, not only in some member states, as the merger of the Allianz insurance company and the Dresdner Bank in Germany shows, but also in Europe. Yet the European Commission does not go so far as to propose a mandatory supervision by one national cross-sectoral regulator, and even less by such a European one. It is true that a European securities commission shaped after the U.S. American Securities and Exchange Commission has been called for. But political reality after the Lamfalussy proposals is not yet ripe for this. In any case, combined supervision makes sense on the national level as well, though it does not require a single cross-sectoral regulator, but can also be carried out in a cooperation model. Even in the case of one single cross-sectoral regulatory body, it would make a big difference whether there is just a holding structure with three fairly separate supervisory departments of this body, or whether a real merger is envisaged and, more important, achieved. Much of this depends, of course, on the persons in charge of such cross-sectoral regulation, as Anton Schnyder as rightly observed.

The following are examples of other important questions:

---

[17] Cf. *Association Européenne pour le Droit Bancaire et Financier–Belgium* (ed.), Bancassurfinance (Bruxelles, 2000).

- State regulation versus self-regulation:[18] There have been good experiences with front regulators, as Susanne Bergstraesser has reported from German experience with international securities cases.
- Independence of regulators, both from the state and politics as well as from the supervised industry:[19] The latter is the well-known problem of captive agencies, which has been mentioned as a problem by both Klaus-Dieter Scheurle and Yasuo Hasebe. Susanne Bergstraesser has presented the question of how independent a stock exchange supervisory authority can be if it is part of the ministry of economics, such as the Hessian stock exchange supervisory authority looking after the Frankfurt Stock Exchange.
- Regulation at what level? There is much disagreement over whether a more centralized or a more decentralized supervision and regulation is more promising. This disagreement already concerns the division of jurisdictions within a nation state, such as in Germany between the *Länder* that want to maintain stock exchange supervision and the federal securities supervisory office (*Bundesaufsichtsamt für den Wertpapierhandel*). It goes further concerning member state supervision or supervision on the level of the European Community. In some areas there are already even global standard setters, such as the Basel Committee or FESCO and FESCOPOL, and most recently the Committee of European Securities Regulators (CESR) with important tasks under the Lamfalussy proposals. Of course, this discussion is linked to the more fundamental dispute on regulatory competition[20] and on the merits of

---

18 Cf. *Wegner*, Wirtschaftspolitik zwischen Selbst- und Fremdsteuerung (Baden-Baden, 1996); *Hopt*, Self-Regulation in Banking and Finance – Practice and Theory in Germany, in: La Déontologie bancaire et financière/The Ethical Standards in Banking & Finance (Bruxelles, 1998), p. 53.

19 Cf. more generally *Viscusi*, Regulating the Regulators: (1996) 63 University of Chicago Law Review 1423.

20 Cf. *Bratton/McCahery/Picciotto/Scott* (eds), International Regulatory Competition and Coordination: Perspectives on Economic Regulation in Europe and the United States (Oxford, 1996); *Cassel* (ed.), Entstehung und Wettbewerb von Systemen, Schriften des Vereins für Socialpolitik vol. 246 (Berlin, 1996); *Esty/Gerardin* (eds), Regulatory Competition and Economic Integration, Comparative Perspectives (Oxford, 2001); *Esty/Gerardin*, Regulatory Co-opetition: (2000) Journal of International Economic Law 235; *Kerber*, Interjurisdictional Competition Within the European Union: (2000) 23 Fordham International Law Journal 217; *Monopolkommission*, Sondergutachten zum 'Systemwettbewerb', 30 June 1998; *Siebert*, Zum Paradigma des Standortwettbewerbs (Tübingen, 2000).

distribution of jurisdictions between a federation and its member states. The results projected by the two factions are the race to the bottom or the race to the top. In my opinion, the truth is much more nuanced. Either result can emerge as an outcome depending on the particular cases, issues, and transnational problems.

– Home country control versus host country control:[21] This vast and multifaceted problem has been mentioned by Susanne Bergstraesser, Wulf-Henning Roth, and other participants. The European Union directives in bank, securities, and insurance supervision, for example, have made wide use of this kind of division. Most recently a similar division was proposed in the 13th directive on takeovers as advocated by the national securities commissions but questioned by many practitioners. A major challenge to such a division is the need for quick decisions, for example, in urgent cases of takeovers, market abuse, bank failures, etc. It is also difficult to achieve adequate and well-informed consumer protection in any country if a foreign regulator and supervisor has jurisdiction. There is disagreement on whether better solutions can be achieved by harmonization of substantive protective provisions or rather by supervisory cooperation. On the other hand, it seems doubtful whether the old conflict-of-law approach can deal with these problems satisfactorily. Anton Schnyder has asked for conflicts of law with new ideas. But what are they?

F. Enforcement

There was agreement that regulation without enforcement[22] is self-deceiving or even chimerical. For effective enforcement, of course, more personnel and financial means are needed. Regulation becomes increasingly difficult as examples of in-house risk models in capital adequacy and liquidity of banks under the recent Basel approach show. Is a state supervisory body able to attract good enough experts for state service if the pay differs so much from what these experts might get in private practice?

But staffing, financing, and organizing regulatory bodies is not enough. There is an important role for private law, in particular for liability and

21 Cf. recently *Callies*, Heimatstaatprinzip und Europa-Pass (single licence principle) im europäischen Finanzmarktrecht: (2000) EWS 432.

22 Cf. *Polinsky/Shavell*, The Economic Theory of Public Enforcement of Law: (2000) Journal of Economic Literatur 45.

private actions. This leads to the expertise of the courts and the possible need for specialized courts or specialized chambers and senates of the courts.

In view of all these factors that are necessary or contributing to an effective regulation, one is led to increasingly emphasize the role of transparency, of disclosure, and of information and information-sharing. By this the forces of the market are used for regulation. This is possibly the most important way of regulating, and certainly the one that is most compatible with competition and individual freedom.

SUMMARY OF DISCUSSIONS

by Harald Baum, Hamburg

The various discussions during the conference were bound together by two overarching themes: the search for a *general theory* as well as an adequate *concept* of regulation.

It became increasingly clear that in Japan as well as in the continental European countries represented at the conference, a comprehensive theoretical approach has not yet been fully developed; instead, it seems to be in the process of formation. *Hopt* emphasized this point especially with respect to the theoretical discussion of self-regulation in Germany that is still in its infancy. There was agreement among the participants that self-regulation must be included in a general theory of regulation, because it is very often merely a substitute for state regulation and in most cases has far-reaching consequences for the freedom of market participants bound to it. Furthermore, it may have relevance even for potential new competitors not yet bound to the self-regulation in the pertinent market, because it is often implemented as a barrier to market entry. *Basedow* pointed out that economists obviously have a broader concept of regulation than traditional lawyers, and their perspectives on that issue differ significantly from each other. Because lawyers lack the broader perspective of economists, an interdisciplinary approach for developing a joint theory of regulation including state as well as self-regulation will be of great importance.

There was also an (almost) unanimous consensus that the market and its self-disciplinary functions must be the starting point for any theory on regulation. This assumption was presented in the introductory lecture by *Basedow* and taken up later by various discussants. While stressing a presumption of freedom, *Köndgen* regarded today's differentiation between state, self-, and mixed forms of regulation to be no longer sufficient, calling

J. Basedow, H. Baum, K. Hopt, H. Kanda and T. Kono (eds.), Economic Regulation and Competition, (321-326)

instead for new theoretical concepts to be developed from scratch. Although the various forms of market failure are widely accepted as a justification for regulation, *Hopt* cautioned that they have to be weighed against the costs of government failures, such as captured regulators, incentive problems, rent-seeking behavior, and others.

Interestingly – and quite contrary to the common stereotype that regulatory competition leads necessarily to the infamous 'race to the bottom' with its assumed intolerable lowering of regulatory standards and legal protection – *Bergsträsser* pointed out that in practice, at least among institutional investors, there is a clear awareness of the quality of regulation in a given jurisdiction as part of the investment decision. Only if the standards of transparency, legal protection of shareholder rights, and supervisory efficiency are regarded as sufficiently high from the investor's perspective will money flow in that jurisdiction. Thus regulatory competition in practice may obviously lead to an *improvement* in regulation and enforcement, which should come as no surprise to those who believe in the disciplinary as well as the innovative potential of competition, regardless of the social context in which it works.

Concerning the concept of regulation, it was asked whether administrative interference is a necessary structural element of regulation. As previously with self-regulation, this question was also answered in the negative for mandatory private law. Although *Köndgen* saw a clear borderline between public regulation and mandatory private law – which was described as 'intermediate law making' – he had no doubts about qualifying civil law rules protecting consumers (for example) as regulation in its purest form. Another example raised by *Basedow* are the German labor laws. The German market is among the most intensely regulated labor markets in the world; however, most of the pertinent regulation is not public law but mandatory private law enforced by civil actions. *Hopt* emphasized that a theory of regulation must explain why labor market regulation is mainly based on private norms in the case of Germany.

Roth added that, for nearly a century, the German insurance market as such had been the central focus of public insurance regulation. The protection of policyholders was also an instrument to create confidence so that policies would be bought and the market would function. This becomes also true for the EU, where prudential regulation is regarded also as a form of industrial policy. However, the regulatory concept with regard to insurance products has changed dramatically: the regulatory focus on individual policies is on a post-market control of unfair terms by the courts, having replaced the former pre-market product regulation by the (German) supervisory agency. Thus, we now see a deregulation through the strengthening of private law enforcement.

A shift from public to private law with a similar content and regulatory aim – i.e., a change from direct to indirect regulation – can presently also be observed in Japan. *Kanda* pointed out that Japan had developed an enormous speed of de- and re-regulation in this sense. Additionally, much of the country's soft law drafted by international institutions was transferred in this process into hard law.

Besides the distinction between regulation by public and mandatory private law, the role of self-regulation figured prominently in the discussion about regulatory concepts. While there seemed to be a generally positive view of self-regulation – given that the two main preconditions of experience and incentives are working (*Köndgen*) – some were more skeptical. *Schnyder* expressed doubts in principle that self-regulation can work from the perspective of competition law; instead, he saw it as a regulatory instrument for periods of transition during which the state regulator does not yet have enough expertise and know-how. *Basedow* reminded participants that the links between self-regulation and state authority vary greatly in different eras, thus leading in effect to different types of self-regulation.

The regulation of exchanges was discussed especially intensely. Some regarded exchange services as a special product that called for specific regulation. *Kalss* stressed this aspect, particularly with new developments where investors have no experience and competition may accordingly not work properly. This view was rejected by others who basically saw no need for specific exchange regulation in addition to the usual market regulation (*Kanda*) or rules governing auctions in general (*Kono*). *Hopt* proposed that trading systems, for example, should have the choice to opt up to a higher level of regulation from minimum state regulation and/or self-regulation. This would leave room for regulatory flexibility and, at the same time, create an incentive for adopting a higher standard of regulation and supervision as a specific proof of quality. This in turn could be used as a marketing instrument. *Köndgen* also saw a strong incentive for exchanges to protect their integrity and reputation by effective regulation.

Another aspect that permeated all discussions was the growing internationalization of markets, players, and regulatory standards. *Basedow* emphasized that globalization has extended our personal reach by lowering costs of travel, communication, freight, et al. As markets have become wider, costs have sunk. Any attempt to limit globalization by closing markets is doomed to fail; he saw no sensible alternative to globalization. However, with regulation, this development not only leads to regulatory competition but also the possibility of regulatory cooperation. *Kanda* added that globalization does not mean one market, but multiple markets that are interconnected. At present, he believes that a problem of mismatch exists when the interdependence of markets – such as financial markets – is so often significantly stronger than the interdependence of regulation. He identified three stages in the historical development of regulation: originally it was national; the second stage included – and still includes – an exchange of information between national legislators; and in the future, joint rule-making by various regulators will significantly increase, thus further increasing the importance of cooperation. *Scheurle* added that, from the European perspective, the European Union had discovered that a full-scale regulatory harmonization as initially planned was impractical, causing the focus to shift instead to an institutional cooperation between regulators. In any case, globalization of markets seems to lead to the development of ever larger administrative agencies, as *Schnyder* pointed out.

Bergsträsser cautioned that at the supervisory level, globalized markets are causing problems; in securities trading, for example, supervision at the national level no longer works and cooperation is often insufficient and time-consuming, whereas the supervisor must be able to act immediately in cases of market manipulation, insider trading, et al. From this perspective, the principle of home country control without harmonization of national rules was seen as being predominantly in the interest of the industry and not of the investing public. So far, trading supervision of remote members on the German stock exchanges is carried out on a private law basis. The exchanges have required their foreign members trading on a contractual basis to pass on the necessary information to the authorities. However, in practice there are obviously limits to the efficiency of that approach. Looking at the insurance market, *Hohlfeld* pointed out that home country control has been working well so far, even if it means that judges in the European Member States have to apply foreign laws. In this context, *Roth* discussed the issue of state liability for failures of supervision in the context of home country control. Assuming that state liability is to be regarded as constitutionally required, the principle of home country control could lead to the disadvantage of policyholders of the host state; he warned of constitutional problems that might arise if, e.g., policyholders were to sue the supervisory agency of the home country of the insurer for damages caused by failures of supervision in their own courts. The courts of the host state would have to judge the activities of a foreign public institution, which immediately leads to the question of state immunity.

Engel raised the more general question of privatization of regulation and how that could be brought under the shadow of the law. *Kanda* envisioned both difficult and easy scenarios for supervision in globalized markets. He mentioned the 'targeting approach' to securities offerings and trading via the Internet as an easy solution that has grown out of soft law set by IOSCO and is being increasingly adopted on an international level as state regulation. *Baum* cautioned that this approach – under which national laws are applied to a foreign financial institution if it 'targets' that national market via the Internet –is at best a second-best solution, despite its wide acceptance. In its essence, it is not much different from the traditional territorial approach to securities regulation that neutralizes most of the gains of globalized markets, because a firm doing business in various jurisdictions has to respect all pertinent laws. If it does not wish to be subject to a specific national regulation, it must exclude the investors of that jurisdiction from its services.

In the telecommunications markets where state monopolies have long dominated, privatization – together with forced market entry to outsiders by the pertinent regulator – has led to a drastic reduction in prices. However, as both *Hasebe* and *Scheurle* regretted, the national markets in both Japan and Germany are not yet globalized due to problems of access to local loops. A further opening-up is underway, but especially in the case of Japan there will be slow progress: competitors there were forced to file claims against the Japanese telecommunications giant NTT for better market access, and court proceedings are time-consuming. Whereas national regulators might have favored closed markets as a form of protective industrial policy, *Engel* stressed that, contrary to a widespread assumption, the efforts of the European Union to fence globalization were not motivated by protectionist ambitions. Instead, the EU was trying to first make Europe as state-like as possible before opening it up to global competition.

Another constant theme of discussion was the interplay of sector-specific regulation and general competition law as well as the relationship between special agencies supervising individual industries, such as the telecommunications or the insurance market. However, *Scheurle* stressed the need for such a specific regulator for the telecommunications industry, even though the set-up of that agency was highly disputed at the time. *Kanda* reported from the Japanese experience that special regulation for banking, securities, and insurance always had a strong anti-competitive connotation. Thus, clashes between such sector-specific regulation and competition law were frequent. One way to promote competition might be a change from direct to indirect regulation. *Hohlfeld* pointed out that the practical cooperation between the German Cartel Office and the different authorities regulating the financial markets had turned out to be rather problematic in the past.

It remains to be seen what influence the unbundling of services, another trend observed in all areas of services and in all countries, will have in this regard. The traditional classifications and separations of products and markets have almost – if not completely – disappeared, and they are increasingly being replaced by a regulatory look at the function of a given service. *Kanda* pointed out that derivatives and insurance are by now mostly regarded as fulfilling similar functions, and thus should be regulated in a similar way. As an institutional result of this development, *Schilling* mentioned the still hotly debated but probably imminent creation of a unified German supervisory authority modeled on the new British FSA to replace the three existing regulators for banking, insurance business, and securities trading.

Japan, on the other hand, had always had its supervision of financial markets centralized at the Ministry of Finance. However, due to numerous problems with that extremely powerful ministry, the Japanese government recently shifted supervisory competencies in particular from the Ministry to a new Financial Supervision Agency. *Kubota* expected a major – albeit slow – change in regulation and supervision as a result of this rearrangement, although he was rather skeptical about copying 'global standards' as an end in itself. He encouraged Japanese lawmakers to try to 'export' specific Japanese features of regulation and thus influence the formulation of internationally accepted standards. In contrast, *Kinoshita* regarded it as positive that Japan had decided to follow the British experience in insurance regulation in the sense that life insurance was to be regulated respecting its investment or saving elements. He also emphasized that the regulatory philosophy of indemnity insurance should further be made clear in the framework of overreaching financial services regulation. *Basedow* thought it was sufficient to take care of national specialties at the enforcement level.

INDEX

European Business Law and Practice Series

1. *Concentration Control in the European Economic Community,* P.V.F. Bos, J.H.V. Stuyck and P. Wytinck. ISBN 1-85333-570-3
2. *Mergers and Joint Ventures in Europe: The Law and Policy of the EEC, Second Edition,* F.L. Fine. ISBN 1-85333-574-6
3. *Intellectual Property and the Internal Market of the European Community,* P. Groves, T. Martino, C. Miskin and J. Richards. ISBN 1-85333-574-4
4. *Privatization in Central and Eastern Europe,* P. Šarčević. ISBN 1-85333-713-7
5. *Harmonization and Hazard: Regulating Workplace Health and Safety in the European Community,* R. Baldwin and T. Daintith. ISBN 1-85333-723-4
6. *European Community Telecommunications Regulation,* S. Mosteshar. ISBN 1-85333-756-0
7. *European Community and International Media Law,* D.B. Winn. ISBN 1-85333-760-9
8. *Corporate Acquisitions and Mergers in Portugal,* R.C. Wolf. ISBN 1-85333-793-5
9. *Corporate Acquisitions and Mergers in France,* C. de Pardieu and N. Weyd. ISBN 1-85333-965-2
10. *Insurance Competition Law: A Handbook to the Competition Law of the European Union and the European Economic Area,* A. Fitzsimmons. ISBN 1-85966-059-2
11. *Federalism and Responsibility: A Study on Product Safety Law and Practice in the European Community,* H. Micklitz, T. Roethe and S. Weatherill. ISBN 1-85966-102-5
12. *Corporate Acquisitions and Mergers in Germany, Second Edition,* D. Beinert. ISBN 90-411-0677-4
13. *A Brief Guide to European State Aid Law,* C. Baudenbacher. ISBN 90-411-0939-0
14. *Intellectual Property and the International Market of the European Community, Second Edition,* P. Groves. ISBN 90-411-0695-2
15. *Customs and Trade Laws of the European Community,* S. Inama and E. Vermulst. ISBN 90-411-9661-7
16. *Modernisation and Decentralisation of EC Competition Law,* 2000. J. Rivas and M. Horspool (Eds.). ISBN 90-411-1442-4
17. *State Measures Distorting Free Competition in the EC,* 2002. C.M. von Quitzow. ISBN 90-411-1466-1
18. *Economic Regulation and Competition. Regulation of Services in the EU, Germany and Japan,* 2002. J. Basedow, H. Baum, K.J. Hopt, H. Kanda and T. Kono (Eds.). ISBN 90-411-1968-X